THEY ALSO WRITE FOR KIDS

Susan Honeyman, Series Editor

THEY ALSO WRITE FOR KIDS
Cross-Writing, Activism, and Children's Literature

Suzanne Manizza Roszak

University Press of Mississippi / Jackson

The University Press of Mississippi is the scholarly publishing agency of
the Mississippi Institutions of Higher Learning: Alcorn State University,
Delta State University, Jackson State University, Mississippi State University,
Mississippi University for Women, Mississippi Valley State University,
University of Mississippi, and University of Southern Mississippi.

www.upress.state.ms.us

The University Press of Mississippi is a member
of the Association of University Presses.

Copyright © 2023 by University Press of Mississippi
All rights reserved

First printing 2023

∞

Library of Congress Cataloging-in-Publication Data

Names: Manizza Roszak, Suzanne, 1985– author.
Title: They also write for kids : cross-writing, activism, and children's
literature / Suzanne Manizza Roszak.
Other titles: Cultures of childhood.
Description: Jackson : University Press of Mississippi, 2023. | Series:
Cultures of childhood | Includes bibliographical references and index.
Identifiers: LCCN 2022039142 (print) | LCCN 2022039143 (ebook) | ISBN
9781496842916 (hardback) | ISBN 9781496842923 (trade paperback) | ISBN
9781496842930 (epub) | ISBN 9781496842947 (epub) | ISBN 9781496842954
(pdf) | ISBN 9781496842961 (pdf)
Subjects: LCSH: Children's literature—History and criticism. | Children's
literature—Authorship. | Children—Books and reading. | Children's
literature—Moral and ethical aspects.
Classification: LCC PN1009.5.M34 T54 2023 (print) | LCC PN1009.5.M34
(ebook) | DDC 813/.509352951—dc23
LC record available at https://lccn.loc.gov/2022039142
LC ebook record available at https://lccn.loc.gov/2022039143

British Library Cataloging-in-Publication Data available

CONTENTS

3   Introduction

17   **CHAPTER 1**
        Sophisticated Children: Reading "Child-Poems" with Hughes and Tagore

37   **CHAPTER 2**
        Subversive Adventures and Intrepid Kids: Cross-Written Activism in Baldwin, Puzo, and Achebe

65   **CHAPTER 3**
        Redefining Terms, Rethinking Concepts: Anticolonialism for All Ages from Erdrich to Santiago

93   **CHAPTER 4**
        Embracing Ambivalence: Cross-Reading the Children of Desai, Danticat, and Morrison

113   **CHAPTER 5**
        Kids Beyond Borders: Soto, Alvarez, and Cross-Cultural Cross-Writing

137   **CONCLUSION**
        Adaptations and Rewritings: Tan, Shange, and More

145   Acknowledgments

147   Notes

155   Bibliography

171   Index

THEY ALSO WRITE FOR KIDS

INTRODUCTION

When it was published in 2011, *The Cambridge Introduction to Toni Morrison* offered an expansive overview of Morrison's works, placing short stories like "Recitatif" and essays like "What the Black Woman Thinks about Women's Lib" alongside novels from *Beloved* to *Tar Baby*. A quick perusal of the book's index reveals the inclusion of these titles within a list of more than thirty texts by Morrison. The list, however, does not include children's books such as *Remember: The Journey to School Integration*, which had been published in 2004. Instead, in a different part of the index, a single item titled "books for children" stands in for the many works within this category that Morrison had already written on her own or in collaboration with her adult son, Slade Morrison. We learn that they appear in only three pages of the otherwise comprehensive and detailed introduction to Morrison's oeuvre, which features insightful, extended readings of novels including *Sula*, *Jazz*, and *Paradise*. While there has been other research focused on these children's books, it is typical for them to be omitted from or marginalized within broader studies of Morrison's writings. Often, outside the more specialized world of children's literature studies, children's books by authors of well-known texts "for adults" are forgotten or sidelined, or else they are left unmentioned because they are simply unfamiliar to readers. This can be as true in the classroom as it is in published scholarship; such books are not infrequently assigned as part of children's literature courses, but beyond those pedagogical contexts, they tend to be omitted from lectures and syllabi.

The absence of children's literature from broader academic conversations is an unsurprising and often unintentional byproduct of the notion that writing for children is not "real" literature or is not adequately serious for in-depth study. This exclusionary attitude has persisted despite the great many adults who are reading contemporary children's and young adult fiction for pleasure, with popular franchises like the *Harry Potter* and *Hunger Games* series drawing fresh attention to the "far from ... new phenomenon" of "child-to-adult crossover fiction" (Beckett, *Crossover Fiction* 85). Whether inside or outside academia, skeptical or uninitiated adults have not necessarily become any more likely to have cross-read or even heard of children's books that were themselves cross-written by authors such as Chinua Achebe, Anita Desai, Joy Harjo, or Amy Tan. Yet readers who do spend time with these texts will discover that they are complex, richly artistic, and unabashedly political, and that at their core, they and their supposedly adult counterparts operate in very similar ways. From Achebe's chapter book *Chike and the River* to picture books targeted to younger children, like Edwidge Danticat's *Mama's Nightingale*, they form part of a larger body of activist children's literature that has long challenged assumptions about the seriousness of writings "for children" and about who, in fact, should read them.

They Also Write for Kids grew out of my own encounters with colleagues and students who were familiar with these writers but who had no idea—and were often delighted to learn—that they had also written works of children's literature. I wanted to offer an easy means of locating these works and some ways of situating them within the context of their authors' other writings. At the same time, I was hoping to help change the minds of readers who might remain unconvinced of what children's literature can accomplish or about its intellectual, aesthetic, or political heft. I found that the project of reading an author's children's books side by side with their books "for adults" provided a generative opportunity to frustrate received notions of children's literature as intellectually or artistically unsophisticated in comparison with books that are assumed to be meant for older readers. Texts like N. Scott Momaday's *Circle of Wonder* and Esmeralda Santiago's *A Doll for Navidades* are rich in the same powerful ideas and intricate writing strategies that make activist children's literature in general so exciting to read, and because they come with a built-in set of "adult" companion texts with which they share these strategies and concerns, they make it easier to deconstruct and resist othering conceptions of the realm of children's literature as a world apart from these ostensibly grown-up works. This manner of thinking, in turn, opens a door to more fluid ways of understanding audience that are prevalent in children's literature studies but that still haven't quite taken hold outside the field, where the belief that children's books are not for adults has continued to limit the extent to which they are read, taught, and discussed, and where restrictive definitions of age-appropriateness have conversely led some to conclude that difficult and complex children's books must in reality be miscategorized adult texts. This book aims to demarginalize these compelling works for a broader audience and to consider how their authors' cross-writing encourages less binaristic, more nuanced ways of thinking about children's literature and its readerships.

The term "cross-writing" has often been invoked to describe texts that were or might have been "intended to speak to both young readers and adults reading over their shoulder" (Smith, "Cross-Written" 142), where authors who "address younger and older audiences with equal care and respect" (Flynn, "'Affirmative Acts'" 121) employ what U. C. Knoepflmacher and Mitzi Myers call "a dialogic mix of older and younger voices" to reach them (vii). For Sandra L. Beckett, in contrast, "Crosswriting refers to the phenomenon of writing for both child and adult audiences but in separate works" ("Crossover Picturebooks" 209). I use this term similarly to refer not just to individual texts with age-diverse audiences but to larger acts of cross-writing in which an author has produced a range of politically engaged works, some of which tend to be classified as "adult" and some of which tend to be identified as children's literature, but all of which make potent and aesthetically rich interventions in discourses surrounding social justice issues. In this way, *They Also Write for Kids* responds to another still-true observation made by Knoepflmacher and Myers in the introduction to their 1997 special issue of *Children's Literature* on "Cross-Writing Child and Adult": that there are a substantial number of "writers whose 'adult' works are much taught and reprinted, but whose work for the young has persistently been segregated" and pushed to the side by those primarily interested in their other writings (xv). The task of recentering "authors crossing over" (Beckett, *Crossover Fiction* 163) promises to assist in demonstrating "the limitations of audience age as a defining category" (Beckett, *Transcending Boundaries* xviii) that has shaped uninterested adults' expectations for what children's books are and what they can do. This approach also promises to disrupt the continuing "low status of children's literature when compared with adult literature" (van Lierop-DeBrauwer 4) or with texts that are received as being for adults, not only because "[d]ual-readership authors ... are responsible for the fact that authoritative adult literature critics now and then pay attention to children's literature" (9), but because of the obviousness with which their books, when examined side by side, contradict belittling visions of children's literature and its purported difference.

In following this strand of thought, I want to make a number of appeals to readers: that we place children's literature in conversation with works more typically understood as being for adults, and that we also read multiethnic US literature alongside books by global writers, consider children's poetry and nonfiction as well as fiction, and read diachronically as well as cross-culturally so that we can better appreciate the longer literary history of such cross-writing projects. None of these is an unprecedented interpretive mode, but several are themselves marginalized approaches. Children's literature outside the Anglo-American tradition tends to be understudied, as evidenced by the 2017 publication of *The Routledge Companion to International Children's Literature*, billed uncomfortably as "the first volume of its kind to focus on the undervisited regions of the world," with a "particular focus on Asia, Africa and Latin America." Nonfictional works remain in the shadows, with Sara C. VanderHaagen's recent study of biographies of African American women serving as a notable outlier. Ask someone with a specialty outside "kidlit" if they are aware that Rabindranath Tagore or Mario Puzo wrote children's books decades before more contemporary writers like Ntozake Shange and Gary Soto began doing so, and you'll likely find them to be surprised. In fact, not a single academic article about Puzo's *The Runaway Summer of Davie Shaw* has appeared in print since the narrative was first published in 1966.

The authors included in this book are unflinching in their activism, working in ways that counter the image of children's literature as more tepid or less aesthetically sophisticated in its political engagement. If "[r]ecently children's literature scholars, creators, and activists have . . . given more critical space" to "politically 'radical' or 'committed' texts with clear didactic dimensions," encouraging people to acknowledge the political in children's literature without assuming that it must be accompanied by "a lack of aesthetic merit or readerly pleasure" (Beauvais 60), their efforts have been vital precisely because such ideas continue to proliferate; even in 2019 it was considered news that "children's books are getting political" (Graves) and that they might actually be of high quality. In this reception context, writings ranging from Langston Hughes's *The Dream Keeper* to Harjo's *For a Girl Becoming* and Julia Alvarez's *Return to Sender* turn out to have quite a lot to say. Many spotlight the connections between the global specters of white racism and white supremacy; colonialism and its neocolonial afterlives; and histories of genocide, slavery, and segregation in the United States—they demand a transnational orientation while reinforcing Lucia Hodgson's assertion that "critical race theory is an essential component of a viable childhood studies methodology" (38). Some explore the specific roles of educational inequality, gentrification, or immigration policy in upholding institutional racism in the US or elsewhere. Others intersectionally resist depictions of girls and women of color that have been used by imperial forces to justify colonial governance. Still other books tackle environmental injustice, western-centric views of economic "development," nationalist and exceptionalist doctrines, and prejudice against multiracial and multilingual identities. This diverse array of concerns speaks to the "myriad ways" in which "children's literature and activist literacies are inextricably wed" (Graff 136). In fact, whether they were published in the previous century or in this one, these books exemplify the qualities that Julia L. Mickenberg and Philip Nel referred to in their 2011 article on "radical" early twenty-first-century children's literature:

> [C]hildren's literature, as well as being a tool of *embourgeoisement*, has been and continues to be an important vehicle for ideas that challenge the status quo and promote social justice.... We have looked for works that cast aside many of the traditional assumptions about what is appropriate for children, acknowledge pressing concerns of the day as relevant to children's lives, and refuse to whitewash difficult truths, but which also display literary and aesthetic quality and recognize the cognitive and emotional capacities of children. Such "radical" children's literature models and encourages activism by children as well as adults, and exposes unjust uses of power. It addresses the reality that the white, middle-class, all-American norm is a myth. (445)

While some have questioned the quality or suitability of children's books like James Baldwin's *Little Man, Little Man*, Mickenberg and Nel's account is a fitting description of all of these cross-written texts, which deploy such methods quite as skillfully as other children's books by writers who are not known for their work "for adults."

Varied writing strategies turn out to be essential to these efforts. Recognizing children as sophisticated in their intellectual and emotional depth, our cross-writing authors subversively repurpose expected tropes and conventions from canonical genres of children's literature such as the adventure story; invite readers to participate in redefining terms and concepts from "civilization" to colonialism and cultural belonging; embrace an epistemology of children's literature that emphasizes ambiguity and complexity; engage in intricate acts of cross-cultural representation; and reenvision their own earlier works in new forms tailored or marketed to younger readers, forms that nevertheless turn out to be very similar to their original versions. Each chapter of *They Also Write for Kids* focuses on one of these methods. With the exception of the last writing strategy, which is its own specific form of cross-writing, none of these techniques is unusual within the world of "radical" children's literature. There are lots of activist children's books by authors not known as writing for older readers that do these things. Yet we stand to gain something unique from scrutinizing these particular examples, especially in combination with the "adult" companion texts that also share in these strategies. If they are so reminiscent of and work so symbiotically with one another, might skeptics then need to rethink their assumptions about what children's literature is and who it is for?

For those who are already passionate about children's literature, it won't be news that children's books are capable of grappling so strategically, effectively, and boldly with a demanding and urgent array of concerns. In her new book *Twenty-First-Century Feminisms in Children's and Adolescent Literature*, Roberta Seelinger Trites explores intersectional feminist approaches to race, gender, religion, environmental justice, queerness, and disability in contemporary books like Jacqueline Woodson's *Brown Girl Dreaming* and Marissa Meyer's *Cinder*. Amina Chaudhri's *Multiracial Identity in Children's Literature* is fine-grained in its analysis of how children's books deconstruct the fallacy of the postracial society and examine the intricacies of racial passing for multiracial children. Kekla Magoon's *Camo Girl* and Margaret Chang's *Celia's Robot* form just two examples of the range of works covered in Chaudhri's study, which mainly centers on authors who haven't written well-known books "for adults"; Erdrich, for instance, is not represented there despite the *Birchbark* series's inclusion of characters who identify as biracial. While Chaudhri cites the skepticism of some of her own undergraduate and graduate students about the feasibility of locating "ideological perspectives" in children's literature (6), and this is a current of doubt that I, too, have encountered in the classroom, research like Trites's and Chaudhri's testifies to the conceptual depth that activist children's literature embraces as it pushes forward for justice.

Meanwhile, previous research on the cross-writing projects of the authors in this book has tended to center on individual writers. Katharine Capshaw Smith has written on Langston Hughes's and Edwidge Danticat's cross-writing, while Maya Socolovsky's and Tiffany Ana López's essays on Julia Alvarez are two additional examples focused on contemporary Latinx literature. Often, as in Trites's and Elizabeth Gargano's research on Louise Erdrich's *The Birchbark House*, the writer's literary production outside the realm of children's literature understandably fades into the background. *They Also Write for Kids* is different in that it looks at a large and multiply varied group of cross-writing authors while foregrounding both their children's books and those books' purportedly adult counterparts. Sometimes, this means scrutinizing how writers reframe their themes for child readers, as there are moments when extreme depictions of violence or emotional distress are made milder, when endings are made happier or more satisfying, or when protagonists are made more admirable, with secondary characters carrying more of the weight of a narrative's ethical ambiguity or complexity. Mostly, however, examining the two sets of texts side by side does demonstrate how little changes from one to the other. Putting them into conversation stresses the depth of sophistication expected of child readers and the seriousness with which their books ought to be taken.

Because the idea of a work of literature being for adults or for children is so problematic, when I use these phrases myself, I mean to indicate how the text was conceived by an author or publisher or how it is now typically classified, rather than commenting on how it should be understood or how it is actually consumed in a cross-reading world. Interest in troubling the readerly categories of adult and child has continued with the publication of books like Teresa Michals's 2016 volume *Books for Children, Books for Adults*, which examines how canonical texts like Defoe's *Robinson Crusoe* came to be received as adult literature. Beckett likewise reminds us that the "texts of even earlier authors, such as Charles Perrault, Jean de la Fontaine, Fénélon, John Bunyan, and Jonathan Swift, have traditionally had a dual audience of children and adults" (*Transcending Boundaries* xii). This problematizing impulse is important when we are working with Tagore's self-translated poetry collection *The Crescent Moon* or with Baldwin's *Little Man, Little Man*, whose legitimacy or appropriateness as works of children's literature critics have sometimes called into question based on more rigid conceptualizations of these categories of audience. Conversely, with novels like Morrison's assigned in so many US high schools that there is now a sample sentence in the Barron's AP English test preparation guide that reads, "She taught the novel *Beloved* to our ... class with enthusiasm" (Ehrenhaft 146), to claim that even the most difficult "adult" works included here should be understood as exclusively for people over the age of eighteen would be an oversimplification of the diverse ways in which books are treated in both educational and nonacademic contexts. Just as childhood "is not an essentially definable position but a cultural construct" (Honeyman 5) whose perceived meanings are shaped by "much variation on the basis of class, region, gender, and race" (Sánchez-Eppler xx) as well as by adults' externally imposed imaginings of youth in general, children's literature is far from an immutable category of literary production.

As we can see, questioning rigid conceptions of audience where children's literature is concerned involves not just reexamining what sorts of books might hold the interest of adults but reinterrogating stereotypical notions of appropriateness for children: expectations that have roots in Enlightenment-era cultural constructions of childhood as a "primitive" state that required "protective patronization," and which provided a blueprint for "imperial domination" itself (Honeyman 111). Resisting the belief that children's literature must meet certain criteria for lightheartedness or gentleness is also a way of paying tribute to the long tradition of protest-oriented children's literature by writers of color who have been necessarily frank with child readers. As Mickenberg and Nel remind us, "Neither children nor literature for them can be extricated from politics," since by "choice or by default, children often get drawn into the 'adult' worlds of politics, violence, and power struggles" (445). The literary history of the Harlem Renaissance, for instance, is steeped in the recognition of this idea, as writers like W. E. B. Du Bois argued that "the middle-class home [could not] be a place of protection from prejudice" but instead "should become a site of education about how to contend with it" (Smith, *Children's* 19), with children's literature playing a vital role. Contemporary children's books by multiethnic US and postcolonial Anglophone writers have embodied similar convictions in addressing injustices that children were already experiencing and continue to experience in their everyday lives. Finally, defining what is "suitable" for children as including controversial writings by Tagore or Baldwin subverts one of the foundational tenets of white supremacist thought by resisting false images of some (read: white) children's greater innocence and need for protection.

One additional benefit of assembling this range of cross-written texts is that it opens up the possibility of bringing writers and literatures together that are infrequently considered alongside one another but that have potent, illuminating connections. Books like Michelle Pagni Stewart and Yvonne Atkinson's edited collection *Ethnic Literary Traditions in American Children's Literature* are important because of their emphasis on diverse writers of color within the US literary landscape—including some writers, like Erdrich and Danticat, who also appear in this volume. *They Also Write for Kids* builds on that study by reaching across ethnonational borders in its broader vision and in individual chapters, too, where reading Hughes and Tagore or Momaday and Santiago in such close proximity illuminates shared cross-writing strategies as well as interrelated patterns and systems of injustice. It can be freeing and revealing to resist traditional ways of writing about multiethnic US literature or postcolonial Anglophone literature to the exclusion of one another, especially when we consider writers like Desai, whose children's books sometimes seem to be left unmentioned because her identity frustrates these acts of categorization. Desai was born in India but for decades has lived and worked in the United States, and her diasporic positionality seems to have consigned her writing to a liminal space between two categories, so that her middle-grade novel *The Village by the Sea* is treated as though it falls too far outside the scope of *Ethnic Literary Traditions* and the *Routledge Companion* alike. Treating *The Village by the Sea* as a fitting counterpart to Morrison's *Remember: The Journey to School Integration* reveals how an epistemology that centers ambiguity and ambivalence enriches both Desai's critique of post-independence economic "development" initiatives in India and Morrison's portrait of Black children's struggles for civil rights within the US public education system. At other times, bringing writers into dialogue with one another across these various barriers can helpfully illuminate difference within similarity, as when the Italian American Puzo and the Nigerian Achebe create narratives of childhood adventure, with Puzo satirizing a surreal, youthful world of white male privilege and Achebe bringing to life a portrait of

Black childhood that is both conscious of and invested in subverting various architectures of oppression.

Although *They Also Write for Kids* won't be able to offer a comprehensive history of every activist writer working in English whose literary production has included children's books as well as books "for adults," I do hope to highlight some of the most compelling and exciting examples of this boundary-crossing while thinking through their implications for perceptions of children's literature and its audiences. In many cases a writer could have fit into more than one chapter; Danticat's *Mama's Nightingale* could be read alongside Erdrich and Sandra Cisneros in chapter 3's discussion of bilingualism and linguistic conceptions of belonging, while Cisneros's own *Hairs/Pelitos* or Momaday's *Circle of Wonder* could take its place alongside Tan's *The Moon Lady* and Shange's *ellington was not a street* in our concluding exploration of adaptations of texts originally marketed to adults or older children. In these instances, I have located each book in the chapter where I feel it works best to illuminate the author's activist approach.

Chapter 1, "Sophisticated Children," draws together Tagore's short stories with poems that the author wrote in Bengali and then translated into English, examining them in conjunction with short stories and poems from Hughes's collections *The Dream Keeper* and *The Ways of White Folks*. Produced around the first few decades of the twentieth century, these texts do important antiracist and anticolonialist work, operating from an intersectional vantagepoint that accounts for accompanying issues of class and gender and that locates their common roots in globally interlinked systems of oppression. Tagore's and Hughes's cross-writing displays a shared construction of their child characters and readers as emotionally and intellectually sophisticated: as more than capable of confronting and disrupting these systems. The thematic and aesthetic echoes that reverberate across their writings speak to our need for more fluid and nuanced ways of understanding what children's literature is and who it is for. Working from these textual examples, this first chapter also gestures toward the transnational aims of this research.

Chapter 2 turns its attention to three postwar writers whose children's fiction is much less well-known than their other books. Titled "Subversive Adventures and Intrepid Kids," this chapter scrutinizes resistive narratives whose settings stretch from the midcentury United States to colonial and post-independence Nigeria, and which draw on and repurpose conventions from within the vast and historically problematic genre of the children's adventure story. Taking part in a contemporary movement that has used stories of children's adventurous confrontations with danger as a vehicle for protest, Baldwin, Puzo, and Achebe tackle subjects ranging from toxic masculinity to the overrepresentation of white identities in children's literature. Inconsistencies in the reception of Baldwin's, Puzo's, and Achebe's work for age-diverse audiences prove nonsensical in light of the very real, thought-provoking, and aesthetically complex interventions that their children's books make, as well as in light of the ways that their purportedly adult texts also center and privilege stories of adventurous childhood.

Chapter 3 is titled "Redefining Terms, Rethinking Concepts" and spotlights writings by a suite of Latinx and Indigenous authors whose work spans the 1960s to the present day. This chapter argues for a comparatist reading of these five writers that recognizes how their cross-writing has deconstructed and redefined the concepts of colonialism, "civilization," and cultural belonging, drawing on the familiar definitional work that young students are asked to do in the classroom but turning it on its head by making children into agents for rethinking, not just acquiring, definitional knowledge. Children's books by Cisneros, Erdrich, Harjo, Momaday, and Santiago expose the centrality of settler colonialism to US history while examining its relationship to gentrification, western models of environmental violence, and racist patterns of white flight. They also validate the hybrid cultures of resistance that have developed in response to these pathologies of whiteness, relying on the agency of independent, confident child protagonists who rework notions of identity and history from an actively anticolonial perspective. In the process, these books stand to engage us all, adults as well as children, with a constellation of vital questions.

Chapter 4, "Embracing Ambivalence," explores acts of cross-writing by Desai, Danticat, and Morrison. Across boundaries of expected audience, these writers' works tend to embrace ambiguity and the ambivalent feelings it inspires, representing experiences that are far from black-and-white and that call for an epistemologically sophisticated approach to understanding them. The narratives in this chapter unearth discomfiting complexities and contradictions that reside in histories of decolonization, immigration, and desegregation and their private and public aftermaths. Economic "development" in post-independence India seems inevitable yet disastrous for many involved; the US criminal justice system is by turns unethical and occasionally upright in its responses to undocumented immigration; and child protestors confronting white racists as well as white allies in desegregating US public schools must process intensely reasonable feelings of anger, resentment, and even hatred, without being held back by the warped logic of respectability politics. In offering up a framework for embracing these challenging topics, the books introduced in chapter 4 stand to further undermine popular conceptions of activist children's literature as blandly rather than richly and powerfully didactic.

Chapter 5 has a special interest in authors whose writing "for children" and "for adults" takes on issues of cross-cultural dialogue, exchange, and representation. Titled "Kids Beyond Borders," this chapter places Soto's poetry and fiction in conversation with Alvarez's fictional cross-writing, showing how they employ cross-cultural approaches that both reflect and move beyond their authors' transnational and otherwise multilayered identities. Read in the context of the #OwnVoices movement, this suite of texts presents a multifaceted activist project: they undermine mythologies of US nationalism and exceptionalism, critique the tendency of white people to reward white children's book authors for culturally appropriative and inaccurate depictions of nonwhite communities, exemplify the efforts of contemporary Latinx writers to engage in sophisticated cross-cultural modes of representation while acting as #OwnVoices creators, and continue to problematize notions of children's literature as unequipped to engage with these sorts of literary and sociopolitical nuances.

Readers will hopefully finish this book with a better familiarity with these authors' contributions to the world of children's literature and the literary methods that they employ. At the same time, it is worth repeating that the majority of these writing strategies are not exclusive to writers who work across audiences in this particular way. The childhood adventure story, for instance, is a genre shared across a diachronic, ethnonationally diverse body of children's literature. While the "generic label, adventure story, signifies a loose, catch-all category of children's literature," its defining features of "danger," "excitement," and "descriptions of tactical maneuvers" in settings fraught with risk (MacCann 97) have made it a primary site of imperialist mythologizing within "a heroic-quest narrative structure" (O'Sullivan 19). Like other politically-minded producers of "radical" children's adventure narratives, Baldwin, Puzo, and Achebe flip the script by using the adventure story toward anticolonialist and antiracist ends, rather than employing it as a tool for consolidating imperialist values as so many previous Euro-American authors did. In the world of children's novelists who are not necessarily known as writers for adults, key examples of these types of subversive adventure stories might include Cassie's often painful but exciting escapades in Mildred Taylor's series of novels about the Logan family, or Pam Muñoz Ryan's depiction of childhood migration and its dangers in *Esperanza Rising*, which since its publication in 2000 has become a staple of upper elementary education in California schools. Both of these books have been described—not only by adult critics but by child reviewers as well—as adventure stories with resistive political implications. Considering a writer like Baldwin or Achebe in this light helps to illuminate their membership in a broader collective of authors engaged in social protest through the writing of children's literature.

While giving credit where it is due, this line of thinking is also significant given the suspicion that acclaimed authors have sometimes attracted in beginning to write more explicitly for children. Although in some cases the task of actually publishing a children's book may have been easier for writers with the visibility granted to them by their popularity with adult consumers, this popularity has proven to be a double-edged sword, with detractors expressing doubt about the ability of authors like Baldwin to write "kidlit" and suggesting, with varying degrees of explicitness, that they ought to stick to composing stories for grown-ups. This was one of the primary objections when Baldwin's *Little Man, Little Man* was first published in 1976, and such skepticism might have permanently suppressed readers' knowledge and appreciation of the book were it not for Duke University Press's republication of the "story of childhood" in 2018. Today, representatives of the publishing industry tend to speak about this form of cross-writing in ways that gesture toward the persistent possibility of such reactions: "What an adult trade writer brings to the table is a built-in audience," one editor suggested, adding that it "doesn't do anybody any good, if we don't think the writer *is a good children's author*" (Seo qtd. in Rosen, my italics). If we wish to deconstruct and frustrate critiques like the ones that greeted the publication of *Little Man, Little Man*, it can be helpful to locate the strategic affinities between this group of cross-writing literary artists and their colleagues who may not appear to write "for adults," as these affinities help to signal that our cross-writing authors are savvier than skeptics expect them to be: that they, too, know what they are doing as they write with kids in mind.

Like other writers of activist children's literature, the authors in this book project an attitude of complete confidence in their younger readers and characters. Children are figured as sophisticated people: as intellectually and emotionally capable. They are envisioned as powerful in both their internal and their external lives, exhibiting "public forms of agency" and resilience (K. Alexander 122) as well as private, introspective forms of self-determination that stem from meaning-making confrontations with challenging worlds. They often reject social expectations for "emotion work" that dictate that children, especially girls and children of color interacting with white power structures, must "mask" their feelings and "act . . . cheerful" to please family members, teachers, or other vectors of adult authority (125). In addition to enacting their own creative and rigorous reasoning about social justice, they also express complex and understandably contradictory depths of feeling, capitalizing with equal conviction on the political potency of righteous anger, tolerance, and conscientiousness. With these modes of representation and address, our writers embrace ways of thinking about and responding to childhood, both as an ever-shifting set of lived conditions and as a cultural invention, that have long made "radical" children's literature far more interesting than some are willing to admit. By writing these attitudes into their works for age-diverse audiences and tempting readers to experience them side by side, they offer those who need it a chance to think differently about children's literature in general: about who it is for, where it belongs, and what we can see it accomplishing if we zoom in far enough, unencumbered by received ideas of what it means to write for adults or for kids.

CHAPTER 1

SOPHISTICATED CHILDREN
Reading "Child-Poems" with Hughes and Tagore

With the inaugural issue of the children's magazine *The Brownies' Book*, which appeared in January of 1920, editor W. E. B. Du Bois made plain his intention to provide African American children with a global framework for understanding experiences of oppression and resistance that echoed across national boundaries. Despite the magazine's stated "aim to be a thing of Joy and Beauty, dealing in Happiness, Laughter, and Emulation," Du Bois did not hesitate to acknowledge these sobering topics within the pages of the new periodical written "for all children, but especially for *ours*" (italics in the original). This emphasis became apparent in the magazine's monthly column "As the Crow Flies," which, in that first issue, provided readers "from Six to Sixteen" with a wide-ranging overview of current events in the wake of the Great War:

> There is unrest in Ireland because the Sinn Fein, (pronounced "Shin Fayn") representing most of the Irish, want Ireland to be an independent Republic.... Large numbers of Indians want to be an independent country and not a part of the British Empire. The English are seeking to suppress this desire by harsh laws and some concessions.... Egypt, the oldest civilized country in the world, inhabited by mulattoes, has been declared a Protectorate of England since the war. Egypt does not like this, and many riots have taken place. (24)

This final reference to Egypt speaks to an important goal of the magazine: to foreground the precolonial history and contemporary affairs of a transnational community of African-descended people who were continually marginalized in white, western-centric narratives. The topic of colonialism in India would also reappear in future issues, which would address developments like, in February of 1920, "[t]he brown people of India" having been "given a share in their own government by the English," as well as acts of revolutionary violence such as the ones reported on in the October 1921 issue, in which "[r]ioters in the Malabar districts . . . looted a treasury of $190,000, freed convicts, and murdered an auto bus crew" (63; 296).

This emphasis was natural given the parallels between the nationalist struggles taking place in India, the colonial history that had preceded them, and the US histories of slavery and segregation, as well as the larger system of white supremacist violence and oppression on which all of these histories had been built. Du Bois and other writers of the Harlem Renaissance were deeply conscious of the "continuum of subalternity and exploitation in which India's experience of colonialism marks one moment and the African American experience of slavery another" (Basu 238). At the same time, for Du Bois and his contemporaries, Indian society posed a substantial challenge to preconceived white notions of racial identity. As Andrea M. Slater has noted, "Blacks and Asian Indians . . . share complicated color-caste systems internally that are reflections of a dominant white culture rooted in the early 18th century that impacted wide-scale economic development and social mobility" (146–47). Together, they also constituted a global majority, unsettling ideas of white American and European culture as globally dominant. With all this in mind, Du Bois's journalism for children in *The Brownies' Book*, like his novel *Dark Princess* and his nonfiction writings in *The Crisis*, gestured toward the interconnected struggles of people of color from New York City to Agra.

This convergence of cultures poses a generative rationale for reading a writer like Du Bois's collaborator Langston Hughes in conversation with Rabindranath Tagore,[1] the prolific Bengali author and activist who, though he was born four decades before Hughes, wrote some of his most exciting works as Hughes was beginning to emerge on the US literary scene.[2] Tagore and Hughes were visionary writers of short stories and other prose that today tends to be viewed as writing for adults. As prolific poets, they also published collections of verse that were directed at child or mixed child-and-adult audiences and that took the experiences of children as their subject, drawing on shared constructions of sophisticated childhood that would resist the global reach of white supremacy. While we tend to be familiar with Hughes's children's poems from foundational studies like Katharine Capshaw Smith's, similar texts by Tagore have received sparse attention, with Supriya Goswami's essay in the *Routledge Companion to International Children's Literature* serving as one of the first to consider Tagore within this broader milieu. The omission is unsurprising given that much of the field has remained focused on "the well-worn path of Anglophone and European scholarship" and literary production ("Introduction" 1). The editors of the Routledge volume rightly suggest that "children's literature and its associated scholarships are, or ought to be, challenged by local knowledges" that frustrate universalist understandings of writing for kids based on western critical frameworks. Yet this crucial historical moment in the relationship between African American and Indian writers also created a shared "glocal" frame of reference (3) that is vital to Tagore's and Hughes's cross-writing, inviting us to examine them in tandem across both geographic and disciplinary boundaries—and, in the process, to resist the persistent marginalization of Tagore's "child-poems."

Within their transnational sociopolitical context, Tagore's poetry collection *The Crescent Moon* and Hughes's collection *The Dream Keeper* share an interest in antiracist and anticolonialist work that accounts for accompanying issues of class and gender. Within these intersectional interventions, the two collections foreground ethnic histories that run counter to western-centric narratives and make vital expressions of cultural pride. The aestheticized images of dreams and sleep, visions of natural beauty, and performative invocations of song and dance throughout both collections offer up these same politically charged ramifications. Tagore's collection takes a gentler approach at times, avoiding overt descriptions of state-sanctioned violence, for instance. Nevertheless, there are powerful correspondences across Tagore's and Hughes's writings for age-diverse audiences that challenge othering conceptions of children's literature. Tagore and Hughes infuse their children's poetry with the same subversively alternative ways of seeing culture, ethnicity, and power that are present in their other works, while posing alternative renderings of childhood itself that counter racist ideologies and oversimplifying views of children's identities more broadly. Their acts of cross-writing frustrate the purported boundary between the "primitive," instinctual child and the intellectual, evolved adult—a mythology with its own roots in imperialist thought (Rose 44).

Of Moons and Mothers: Tagore's "Child-Poems"

British constructions of childhood in India in the early twentieth century were inseparable from the colonial project, which used the figure of the imagined Indian child in attempts to rationalize the structures of imperial power. Much as questions of women's rights in India were distorted and manipulated by British imperialists who cast themselves in the role of savior of Indian women and girls, the putative gap between the ideal western childhood and the experience of this imagined Indian child became an insidious and faulty justification for empire, even as the colonial apparatus established a revealingly oppressive set of rules for Indian children. Sarada Balagopalan points out how subsets of Indian society were targeted by the imperial imagination and their children singled out in this manner. Children placed in juvenile reform schools, for instance, were cast as having "native parents" who were "ignorant, neglectful and criminal," creating a need for young people to be raised apart from families that "lacked the necessary skills to properly socialise them" (Balagopalan 31–32). In parts of India where agricultural workers had shown great interest in sending their children to school, this interest was "deliberately misread" as an artificial show of feeling intended "only to please government officials" (35). Balagopalan notes that within the colonial administration, "[s]chooling began to be discussed as that which these communities believed made their children 'unfit' for manual labor since it deprived them of 'the hardening effects of work in the fields at an early age'" (35). This forced reasoning provided the British with a logic for offering only an agriculturally focused curriculum in such communities—a curriculum that families turned out not to be interested in, as evidenced by their withdrawal of children from schools with this focus. It also reinforced an imperialist discourse that maligned Indian cultural traditions and their impact on children's future lives, while allowing colonial authorities to claim that they had been generous in compromising with these conveniently fabricated local values. In short, these mythologies became entrenched because they accorded with racist notions of western cultural superiority and legitimated the existence and daily operations of colonialism.

Tagore's own image of children and childhood is important because of how it undermines this imperial picture of the Indian child. Tagore was interested in childhood experiences of play and learning across social strata, a fact that we can see, for instance, in his interest in the nursery rhymes and folktales that he remembered being told during his own childhood, and which he would become among the first in Bengal to compile and publish.[3] Tagore's orientation toward childhood also seems to have been shaped considerably by his later educational experiences, including the sense of intellectual and social independence that led him to reject the colonial framework for education and drop out of formal schooling around the age of fifteen, when he began to be educated at home.[4] Tagore recalled having despised strategies like rote memorization, which he believed expressed contempt for children as independent people and which proliferated in colonial schools despite the lip service paid by high-ranking officials to the task of moving beyond such pedagogies. British authorities sometimes criticized the use of rote memorization in Indian colonial education because they feared that such strategies might not sufficiently "transform" Indian colonial subjects (Seth 32). Inversely, Tagore objected to how western educators used these techniques to inundate Indian pupils with foreign cultural artifacts, such as a "caricature of a song in English" that he remembered having had to memorize as a child (Bhattacharya 64).

For Tagore the adult writer, the necessity of countering this assimilationist paradigm seems to have made it vital to recognize children's independent abilities. As Ranjan Ghosh has suggested, "[c]haracter formation then for Tagore . . . owes as much to the child's independence and creativity as it does to the teacher" (409). Tagore's insistence on taking children seriously as thinkers and artists is visible not just in the child figures he depicts in *The Crescent Moon* but in its engagement with complex, serious concepts that he trusted child readers to be quite capable of absorbing. Like the twenty-first-century authors whom Mickenberg and Nel describe, Tagore "cast aside many of the traditional assumptions about what is appropriate for children," producing a work of "literary and aesthetic quality" with strong political investments that he specifically hoped children would read. In this way, Tagore's writings invalidate the constructions of Indian childhood that typified the colonial education system and on which the colonizer ideologically relied. Tagore's depictions of childhood also disrupt the false imperialist narrative of Indian family life, especially outside the upper castes, as exploitative of women and children and thus as a rationale for the imposition of colonial governance. Finally, they ask suspicious adults to reenvision what children's poetry can accomplish, who it is for, and what it means for a book of poems to be suitable for or tailored to kids, as these are not poems whose "subject matter" has stereotypically obvious "child-appeal" or any "lack of appeal for adults" (Pullinger 5).

The Crescent Moon contrasts the wisdom of Tagore's child characters with the shortsightedness of adulthood and, in doing so, makes an intricate, resistive response to British imperial ideology. In many poems, the collection yokes childhood with a class consciousness that rejects received notions of adult accomplishment through materialism. Tagore's textual children are wise in their detachment from class elitism and their refusal of the fetishistic view of objects that rules so much of the adult world within Tagore's verse. Wistfully self-effacing, the adult speaker in the poem "Playthings" contrasts how they "seek out costly playthings, and gather lumps of gold and silver" with how a child sits "happy . . . in the dust, playing with a broken twig all the morning" (23). The ruefulness in the speaker's lament signals that the child is indeed the wiser of the two: "With whatever you find you create your glad games," the adult reflects, adding, "I spent both my time and my strength over things I can never obtain" (23). With the singsong, stereotypically childish quality of the speaker's rhyming words, Tagore underscores this act of inversion. The adult, despite or even because of his apparent worldliness, has been so seduced by objects that he cannot act on what he already knows: that his quest for material satisfaction is futile.⁵ We might think here of Alison Lurie, who describes how the "great subversive works of children's literature suggest that there are other views of human life besides those of the shopping mall and the corporation" (xi), though Tagore's perspective predates the advent of the shopping mall as the "ultimate architecture of late capital ... designed to serve India's growing consumer classes" (Athique and Hill 73).

In her study of other Tagore poems with similar themes, Josephine A. McQuail suggests that Tagore's view of childhood stemmed from his admiration of the British Romantic poets, with their emphasis on what they envisioned as children's relative purity and innocence. While this interpretation casts Tagore as an imitator more than a critic of British culture, I read these poems as making a different intervention in the cultural dialogue between the metropole and the colonial space. In a sense, "Playthings" calls into question the very notions on which British imperialism in India was based, with its both literal and figurative investment in profiting from the natural and human resources of the colonized. By privileging the child's antimaterialist stance over the adult's fetishization of meaningless, often unattainable objects, not only does Tagore's poem cast children as intellectually independent in a way that would have challenged colonialist efforts to uphold the structures of empire through assimilationist forms of education, but Tagore also undercuts the larger system of values on which the colonial project was predicated. Tagore's verse thus paints a very different picture from the classic "rags-to-riches" narratives of the metropole: children's books like Frances Hodgson Burnett's *A Little Princess*, whose backstory is set in India and which sees the title character united with a rich benefactor who restores her rightful inheritance by the novel's conclusion.⁶ Whereas *A Little Princess* paradoxically suggests that the reward for antimaterialism should be a great fortune, Tagore casts the absence of material excess not as a temporary state to be surmounted but as a philosophy of living that comes easily to children in their wisdom. In the process, "Playthings" invites both children and adults to resist interlacing structures of valuation, domination, and oppression.

Other poems undermine the metropole from additional angles, working with a subversive subtlety that would have been fitting given the translated collection's range of potential English-speaking readerships. There might have been little chance of the book proliferating among a British audience, for instance, if Tagore's anticolonialism had been more legible to "adults reading over" young shoulders. Instead, like the body of Cold War-era US children's literature in which "popular books by radicals [were] decidedly *not* revolutionary" in the most obvious or expected respects (Mickenberg 17), Tagore's poems seem to have been cross-written to address a cross-cultural mix of adults and capable, savvy children, operating with oblique sophistication. Take the speaker in

"The Unheeded Pageant," who revels in sensory imagery that sets the poem apart from the "civilizing" impulse of the colonizer: "She claps her hands and her bracelets jingle, and you dance with your bamboo stick in your hand . . . / The wind carries away in glee the tinkling of your anklet bells" (9–10). These aesthetic references are casual and fleeting. Yet like Tagore's original decision to write these poems in Bengali, a gesture of cultural pride that disrupted the false narrative of British superiority and resisted the demand for assimilation, Tagore's refusal to mark the woman's body as properly Anglicized resists Eurocentric ideas about what is proper and who is worthy of literary attention.

Something similar happens in "The Champa Flower," whose child speaker recalls how "after the midday meal you sat at the window reading *Ramayana*," and in "The Sailor," where the child proclaims that he is "not going into the forest like Ramachandra to come back only after fourteen years" (30, 40). Valmiki's *Ramayana*, the most famous version of a story that remains widely read, adapted, and performed in contemporary India, has such enduring standing as a work of classical Indian literature for both children and adults that this metatextual reference takes on a special significance.[7] As Makarand R. Paranjape notes, by this time, the eighteenth-century British interest in "classical Indian studies" had given way to attitudes like those enshrined in Thomas Babington Macaulay's 1835 "Minute on Indian Education" (107). The latter, of course, had asserted that "a single shelf of a good European library was worth the whole native literature of India and Arabia" (70). In this context, Tagore's method has a palpable, provocative urgency. Through its repeated classical references, Tagore challenges the colonialist tendency to erase precolonial literary and cultural history, inviting recognition of twentieth-century India's classical inheritances.

Tagore's poems use references to nature in a similar fashion, reveling in untranslated and in some cases untranslatable vocabulary with more global implications. In "The Champa Flower" and "Sleep-Stealer," the "shadow of the *champa* tree" and "the shadow of the *banyan* tree" may not always be decipherable for English speakers (29, 12). What should be universally legible, however, is the image that the poems generate of a culturally independent India with its own languages as well as its own ecosystems. Even while writing—or at least translating—for a potential audience that would have included foreign children, Tagore makes no effort to define these words. There is no glossary, there are no footnotes that expand on them, and there is no descriptive language in the main text that explains what a champa flower or a banyan tree looks like. In withholding this information, Tagore literally requires readers to meet each poem on its own terms, unsettling the assumption that white, English-speaking people who are unfamiliar with this vocabulary should be prioritized by default in the composition of literary art. Tagore trusts young people with these positionalities to take an interest in a reality that is marked as lying outside their own world, even if some elements of that world prove difficult to parse. He suggests that he expects much better from a new generation of children who, through acts of intellectual discovery, might do better than their parents at resisting discourses of cultural supremacy and their political effects, and who might even accept the responsibility of educating themselves rather than expecting writers of color to coddle them or cater to their existing frame of reference. Meanwhile, for both Indian and Anglo-American readers, the poet's words reverse the power dynamic in which colonial children were expected to embrace highly localized works of literature from the metropole with more interest than literature set in their own communities.[8] In upending this typical relationship between the colonizer and the colonized, Tagore sends a powerful anticolonialist message and asserts that these types of big intellectual ambitions are the province of children's poetry.

Images of mothers also proliferate throughout these "child-poems." "My Song" invokes a mother's wishes for her own child: "My song will be like a pair of wings to your dreams, it will transport your heart to the verge of the unknown. / It will be like the faithful star overhead when dark night is over your road. / My song will sit in the pupils of your eyes" (78). Motherhood here is tenderly performative, artistic, and celestial as the speaker explores the nighttime natural world alongside the familiar role of song in lulling a child to sleep. What is most remarkable is the way that this cross-culturally recognizable tradition of mothering contradicts propagandistic renderings of Indian girlhood and womanhood that were used to justify British colonial rule. As Mrinalini Sinha notes, the "practices found among particular groups and in particular regions of India," such as *sati*, female infanticide, and child marriage, "were treated as emblematic of all India and of Indian culture as a whole . . . a basis not only for the ideological justification of the 'civilizing mission' of British imperialism in India but also for arguments about the 'barbarity' of Indian culture" (29). Against this backdrop, the ever-present figure of the mother in *The Crescent Moon* does more than evoke a "universalized female presence" (Ritter 235) or even testify to Tagore's grief at the premature loss of his own mother.[9] "My Song" rewrites the British mythology of Indian girls' and women's lives to include a very different perspective on motherhood and the loving bonds between Indian women and children. Other poems, such as "Superior," accomplish similar things while specifically referencing girls. Even when motherhood ends in sadness, as in a series of poems that hint at the death of a beloved child, it persists in countering these racist stereotypes. Tagore's portrayals are consistent with his stated interest in what he referred to as "the rhymes that women in Bengal use to amuse children," his interest in and respect for Bengali "women's work," and his awareness of the importance of capturing this work in writing (qtd. in McQuail 493).

It seems clear that those who believe that children's literature is just now "getting political" have not been reading Tagore. As I have suggested throughout this discussion, Tagore's manner of thinking about childhood is politically significant because, unlike British imperialists in their imaginings of Indian children, Tagore viewed *all* children as independent, creative, and intellectual beings, resisting the assumptions on which the colonial apparatus was based. *The Crescent Moon* exemplifies this attitude by engaging child readers in serious ways about complex subjects and by highlighting children's wisdom. Another place where these views of Tagore's are reflected is in his earlier stories, which tend to be received as being for adults although as always, such assumptions about potential audiences are reductive. The short stories share the activist emphasis of Tagore's verse while depicting childhood in fundamentally progressive ways. Revisiting them becomes a way of rendering doubly visible the thematic and formal strategies of Tagore's cross-writing. Telegraphing complete confidence in his younger readers, Tagore proves to have been willing to transmute ideas from his stories to *The Crescent Moon* with few modifications, save a more oblique approach to physical and emotional violence that is described in somewhat graphic detail in his early short prose.[10] These close resemblances become a testament to Tagore's distinctive vision of childhood and its challenge to infantilizing colonialist practices pushed on children. They also force a confrontation with stereotypical conceptions of children's literature, including children's poetry, as comparatively lacking in intellectual nuance, aesthetic richness, or activist power, making it difficult to maintain these distinctions.

First there is "The Postmaster," a meditation not just on love and loss but on the intersections of class, gender, colonialism, and childhood. "The Postmaster" begins with a sardonic description of the British colonial administration, which has "with much effort established a new post office" in a rural village without considering practical matters such as how the new postmaster will support himself—his salary is "meager"—or what he will do with his time—he has "very little work," presumably because there was little need for a post office in the first place (42). The post office quickly becomes a symbol of the dysfunction of colonial governance, whose resounding, self-centered egotism is paired with a stubborn lack of local knowledge. Anticipating so many of the poems in *The Crescent Moon*, this opening passage counters the logic of British cultural superiority and thus of British rule.

As the narrative progresses, a child character becomes central to it. Most striking is how the postmaster's teenage servant Ratan, who is emotionally invested in her relationship with the postmaster, refuses to allow him to pay her when he leaves the village: "I beg you, Dadababu, I beg you—don't give me any money," she protests (46). While Ratan's words can be read as a function of her teenage love for the postmaster, whose family she has started referring to "as if they were her own" (43), they also say something about the persisting value of human relationships in a world seeking to resist and reject the colonizer's materialism. Like the child in "Playthings," Ratan is much wiser than the "educated" young postmaster from Kolkata, who allows the imperial value system to pervade his consciousness in prioritizing the city's "rows of tall buildings" over human connection and in stifling the "sharp desire" he feels to return for her (46, 42). Declining to sanitize the postmaster's betrayal through an exchange of money for services, Ratan effects a larger act of resistance to the materialist, imperialist values that his actions represent, and the story begins to challenge British constructions of unthinking, inferior Indian children.

Gender widens the gulf between Ratan and the postmaster, intensifying Ratan's economic insecurity: "It seemed unlikely that she would get married," Tagore's narrator muses (42). Like *The Crescent Moon*, then, "The Postmaster" takes up the question of women's position in colonial India, this time revealing how issues in Indian girls' and women's lives are created and intensified by the colonial machine and its overvaluation of "civilized" urban spaces—which Tagore personally resisted, as he "disliked" the city (Radice 6). Parallel themes arise in another short story, "Punishment," in which a woman named Chandara is executed for a crime she did not commit after her husband asks her to lie to save his brother from execution. As Supriya Chaudhuri argues, stories like "Punishment" scrutinize the domestic sphere and how its individual subjectivities are "marked by the contradictions and imbalances of the colonial encounter" (57). The apparatus of colonial justice, which includes a flock of police officers and "barristers" (Tagore, "Punishment" 133), is rendered incompetent when Chandara designs her false confession to ensure her execution. Chandara's determination to die rather than live with a disloyal husband reveals the fundamental ethical fissures of the system. While *The Crescent Moon* never depicts such violent ends, the poems are equally effective in subverting the British imperial narrative of gender in colonial India, and revisiting the short stories becomes a way toward reconsidering and more deeply appreciating this activist work.

Non-western cultural references deepen the links between Tagore's writings. The narrator of "Punishment" recalls how Chandara "kept going to the ghāt" but leaves that term unexplained (130). The narrator of "The Postmaster" remarks that "if a genie out of an Arab tale had come and cut down all the leafy trees overnight," the "half-dead, well-bred" young postmaster would have finally enjoyed his life in the rural village (42). These terms and references serve as reminders, just as in *The Crescent Moon*, that the English language need not be the center of the global literary universe and that British writers have never had a monopoly on the creation of literary art. "The Postmaster" and "Punishment" anticipate the decolonizing strategies of poems like "The Champa Flower" and "Sleep Stealer" and suggest that Tagore expected his various audiences, regardless of age, to cope with terms and concepts that may have been unfamiliar depending on their cultural identities.

Six years after *The Crescent Moon* was published, Tagore wrote to the Governor General of India to renounce the knighthood that he had been awarded by the British government. A group of unarmed Indian protestors had been shot and killed in what became known as the Jallianwala Bagh massacre, with unofficial estimates much higher than the official death toll of 379 recorded by the British. Scholars have characterized Tagore's relationship to Indian nationalism as "ambivalent," colored by an early enthusiasm for English culture that belied his feelings about his colonial education as well as influenced by his concern that, in its quest for independence, India would adopt the European model of nationalism (Tuteja and Chakraborty 2). Yet Tagore was vocal in calling out injustice even as he developed an internationalist perspective that voices such as Gandhi and Nehru would acknowledge as unique.[11] In his children's poetry, Tagore displays an expansive decolonial consciousness, attacking imperial ideas of class and gender while centering and celebrating Indian histories and identities. The poems engage in serious ways with antimaterialism, invoke discourses of cultural history and pride, and resistively represent the bonds between mothers and children, thus making an intricate critique of colonial architectures. Stories like "Punishment" may present these ideas through a more disillusioned and graphically violent lens than the one that comes to life in *The Crescent Moon*. Still, rereading the poems together with Tagore's earlier prose highlights his perception of Indian children as sophisticated and independent intellectuals—a group of people who, where issues of social justice were concerned, could be addressed in much the same way as adults. Given the importance of British imperialist imaginings of Indian childhood to upholding colonial systems, these interventions of Tagore's constitute a subtle but essential form of revolution. They also assert without question that adults should take Tagore's verse seriously—and that this can be true without it making the poems unsuitable for children.

Playing the Blues: Hughes's *The Dream Keeper*

Critics have debated what readership Tagore actually intended for *The Crescent Moon*. For McQuail, "the poems are more obviously aimed at adults" (492), yet

Purnima Mehta reminds us that many of these works had initially been written in Bengali for Tagore's young children to read after their mother's death. This discord speaks to the persistent anxiety surrounding children's interpretive capabilities and the desire to construct clear boundaries between adult and child audiences—even when authors themselves write across these demarcations, producing work that anticipates "a diverse, cross-generational audience that can include readers of all ages" (Beckett, "Crossover Picturebooks" 209). Tagore shared this apparent boundary-crossing with Langston Hughes, whose 1932 poetry collection *The Dream Keeper* had its origins partly in librarian Effie Lee Power's request that Hughes collect and republish those of his poems "that were suitable for children" (Tracy 171). For *The Dream Keeper*, Hughes took verse that often had not been labeled as being for young people—including many of his most iconic 1920s writings—and redefined it as children's poetry. In assembling the collection, he either reproduced the poems without alteration or, in some cases, even intensified their political message. These poems showcase the affinities between Hughes's and Tagore's cross-writing activities and the links between their often similar perceptions of childhood, its localized cultural contexts, and the "glocal" backdrop furnished by white supremacy. Analyzing them in tandem means rethinking disciplinary boundaries based on geographic borders as well as reconsidering age-bound conceptions of children's literature and the people who read it.

As before, attention to systems of beliefs about children's identities is warranted here. Robin Bernstein has noted how the character of Topsy in Stowe's *Uncle Tom's Cabin*

> became the prototype for the pickaninny, an imagined dehumanized black juvenile and a staple of U.S. popular culture from advertising images (such as the Gold Dust Twins) to children's literature, animation, and film (such as *Little Black Sambo*, Bosko, or the Little Rascals, respectively).... The dehumanized pickaninny, contrasted with an angelic white child, argued in a polygenetic vein for irreconcilable differences between black and white youth. (16)

This racist legacy would persist into and beyond the twentieth century, accompanied by a general current of white supremacist thinking that has shaped areas of African American childhood ranging from funding for public education to the treatment of Black children within the criminal justice system. The dehumanization of Black childhood was necessary to a system of institutional racism that relied on white apathy about or even approval of these policies. Meanwhile, the "angelic white child" was conceived of as vulnerable to the threat of Blackness in a vision of childhood that both stemmed from and was used to justify the vilification of Black identities. What is critical to recognize is the transnational correspondences between white supremacist imaginings of African American and Indian children, which Bernstein invokes in mentioning *Little Black Sambo*. This apt reference illuminates the interconnectedness of white racist ideas of African American and Indian culture as they are embodied in the figure of the racialized and othered child; as Hughes himself noted, while it is set in India, *Little Black Sambo* draws on the pickaninny stereotype in ways that vivify the global reach of white racism.[12]

The hyperracialized insistence with which white people in the United States denied Black children's membership in "the category of childhood" created an urgent need for writers like Du Bois, Hughes, and others to construct an entirely different understanding of African American children's identities (16). At the start of her 2004 book, Smith quotes an argument that Du Bois made in *The Crisis* in 1912, proclaiming "Your child is wiser than you think" (1). While asserting the actual childhood of Black youth in contravention to white racist mythmaking, this generation of writers celebrated Black children's brilliance, emotional depth, and sense of ethics. True to this distinctive view of childhood identities, Hughes would submit some of his first poems to *The Brownies' Book*.[13] Hughes was also "sensitive to the formidable presence of white children" among his readers, for whom he hoped to counter racial stereotypes of people of color both internationally and in the US without erasing cultural difference (233). Importantly, Hughes thus resisted the fallacy of the "angelic white child," resting tangible responsibility for the task of deconstructing racist systems at the feet of white children. *The Dream Keeper* would exemplify the aesthetic potentiality of children's verse in the hands of readers perceived in a manner that will already be familiar to us from Tagore.

The first poem in *The Dream Keeper*, which is also the title poem, introduces a duality that will reverberate throughout the entire collection. The poem is fundamentally about hope—about the need to dream and for dreams, especially those of children, to be protected. Yet the poem acknowledges the external threats to hoping and dreaming posed by a racist United States: "Bring me all of your / Heart melodies / That I may wrap them / . . . Away from the too-rough fingers / Of the world" (Hughes, "Dream" 2). What Smith calls a "seed of fear" emerges in these final lines, foreshadowing the poems in the collection that more overtly dissect this "roughness" ("Cross-Written" 133). The poem casts childhood as something that ought to be cherished and protected, to be "wrapped" away from danger—and yet, in acknowledging that danger, Hughes signals his eagerness to be candid with child audiences and his belief in their ability to cope with what he has to say. The rest of the collection will move between these poles of hopeful idealism and frank acknowledgement, recognizing that for social change to occur, it is not enough for literature to reenvision the world: abuses must be catalogued and denounced. Hughes's poems selected for children testify to injustice even as they anticipate its long-awaited eradication, projecting a vision of capable, sophisticated childhood.

We can see this in the famous "I, Too," where before proclaiming how "[t]omorrow, / I'll sit at the table / When company comes," Hughes's speaker reports on the existence of a very different state of current affairs: what Keith Clark calls "the unrecognized native son" being "relegated to the 'kitchen' of America's racial house" (63; 8). The speaker matter-of-factly announces, "I am the darker brother. / They send me to eat in the kitchen" (Hughes, "I, Too" 63). The structure of the piece privileges hope, confining this plain statement of the status quo to a single early half-stanza. It is the last few prophetic lines of the poem that echo in our minds: "Besides, / They'll see how beautiful I am / And be ashamed—/ I, too, am America" (63). Still, those earlier lines evoke a host of sobering associations, from the intersectional oppression of Black domestic workers to the broader mechanisms of segregation that the poem more figuratively recalls in emphasizing the domestic image of the "kitchen." The poem draws attention to the dynamics of class as well as race, casting a critical eye on wealthy white families and their role in preserving racist superstructures as they sit in their grand houses receiving "company." Finally, it is worth noting that Hughes's speaker can be read as a Black child or adolescent who is "eat[ing] well, / And grow[ing] strong" (63). Hughes's words make the intertwined realities of white racism and class inequality legible for Black and white children alike while affirming Black childhood as a capable position of power. Although this poem has been widely interpreted, part of what is exciting here is the way that Hughes's investment in unpacking issues of class echoes similar rhetorical moves by Tagore in poems like "Playthings," where anticolonialism and antimaterialism are linked and where, again, child figures are depicted as commanding respect from the adults around them. Faced with how racialized ideas of US childhood both reflect and are deployed to prop up racist ideology, Hughes and his speaker refuse to accept these constructions of childhood or their weaponization against Black communities. In this act of resistance, "I, Too" makes its own intervention in questions of children's literature and its capacities.

For a writer with Hughes's international vantage-point, this conversation would be incomplete without some link to a transnational African past. And indeed, a striking number of poems in the collection reference this history shared across the diaspora. In "African Dance," the speaker describes how the "low beating of the tom-toms, / The slow beating of the tom-toms, / . . . Stirs your blood" (72). The repeated percussive echo evokes the diaspora's musical heritage and its affective power, illustrating Hughes's interest in challenging cultural myths and inequalities—such as the unearned emphasis on western music history and heritage over non-western musical forms in Eurocentric societies—while rejecting "color-blind" strategies for seeking racial parity (Smith, *Children's* 234). Hughes's poem has a clear kinship with poems from *The Crescent Moon* like "The Unheeded Pageant," which uses aural imagery and performative references to sound (the "bracelets [that] jingle" and the "anklet bells") to rewrite western-centric accounts of artistic production that were equally implicated in British colonialism and in the racial inequities of the postbellum United States.

"The Negro Speaks of Rivers," which was published in *The Crisis* before its inclusion in *The Dream Keeper*, invokes the Congo, the Nile, and "the pyramids above it" with similar results (62).[14] In this associative succession of images, which unites locations throughout the African continent, Hughes's speaker recognizes, valorizes, and celebrates the millennia-long reach of African civilizations (62). For someone who might not otherwise connect Egypt or the Congo with "the singing of the Mississippi," the poem sends a strong message that the history of Black America is deep and irrepressible and that it reaches beyond borders to encompass these geographic and temporal spaces (62). At the same time, in referencing the specter of "the Euphrates when dawns were young," Hughes claims a fuller transnationalism and an even more profound transhistorical identity for the diaspora (62). Rejecting the severance of Black Americans' genealogical connections to a precolonial African and global past by the Middle Passage and American slavery, the poem asserts that these connections and this legacy are unbreakable. As in Tagore's "The Champa Flower" and "Sleep-Stealer," referencing the topography of these localized natural settings becomes a means of upending received notions of western cultural dominance and recovering histories obscured by racist and imperialist ideology and violence, while trusting in the ability of sophisticated child readers to unpack these diverse references in a cross-written text with historically shifting and multilayered readerships.

It is unsurprising that Hughes's poetry selected for *The Dream Keeper* would sometimes proclaim intense racial pride through descriptions of physical beauty, as in "My People." There, Hughes's speaker affirms, "The night is beautiful, / So the faces of my people. // . . . Beautiful, also, are the souls of my people" (60), creating through repetition "a paean of praise to the beauty of blackness" and countering racist Eurocentric ideals (Berry 30). In the context of this chapter, what I find most exciting is how the poem's approach recalls the aestheticized, admiring images of Tagore's "The Unheeded Pageant." While it is the woman and child's choices of clothing and their quotidian acts of performance that enthrall Tagore's speaker, and while they are described using more specific images than "My People" employs, the two poems share an investment in dismantling systems of racial and colonial oppression through literary depictions of "unheeded" beauty that rewrite aesthetic codes. As artistically rendered as they are politically powerful, with flourishes that reflect Hughes's distinctive "modernist vision" (Komunyakaa 50), poems like "My People" work together with ones like "The Unheeded Pageant" to frustrate the expectation that "appropriate" children's poetry will lack aesthetic nuance and conviction, being "simplistic in form and content" rather than having "depth and craft" (Apol and Certo 283).

Hughes's explorations of motherhood serve a similar function: they reaffirm the rights and identities of Black mothers and children in a sociopolitical environment that has continued to threaten and invalidate them. One poem, "Lullaby," calls up a mother's voice as she addresses her "little dark baby," referring to him tenderly as "little black baby" and "night black baby." Echoing the mother in Tagore's "My Song," Hughes's mother-speaker offers her baby a lullaby composed of "Stars, stars, / Moon, / Night stars, / Moon" (50). The song has a gentleness that is punctuated by a final triumphal exclamation: "For your sleep-song lullaby!" (50).[15] There is a tone of forceful pride in the mother's voice as she claims her right to create her own tender music for her "dark body's baby" (50). "Mother to Son" sounds a different note as the speaker exhorts her child not to "set down on the steps / 'Cause you finds it kinder hard" (64). This "blues poem" is a testament to struggle more than a quiet ode to gentleness, yet its insistent vernacular also proclaims the importance and the resilience of this bond between mother and child, negating dehumanizing white stereotypes of Black childhood and motherhood just as Tagore undoes imperialist mythologies in his "mother-and-child" poems (See 810). For both Tagore and Hughes, then, mother-child relationships within children's poetry become a site of resistance that invites expressions of ethnic pride inflected with an intersectional grasp of the need to acknowledge gender—and reconceptualize childhood—in doing antiracist and anticolonialist work.

Where Hughes departs from Tagore is in the frankness with which *The Dream Keeper* records human rights violations by white people at home and abroad. Terrifying acts of white violence emerge in "The Negro," which laments, "I've been a victim: / The Belgians cut off my hands in the Congo. / They lynch me now in Texas" (59). A decade before it was included in *The Dream Keeper*, "The Negro" had appeared in *The Crisis* with this exact same diction. In comparing patterns of racist violence across national borders, the poem challenges the fallacy of US exceptionalism through a transatlantic gesture of witnessing. The poem also talks to children via a single first-person speaker who tells of having experienced both acts of violence and who lays claim to both of these personas. The poem thus gestures toward a transnational network of Black identities that is at once multifaceted and unified; it does in verse what *The Brownies' Book* did in prose in covering news from African and African diasporic communities outside the US. "The Negro" brings to light the horrific consequences of white supremacy for child readers while pointing out the power that lies in the diaspora as the speaker claims "the depths of [his] Africa" for his own. Following the poem when it was published in *The Crisis* was a short, hopeful article about the progress of the Dyer Anti-Lynching Bill, which would be passed by the House of Representatives but filibustered by Southern Democrats in the Senate. The interplay between the poem's reference to lynching and this surrounding material echoes the push and pull of hopefulness and testimony throughout Hughes's collection.

Instances like this one illustrate *The Dream Keeper*'s commitment to the concept of childhood "wisdom" espoused by Du Bois and others while helping to situate Hughes's writing within a much larger tradition of activist children's literature determined to "tak[e] children seriously as political actors in their environment" (Hayward 3). The fluidity with which Hughes moved this material between publication venues speaks volumes about his image of childhood and of children's abilities—their intellectual and emotional depth as well as their ethical capacities. As before, Hughes's work also presents us with a unique opportunity because it invites us to bring children's poetry into direct conversation with texts that are purportedly for adults. Stories like "The Blues I'm Playing," published two years after *The Dream Keeper* and included in *The Ways of White Folks*, share affinities with Hughes's children's poetry that speak to the maturity of the latter's themes. Like Tagore's "The Postmaster" and "Punishment," Hughes's stories feature adult content as traditionally conceived—including, in this case, some frank discussions of sexuality that are absent from *The Dream Keeper*. At the same time, the stories echo the poems in ways that reemphasize the poems' sophisticated construction of childhood and its activist ramifications. Sometimes, they even back away from the types of violent, arresting content that the poems include, bringing into relief the bold frankness of *The Dream Keeper* and Hughes's confidence in children's emotional resilience.

"The Blues I'm Playing" centers on Oceola Jones, a brilliant musician whose connectedness to the African diaspora is merely tolerated by her white patroness Mrs. Ellsworth. These connections manifest in Oceola's commitment to "the soft and lazy syncopation of a Negro blues" that she proclaims "is [hers]," as well as jazz and "her own variations on the spirituals," all of which tie Oceola to a collective, transnational project of resistance (Hughes, "Blues" 122, 118). The linkages increase in visibility when Oceola goes to Paris, where she entertains Black artists and intellectuals with blues songs and makes "the bass notes throb like tom-toms" as "the black colonials dance . . . the beguine," a dance with Franco-African roots (113).[16] Like "The Negro Speaks of Rivers" and "African Dance," "The Blues I'm Playing" brings this transnational diasporic community to life and celebrates its power, although the story does acknowledge its potential limitations. In his letters to Claude McKay, Hughes lampooned the "returned natives" who had come back to the United States from France, commenting that "at least ten million colored schoolteachers have been, seen Paris, and returned" (*Selected Letters* 98). Oceola feels similarly suspicious of the people she encounters abroad, with their "interminable arguments ranging from Garvey to Picasso to Spengler to Jean Cocteau" ("Blues" 112). This cynical nuance of Hughes's transnationalist vision is less visible in *The Dream Keeper*. Yet both Oceola's preferred musical genres and the "tom-toms" evoked by Hughes's narrator recall similar details of "African Dance," upending Eurocentric notions of history, art, and culture.

Amid all this, the pianist's patroness stands apart as a symbol of white attempts to control, possess, and violate Black identities. The desire for possession manifests in Mrs. Ellsworth's determination to remove Oceola from her Harlem apartment, which casts Oceola as an object to be shuffled from one location to another and Harlem as "worse than Chinatown" (108). Like her conviction that Oceola should play Chopin rather than the blues, Mrs. Ellsworth's beliefs about Harlem fuse white supremacist ideology with class elitism and recall the collisions of racial and socioeconomic identities in "I, Too." Mrs. Ellsworth also attempts to distance Oceola from her long-time lover and eventual fiancé, "the Pullman porter at Meharry," by sending her abroad (112). Mrs. Ellsworth's strategy chillingly echoes the historical fracturing of Black families in the United States by white legal and social structures: first under slavery, then through racial profiling and incarceration. Even endeavoring to control Oceola's reproductive identity, the "aging white lady" pressures her not to "marry and be burdened with children! Oh, my dear, my dear!" (114, 117). Mrs. Ellsworth's attempt to become the arbiter of Oceola's reproductive future recalls and foreshadows a sordid United States history in which racist laws and policies—ranging from forced and coerced sterilization campaigns to biased drug laws—have disproportionately endangered Black women's reproductive rights.[17] Put in dialogue with "The Negro," this popular and often anthologized story takes on new significance. Because its political references lack that poem's overtly violent imagery, they drive home a point that I hope to make by contrast. In addition to its deep-running affinities with Hughes's other work, *The Dream Keeper* is even more daring in the way that it handles this sort of material, challenging elitist conceptions of poems "for children" as watered-down, less potent versions of more "significant" works perceived as being for adults. In the process, *The Dream Keeper* communicates a vision of childhood that emphasizes children's intellectual depth and personal power—with specific implications for a United States that ignored these qualities in Black children in particular.

Much like "I, Too," the story of Oceola's relationship with her patroness ends on a triumphal note. Oceola decides to marry on her return to New York, unwilling to give up blues, jazz, or her dreams of love, although this will mean the loss of Mrs. Ellsworth's financial support. "Listen!" she commands. "How sad and gay it is. Blue and happy—laughing and crying. . . . How white like you and black like me. . . . How much like a man. . . . And how like a woman. . . . Warm as Pete's mouth. . . . These are the blues. . . . I'm playing" (122–23). "The Blues I'm Playing" takes questions of race and diaspora, wealth and its discontents, gender and sexuality and collides them with stunning results, modeling diverse modes of social protest and fleshing out ideas that recur throughout Hughes's writing. But what is most intriguing to me as a reader of children's literature is how *The Dream Keeper* anticipates some of these ideas and the formal strategies deployed to communicate them, often in more sobering forms. Like Tagore, Hughes resists the "[a]ssumptions about children's limited ability to deal with certain topics [that] have often restricted their literary experiences" (Beckett, "Traditional Tales" 66), and laying out Hughes's works for age-diverse audiences side by side makes this resistance palpable.

Cross-Written Poems, Transnational Affinities, and Activism for All

From colonial India to the United States, the transnational architecture of white supremacy in the early twentieth century shaped and relied on constructions of childhood that were used in attempts to rationalize imperialism, anti-Black violence, and other structural, strategic forms of oppression. Taken together, Tagore's and Hughes's poems paint a vivid picture of the place of children's literature—and the role of multiple types of cross-writing—in the equally transnational efforts to dismantle those structures. *The Crescent Moon* and *The Dream Keeper* foreground intersectional antiracist and anticolonialist discourses, emphasizing the critical role of ethnic histories and expressions of cultural pride in supporting resistance movements. Depicting Indian and African American children as sophisticated in their wisdom while treating all children as capable of grappling with complex concepts and issues, Tagore's and Hughes's cross-writing functions to destabilize logics of racism and colonialism that rest on othering visions of children of color, as well as ways of thinking that falsely discriminate between works "for kids" and "for adults."

CHAPTER 2

SUBVERSIVE ADVENTURES AND INTREPID KIDS

Cross-Written Activism in Baldwin, Puzo, and Achebe

Among the works of children's literature included in this book, Hughes's poems are in a special position in that they tend to be some of his most well-known writings. Yet this familiarity with the poems has not always been accompanied by an awareness that Hughes actually wrote for or hoped to reach a child audience, since readers often encounter these short texts in anthologies of "adult" verse, for instance, with no reference to *The Brownies' Book* or *The Dream Keeper*.[1] It is not uncommon for an author's children's books to be so much less popular that most people have never heard of them, or for a text to be comparatively neglected by adults because it seems to be a conventional offering for children rather than a subversively revolutionary one like the author's other works. Then there are children's books that get set aside because they don't conform to stereotypical notions of children's literature at all, seeming to be appropriately tailored neither to children nor to their parents. Such oversimplifying responses are likely when adults have either conscious or unconscious preconceptions about what child readers can handle and how writers will accommodate those capacities.

The books covered in this chapter fall variously into these categories. First there is James Baldwin's *Little Man, Little Man: A Story of Childhood*, written in collaboration with French illustrator Yoran Cazac, which was published in 1976 but had been out of print for decades before it was republished by Duke University Press in 2018, and which Nicholas Boggs was right to call "the most critically neglected of all of James Baldwin's literary works" (118). Then there is

Mario Puzo's *The Runaway Summer of Davie Shaw*, a rather quirky advanced chapter book that was published in 1966, is out of print, and even at the time of its publication gave Puzo only "some critical praise and a total of $6,500," a figure that would pale in comparison to the hundreds of thousands of dollars that he would make from selling the paperback rights to *The Godfather* (Roy). These two books invite us to discover their connections to Baldwin's *Giovanni's Room* and Puzo's *The Fortunate Pilgrim*, which itself is much less well-known than his *Godfather* series but nevertheless was one of the literary-artistic highlights of Puzo's life as a writer. Returning to a more transnational mode, I also want to propose that we scrutinize Baldwin's and Puzo's work alongside Chinua Achebe's 1966 chapter book *Chike and the River* and some of his "adult" writings, from short stories like "Vengeful Creditor," which first appeared in the journal *Okike* in 1971, to his 2012 memoir *There Was a Country*.[2]

When these narratives are read together, one pattern that emerges is their insistent repurposing of genre conventions of the adventure story, through which they upend the precedents established in so much of earlier canonical Anglo-American children's literature. Tales of adventure become vehicles for tackling injustice, representing and enacting forms of social protest, and undermining and destabilizing systems and structures of oppression. These three authors' children's books are populated with child characters who seek out new experiences, throw themselves headlong into "danger" and "excitement," and then are obliged to grapple with the ramifications of both, employing the "tactical maneuvers" necessary to ensure their survival, whether in faraway places or in "their own neighborhoods and towns" (Tribunella 23). Often the danger is socially constructed, and both the adventure and its consequences become sites of subversion as readers are called on to critique and resist the architectures that have put the child protagonist in harm's way. In making use of these reworked conventions, Baldwin, Puzo, and Achebe all participate in a more contemporary tradition of reclaiming the genre for quite different uses than the ones enshrined in imperialist narratives of white boy explorers conquering unfamiliar territories that were penned during the "Golden Age" of British and US children's literature.

What is particularly arresting is how the children's adventure stories pick up thematic and stylistic strands from their authors' "adult" works, which at first glance may not read as adventure narratives per se, but which in fact are populated with intrepid, risk-taking young people whose confrontations with peril uncover the intersecting forms of injustice that shape their worlds. In the three children's books, endings are rosier and hope most often prevails. Nevertheless, underneath these superficial differences lie more meaningful currents of similarity that reveal how these types of cross-writing can leverage familiar plots toward activist ends while destabilizing what many adults believe they know about the differences between children's fiction and its alternatives. As before, because these books have a built-in set of companion texts from outside the world of children's literature, they make it easier to counter othering stereotypes of works "for kids." Our writers continue to challenge conventional ideas about age-appropriateness by crafting politically and aesthetically daring children's books that deserve attention from adults, and at times by creating content for children that adults have had trouble accepting as suitable for them.

Marah Gubar has rightly advocated that Golden Age authors be reconceptualized as "resist[ing] the Child of Nature paradigm . . . in favor of the idea that young people have the capacity to exploit and capitalize on the resources of adult culture," and that they can "be addressed in the same terms as adults" (5–6). Thus understood, authors like Lewis Carroll and William Makepeace Thackeray are not so different from the authors in this book, and they advanced viewpoints that were more revolutionary than not. Still, many Golden Age writers also participated in the trend that made "frequent connections between boys' adventure and empire" (Tribunella 23), with "adventure stories with exotic settings" often centering on "a young English man . . . molded and strengthened by his escapades in the wild and his adventures with the natives" (O'Sullivan 19). As Margery Hourihan reminds us, the adventure story has been critical not just to children's literature but to storytelling more broadly in a western literary tradition dominated by imperial anxieties and agendas:

> Following the success of *Crusoe* the age of imperialism produced a flood of adventure stories in which intrepid British lads struggled against dark-skinned opponents to bring enlightenment to distant reaches of the empire. In post-imperial stories, James Bond and his like defend democracy against communism. . . . This adversarial way of perceiving the world means that conflict is seen as natural and inevitable. The hero is constantly confronted by enemies which he must overcome. . . . (2–3)

These Golden Age norms and their more recent analogues created a tradition against which authors like Baldwin, Puzo, and Achebe would write, strategically resisting such mythologies while working within the genre that had served to proliferate them. Maria Nikolajeva documents how some contemporary US children's fiction has built on and complicated the canonical model, suggesting that books like Gary Paulsen's *Hatchet* "have the marks of adventure . . . while at the same time they are psychological, even existential novels depicting the young protagonist's inner quest for maturity" (114). Baldwin, Puzo, and Achebe go much further, however, as both the external and the internal "quests" of adventurous fictional children spark larger conversations about their real "enemies."

Some of the most acclaimed contemporary children's fiction has been written by authors who have taken up this task of genre reinvention, with historical "adventure books" like Mildred Taylor's, for instance, being recognized for their embrace of "a more liberal ... multiracial and democratic humanism" that has contested US exceptionalist thought by recognizing the more than "troubled" nature of the United States' relationship to issues of race (Butts 16). We might also think of Pam Muñoz Ryan's *Esperanza Rising*, a historical novel that offers "adventure" (as one child book reviewer specified) inflected with political commentary on issues ranging from the Depression-era forced repatriation of Mexican Americans to the "revolution boiling in the background" as exploited agricultural workers in California's Central Valley organized to more effectively resist their employers (Danielle T). Outside the realm of the historical, a similar spirit has shaped Cathy Camper and Raúl the Third's graphic science fiction epic adventure series *Lowriders* as well as Matt de la Peña's *The Living* series, where a YA survival narrative with elements of the "hunted man" adventure story (Hintz and Tribunella 256) becomes a vehicle for exploring a teenager's confrontations with "class, prejudice and romance" (de la Peña and Simon). Among the books designated as suitable for even younger kids, there is Carole Lindstrom and Michaela Goade's picture book *We Are Water Protectors*, whose publisher problematically designated it as "mythological fiction" but which in reality is a contemporary realist narrative. There, a bold Ojibwe child leads the adults of her community as she sets out on a difficult yet exciting quest to battle the corporate forces that threaten "plants, trees, rivers, [and] lakes" by building oil pipelines across "tribal lands and waterways" (Lindstrom and Goade). This is to say nothing of recent activist children's adventure stories hailing from outside the Americas, like Jasbinder Bilan's *Asha and the Spirit Bird*, billed as a "gorgeously original magical-realist Indian adventure" with an investment in the "very strong sense of justice and fairness" that Bilan sees in her child readers and characters as they face "difficult situations created by adults" (Bilan and Eagleton), from economic violence to kidnapping and forced child labor.[3] There are so many diverse examples in this genre that any attempt to summarize them is bound to be incomplete. What these examples do speak to is the range of books by contemporary writers who invert the long-established relationship of the adventure story to imperial ambitions, mythologies of white supremacy, and other instruments of oppression.

Thus situating this chapter's writers gives us a sense of the very real activist literary movement to which they have contributed: a movement that has continued to attract suspicion from adults who are unconvinced of how much complexity children will comprehend. Lindstrom and Goade, for instance, have received online censure on Goodreads from contributors who have tellingly objected that their book's "nuances ... may go over the heads of most children" ("We Are Water Protectors"). This critique, though it has arrived several decades later, echoes the reaction of Julius Lester to *Little Man, Little Man* in his review of the book in *The New York Times*: "Children's literature is a province of its own," he protested, "a fact which the literati do not take seriously enough." Lester's negative attention was focused more on the impressionistic, fragmentary quality of Baldwin's text, a kind of very-late-modernist sensibility that Lester described as making the book lack the "focus" needed "to wholly engage the reader." Nevertheless, what these reactions share is that they critique writerly choices that, when they are deployed in works that are seen as being for adults, tend to receive praise rather than censure. In its "experimental, enigmatic" nature (Alter), *Little Man, Little Man* is not so different from the acclaimed *Giovanni's Room*, and a 1956 review in the same paper feted that novel for its "subtlety" in capturing "the rareness and difficulty of love" (Hicks).[4] Yet to write a good picture book, Lester suggests, one must write an accessible, transparent, and stylistically conventional work, much as one is expected to write children's poetry that is "simplistic in form and content." Considered against the backdrop of these received ideas, Baldwin, Puzo, and Achebe present a distinctive opportunity because their cross-writing breaks down these audience-based distinctions.

A final introductory note concerns the transnationalism of this chapter. One of the advantages of reading Langston Hughes's children's poetry with that of Rabindranath Tagore is that it underscores the affinities between South Asian anticolonial struggles and resistance to white supremacy in the early twentieth-century United States. Placing Baldwin, Puzo, and Achebe side by side works toward a similar end in bringing shared literary strategies into relief, although this method calls for especial care and attention to contextual detail. While it is true that Italian Americans experienced ethnic discrimination and diasporic alienation upon their immigration to the US, Baldwin's writing was formative in forcing the recognition of the essential differences between these experiences of marginalization and the persisting current of anti-Black racism in modern and contemporary US life. As Baldwin wrote in his 1984 essay "On Being 'White' ... and Other Lies," there exists "at least, in principle ... an Italian community" both in the United States and abroad: "Rome, Naples, the Bank of the Holy Ghost and Mulberry Street. . . . No one was white before he/she came to America. It took generations, and a vast amount of coercion, before this became a white country" (178). Baldwin also stipulates that Italian Americans and other white immigrant communities must still be held responsible for opting into this culture of whiteness and for upholding the structures of white supremacy, including white terrorist violence. Such betrayals of people of color and of Black Americans in particular frustrate facile interethnic comparisons and complicate the prospect of allyship between the Italian and African diasporic communities in the US, though such attempts at solidarity have not been uncommon.[5] This historical backdrop gives a different importance to the task of putting Baldwin and Puzo into conversation. Meanwhile, the few comparative studies of Baldwin and Achebe underscore the similar currents of literary-political resistance that run between them, with writers like Eleanor W. Traylor locating a "readerly and writerly kinship" through which both Baldwin and Achebe "call out the liars, the hypocrites, the greedy, the petty" in addition to and as part of their political projects (230, 239). This chapter combines these two approaches, recognizing the children's adventure story as a site of engagement with interconnected sociopolitical issues across contexts with vital distinctions between them. In bringing African American and postcolonial African writers like Baldwin and Achebe into dialogue with a "white ethnic" immigrant writer like Puzo, we can begin to see compelling transnational patterns in their cross-writing—including strategies for grappling with white racism, white privilege, and the realities and lasting after-echoes of imperialist ideology and colonial governance.[6]

Examining these resistive adventure stories reveals how they mold conventional plots to their advantage, unpacking and scrutinizing these entangled issues along with others that range from toxic masculinity to asymmetrical access to education. In fact, while Baldwin's, Puzo's, and Achebe's books may not at first seem to upend the gender paradigms that predominated in many Golden Age works, when adventure stories were "almost synonymous with the term 'boys' story'" (MacCann 97), a detail-oriented interpretation suggests otherwise. *Little Man, Little Man* treats the adventures of both boy and girl characters as worthy of attention while zeroing in on toxic expectations for boys' childhood identities; *Davie Shaw* unearths and critiques a species of white boyhood privilege that proves inaccessible to both girls and children of color; and *Chike* doesn't shy away from violently gendered topics such as domestic violence. In the end, both the children's books and the texts that are ostensibly "for adults" do activist work that responds intersectionally to the racist and imperialist history of the genre. The results demand to be read and appreciated across putative boundaries of audience.

From *Giovanni's Room* to *Little Man, Little Man*: Baldwin's Adventurous Childhoods

The opening pages of *Giovanni's Room* set the stage for much of the tragedy and the social critique that will unfold as the novel follows David, its narrator-protagonist, across the Atlantic Ocean to Paris and eventually to the house in the south of France where he will find himself when his lover, the eponymous Giovanni, is executed for murder. Much has been made of the initial encounter between David and his childhood friend Joey, who revel in each other's bodies in a queer love scene that leads David to muse that "a lifetime would not be long enough for [him] to act with Joey the act of love" (8). For Ernest L. Gibson III, the scene is a way for Baldwin to "disrupt the heteronormativity of American space through same-sex intimacy" (75); for John C. Charles, it "reinforces David's association of homosexuality, female sexuality, and death" within Baldwin's "white-life novel" (127, 7). While all of this is true, what is in a sense the most moving about David's early narration is his tender and sincere account of this exhilarating, risk-filled adventure, which he undertakes when he is "still in [his] teens" (Baldwin, *Giovanni's* 6). While the novel may not read as an adventure story in any conventional sense of the word, it will engage relentlessly with the tension between its narrator's intermittent moments of joyful, subversive risk-taking and the menacing cultural shadows that lead him to flee from it, employing evasive "tactical maneuvers" to protect himself.

The pivotal opening scene begins not with the unknown or unexpected but with the comfort of what has become routine, a variation on the "domestic issue" that Nilay Erdem Ayyıldız cites as a point of departure for many earlier canonical adventure narratives (46). David remembers, "I laughed and grabbed his head as I had done God knows how many times before, when I was playing with him or when he had annoyed me" (Baldwin, *Giovanni's* 7). Still, just as "horsing around in that small, steamy room" of the shower makes David feel "something" for Joey "which [he] had not felt before," Joey's response to his touch is novel, unanticipated, and breathtaking: "And he did not resist, as he usually did," David recounts, "but lay where I had pulled him, against my chest. And I realized that my heart was beating in an awful way and that Joey was trembling against me. . . . Joey raised his head as I lowered mine and we kissed, as it were, by accident" (6, 7–8). The unexpectedness of the two boys' kiss inspires fear—"I was very frightened," David reflects—but also a feeling of "joy" that, as David would tell it, envelops them both (8). For Baldwin's narrator, allowing himself to grapple momentarily with a queerness that he will spend much of the rest of the novel repudiating becomes the consummate adolescent adventure: something uncharted, exciting, and perilous that inspires a rush of emotions and makes him feel alive, as though his "heart would burst" (8).

It is for good reason that David finds this excursion into the unknown as frightening as it is joyous: as much as in any nineteenth-century British adventure story, the journey will require that he "deal with . . . dangerous events and make urgent choices" (Ayyıldız 46). Even before revealing the secret of his time with Joey, David makes clear the current of shame that will flow through him as he remembers their night together. "For a while he was my best friend," he explains. "Later, the idea that such a person *could* have been my best friend was proof of some horrifying taint in me. So I forgot him. But I see him very well tonight" (Baldwin, *Giovanni's* 6). Bound up with these feelings of shame and of "tainted" selfhood is David's awareness of the cultural atmosphere that stigmatized queer identities in the midcentury United States, as well as a more specific source of discomfort in the shape of his father, whom he dreads disappointing with the news:

> I was ashamed. The very bed, in its sweet disorder, testified to vileness. I wondered what Joey's mother would say when she saw the sheets. Then I thought of my father, who had no one in the world but me, my mother having died when I was little. A cavern opened in my mind, black, full of rumor, suggestion, of half-heard, half-forgotten, half-understood stories, full of dirty words. I thought about my future in that cavern. I was afraid. I could have cried, cried for shame and terror.... (9)

In this passage, it becomes obvious that the danger in David's adventure stems from social attitudes that are steeped in antiqueerness and that threaten to paint him as monstrous. This is a heartbreaking depiction of adolescence on Baldwin's part, one that underscores not just a young person's "excitement at encountering" the unknown, as we might expect from a Golden Age tale of adventure (Ayyıldız 47), but his acute and paralyzing consciousness of its life-threatening nature.

As the novel progresses, the echoes and consequences of this opening scene will deepen, with the adult David's fears leading him to forsake his lover Giovanni in Paris just as he has done with Joey so many years before. David's boyish spirit of discovery thus gives way to an intense emotional and physical violence: a desperate Giovanni murders the employer who attempts to prey on him after David's departure, then faces execution himself. The narrative closes with a religious refrain that embodies David's early struggles, their roots in antiqueer ideologies, and their connection to the novel's devastating end. "*When I was a child, I spake as a child,*" David recites, "*I understood as a child, I thought as a child: but when I became a man, I put away childish things.* I long to make this prophecy come true.... I move at last from the mirror and begin to cover that nakedness which I must hold sacred, though it be never so vile" (Baldwin, *Giovanni's* 168–69). To the last, Baldwin's narrator grapples with this false sense of his own "vileness," and as the repudiation of his "childish" experiment in self-expression and self-love, the novel's closing lines reemphasize the brokenness of a world that has made David believe that his queer body "must be scoured perpetually with the salt of [his] life" (169).[7] By invoking his former child identity in the novel's final pages, Baldwin's narrator situates his early and unexpected acts of discovery as an exponent of the "youthful exploration" familiar to us from canonical children's adventure stories (Lee 316), though David's jaded perspective reflects the disillusionment he has undergone since first risking safety in the pursuit of joy.

Originally published two decades after *Giovanni's Room*, *Little Man, Little Man* has been specifically billed by Duke University Press as a story of a child's confrontations with "grown-up adventures and realities." The book was written at least partly for Baldwin's nieces and nephews, recalling the intended role of Tagore's "child-poems" in the lives of his children after the death of their mother. In an afterword to the 2018 edition, Baldwin's niece Aisha Karefa-Smart—the real-life model for the book's character of Blinky, whom Baldwin treats with careful attentiveness in contravention to her friends' skeptical observation that "she a girl"[8]—recalls the delight that the younger members of their family felt on discovering that their beloved uncle had remembered that "a promise was a promise" and had written "a book about [Aisha's little brother] TJ!!!!" (95). In contrast, on the book's original publication, its publisher identified *Little Man, Little Man* as a "child's story for adults" (qtd. in Boggs and DeVere Brody xv), and this phrasing would foreshadow its initial reception; while critics like Lester worried over the book's supposed dearth of "focus," others concluded that its themes were not "suitable for children" (Karefa-Smart and *The Conscious Kid*).[9]

It is true that *Little Man, Little Man* excavates social issues ranging from "poverty, police brutality, [and] crime" to "addiction, racism, and social marginality," all refracted "through the voice and vision of a black child" (Boggs and DeVere Brody xvi). Yet this in no way makes the book "unsuitable" for a child readership. As Karefa-Smart remarked in a recent interview,

> Black children are targeted, treated, and tried as adults more often than white children. In many situations, things are projected onto Black children that are not necessarily projected onto white children, especially in terms of what our responsibility is in society. Black children, especially in urban environments, are perceived as older because of the issues they are grappling with in a society still struggling with white supremacy.... We know what happened with Trayvon Martin and Tamir Rice. How Black boys are perceived as older, bigger, and more adult than they actually are. These are children. That is the reality for Black people and Black children. Our perception in the world is going to be skewed toward more adult themes.

In reflecting and accounting for these realities, *Little Man, Little Man* makes its own challenge to limiting ideas of age-appropriateness in children's literature, working in the tradition of Du Bois, Hughes, and many other Black writers in the United States who anticipated a young audience for their literary production. Reading it in conjunction with a novel like *Giovanni's Room* further deepens our sense of that challenge by uncovering the boundary-spanning continuities in Baldwin's writing. Facing danger, struggling with fear, and diving into the experiences that inspire it, Baldwin's nephew-turned-protagonist encounters issues that are intimately connected to *Giovanni's Room* and its cultural critique, including toxic expectations for childhood masculinity. While the first line of the book characterizes TJ's life as lulling in its humdrum sense of routine—"Music all up and down this street, TJ runs it every day," we learn (Baldwin, *Little Man*)—the stakes of Baldwin's "experimental, enigmatic" book will prove to be as high as those of Baldwin's groundbreaking "adult" narrative as TJ makes his way "from adventure to adventure" (Karefa-Smart 95).[10] But instead of suggesting that TJ's story is "a child's story for adults" alone, these parallels between *Giovanni's Room* and *Little Man, Little Man* help to demonstrate that wonderfully written books "for kids" can look very different from what some adults expect.

Often it is the danger of bodily injury that threatens Baldwin's young protagonist or his friends WT and Blinky, as when TJ falls forward while trying to catch a ball and ends up with a bloody knee, or when the ball that he has just thrown above his head in an attempt to show off "knocks him on his ass" (*Little Man* 11). In both instances, TJ claims that he is not really hurt: "He look at his knee. He don't want his Mama to get worried. It not too bad. It bleeding just a little bit" (8). Wise beyond his years amid all of these incursions into his physical space, TJ is stoic as he faces the blood and the recognition that "it hurt a lot," hoping to avoid showing what he feels not just because he might be embarrassed but because he wishes to shield others from anxiety (11). I will have more to say below about the figure of the stoic child in *Little Man, Little Man*. In the meantime, it is striking how these quintessential childhood moments, though they may be predictably unpredictable, carry the same feeling that we can remember from *Giovanni's Room*. Again we see a child or adolescent—in this case a child who is not yet five years old—throwing himself into life with abandon and then grappling with the consequences.

Sometimes TJ's and his friends' physical adventures have more particularized thematic implications, as when a glass bottle falls from the roof of the building above them and it emerges that the bottle may have belonged to TJ's neighbor Miss Lee, who struggles with alcoholism. TJ's fear is palpable: "He rises up and something comes down, but it is not the ball. It flashes, flashes, flashes over his head like lightning, like thunder it crashes at his feet. It like a big explosion, like a bomb falling on him, and TJ scream and start to cry.... WT got that hole in his sneaker and he done stepped on the glass and his foot be bleeding something awful" (77). If the greatest adventure in *Little Man, Little Man* is simply TJ, WT, and Blinky's everyday explorations of their neighborhood, the danger that emerges from those adventures is woven into the fabric of the neighborhood as well, where one woman's alcoholism collides with another family's economic marginalization—embodied in the hole in WT's shoe—to leave WT with an injury that inspires fear in all of the children. In charting the three children's movements through their neighborhood, with this event as the climax of their daily journeys, Baldwin uses the flight pattern of their adventures to access this collision of social issues and injustices and to witness its influence on the lives of children who are "poor, black, and less than four feet high."[11] Boggs, one of the only scholars to have written about *Little Man, Little Man* before its republication, suggests that this moment marks "a visceral transition from the playful scene of youthful adventure ... into an unexpected scene of trauma that seems particularly ill-suited to a children's book" (127). For Boggs, indeed, that is part of what makes this a "child's story for adults." However, the constellation of texts in this chapter suggests that this type of encounter with danger and even injury is an essential part of the children's adventure story when it is bent on resisting existing power structures rather than consolidating them in the manner of canonical imperialist fictions for children, which often presented danger through a more minimizing white supremacist lens: as something that would be easy for a boy to surmount "with the help of his European knowledge" and his "technological and, most importantly, racial power" (Ayyıldız 47).

There are scenes in which TJ's fears seem to stem mostly from his imagination, whether he is visiting with the elderly Miss Beanpole or waking up alone in the middle of the night with the worry that something awful has happened to his parents. In these cases, too, adventure and fear go hand in hand, with substantive ramifications for *Little Man, Little Man*'s vision of the larger social universe that TJ inhabits. Like the routine in which he "runs this street every day," TJ's visits to Miss Beanpole are habitual, as we can see when Baldwin's narrator describes how she "turn her back to TJ, *like always*" (*Little Man* 45, my italics). At the same time, TJ's fear makes the visits an adventure, as though he is never certain of what may happen to him and this anticipation of uncertainty, even if the visit itself is nothing extraordinary in the end, makes each of their tête-a-têtes exciting. Almost resembling a twentieth-century Miss Havisham, Miss Beanpole brings TJ into a room where "[d]on't nothing never change ... a real weird room. Like a room in the movies or the TV where something happened in the room a long time ago and somebody hid in the room and they saw what happened and they still hiding in the room.... Maybe that why Miss

Beanpole never go out" (46).[12] While they are arresting in themselves, these descriptions of Miss Beanpole and her seclusion as a woman who sits "in that window like she waiting for somebody" function to put into relief the things that TJ is really most afraid of: "sometime in the middle of the night," we learn, "he wake up all of a sudden and he don't hear nobody in the house. Then, he scared. He real scared" (62, 51).

Where this train of thought becomes most profound is in Baldwin's acknowledgment of the pressure that TJ feels to hide his fears and his sadness: "His Daddy say he don't want no cry-baby for a son, so he don't cry, he just lie in bed, stiff and still.... He don't get up and he don't cry or nothing because TJ's Daddy drive a taxi all day and he need his sleep" (60–61). In a child's imagination in which the simple act of waking up in the middle of the night can be an adventure—something emotionally dangerous and fear-inspiring—the real struggle comes from the intersection of gendered and raced expectations for childhood masculinity and the class-rooted realities of TJ's father's profession. With two straightforward sentences, Baldwin captures what bell hooks refers to as "the patriarchal socialization that insists boys should not express emotions or have emotional caretaking," which "is most viciously and ruthlessly implicated in the early childhood socialization of black boys" (86), along with its intensification by economic stratification. These expectations often seem to pose the greatest danger to TJ, much as the greatest danger David encounters is the stigmatization of queerness. Yet as Boggs points out, *Little Man, Little Man* "articulates alternative models of black masculinity and black kinship that are produced by the child characters themselves," models that become essential "counter-narratives" (119). In these alternative renderings, "the network among ... three childhood friends," two little boys and a little girl, becomes a source of comfort, support, and healing (127)—for instance, when WT is injured and his younger and older friends both tend to him, embracing "tactical maneuvers" that secure his physical safety as well as his emotional well-being after the danger has passed. We can see Baldwin tapping into the same source of conviction in children's collective capacities that Taylor draws from in *Roll of Thunder, Hear My Cry*, which was published the same year as *Little Man, Little Man*. There, a crying Black teenager confides in his two friends about the white boys who have forced him to rob a store with them and have threatened to hurt or kill him "if [he] ever told!" (Taylor 245). What most strikes me is how these "counter-narratives" of kinship and healing productively stem from quite realist depictions of children's daily lives as dangerous, anxiety-producing adventures. The genre thus becomes a vehicle for activist convictions that are every bit as complex and vital as those unpacked in an "adult" novel like *Giovanni's Room*, and they are unfurled for child readers—not just adult ones—to see and appreciate. Baldwin's two books turn out to engage the same universe of concerns, since the "patriarchal socialization" that hooks cites and that *Little Man, Little Man* captures is very much connected to the repressive pressure put on Baldwin's adolescent-turned-adult narrator as he attempts to negotiate and resist an antiqueer cultural landscape.

In vivifying the adventure, danger, fear, and kinship in the lives of TJ and his friends, *Little Man, Little Man* testifies to these multilayered textures of childhood and of life more broadly in TJ's community, highlighting injustice at the same time as it celebrates the resilience of Black children, centers and valorizes African American vernacular English, and underlines the importance of Black pride, which TJ's father insists on when he says, in one of the book's relatively few moments of dialogue, "I want you to be proud of your people" (Baldwin, *Little Man* 57). This productive tension between the two tasks of calling out inequities and honoring the public and private agency of Black children is something that Karefa-Smart has been vocal about, commenting on how Baldwin "illustrate[s] a ... lighter side of a Black childhood" through TJ's "whimsical nature," his "adventurous" spirit, and his ability to see "the world as a magical place," even though the book doesn't hesitate to address purportedly "adult themes" (Karefa-Smart and *The Conscious Kid*). A critical intervention, this contribution of *Little Man, Little Man* to the discourse surrounding Black childhood resists both the ways in which "Black children are targeted, treated, and tried as adults" and the tendency of condescending cultural outsiders—often "well-meaning white people"—to paint Black children as hapless victims. Appropriating the conventions of the adventure story becomes the perfect literary strategy for achieving these ends in a children's book that is determined to take children seriously and that, in doing so, has discomfited adults who have narrower methods of defining suitability within children's literature. Rereading the republished children's book in tandem with a novel like *Giovanni's Room* only deepens this sense of it as a seamless part of Baldwin's oeuvre that deserves equal membership there alongside his other works.

Kids on Their Own: Puzo's Children from New York City to the Western United States

The ending of *Little Man, Little Man* in some sense could not be more different from the ending of *Giovanni's Room*. WT ends up laughing at TJ "doing his African strut," and the feeling in the air seems to be that the payoff of embracing childhood adventures—in the form of friendship, joy, and laughter—is worth the socially imposed peril and the feelings of terror that such experiments in childhood living can entail (Baldwin, *Little Man* 93). The two books nevertheless are strikingly consonant with one another in their consciousness of how the new or unexpected, while exciting, can be bound up with danger in the lives of children and teenagers who face marginalization because they are nonwhite, queer, working-class, or some intersectional combination of these identities. Something similar happens in Puzo's depictions of children's lives from *The Fortunate Pilgrim* to his chapter book *The Runaway Summer of Davie Shaw*, which was destined for critical and popular neglect, being both a "literary" work and a children's book by an ethnic American writer whose claim to fame was his pulpier depictions of Italian American violence.[13] Drawing *Davie Shaw* out of the shadows allows us to appreciate its activist contributions and its connections to Puzo's other writings, which challenge stereotypical conceptions of children's literature even when the book, if read in a more superficial way, might seem to uphold them.

Among the children of *The Fortunate Pilgrim*, often it is Lorenzo, the oldest child of the family at the center of the novel, who receives the bulk of the attention. This is understandable given that Lorenzo's character furnishes the "prototype of the immigrant worker turned gangster and eventually culture hero" for Puzo's later novels (Gardaphé 24). Others seem drawn in by some of the captivating scenes of childhood that happen on the street with Gino, a younger son of Lucia Santa Angeluzzi-Corbo, whose everyday life recalls *Little Man, Little Man* despite his supposedly adult audience. Gino has what Thomas J. Ferraro calls a "case of wanderlust" (404); embodying the identity of the "restless family explorer" (Messenger 141), he would be a "wanderer (a picaresque hero whose adventure is defined by travel)" in Martin Green's typology of adventurous protagonists (Hintz and Tribunella 256), even if his journeying is circumscribed by urban boundaries as he runs through the streets of the family's "tenement" neighborhood (Puzo, *Fortunate* 6), encountering mischief and seemingly fearsome things. At the beginning of the novel, Gino runs "crazily in some sort of tagging game incomprehensible to [his] father, as was the child's American speech, as were the books and newspapers, the colors of the night sky" (15). Gino's youthful adventurousness becomes an invitation for Puzo's narrator to recount the feelings of diasporic alienation facing his wearily adult father, taking up an issue that will persist in influencing the Italian experience of migration throughout the Americas. Gino's attempts to evade his compatriots in their game of tag lead him to a more alien environment "at the top of 31st Street," where he glimpses "an old Irish crone" through the window of a first-floor apartment and becomes afraid. He sees how the woman

> rested her head on a furry pillow and watched him move past her down the empty silent street. In that weak yellow light her head was bony with age, her

thin, whiskered mouth bloody with the light of a holy red candle. Behind that feral face, faintly visible in the shadow of her room, a vase, a lamp, and a graven image gleamed like old bones. Gino stared at her. The teeth bared in greeting. Gino ran. (18)

As I have written elsewhere, this gendered description of an aging woman communicates a great deal about the stigmatization of postmenopausal women's identities, with the ethnicity of the "crone"—her Irishness—combining with her age and gender in Gino's mind to encourage him to envision her as monstrous.[14] In bringing to life not just Gino's adventurous games but the sense of danger and fear that they inspire, *The Fortunate Pilgrim* engages an intersectional constellation of prejudices that the novel will scrutinize as it progresses, exploring the historical tensions between the Irish and Italian diasporic communities and the continued, reciprocal othering of older women across these communities. Even in a narrative that is not an adventure story per se, Puzo's "Gino subplot" uses depictions of a daring and adventurous childhood toward political ends, as a means of accessing this constellation of identities, issues, and opportunities for resistance.

Gino is often found running "crazily" through his neighborhood and the city at large during the remainder of the novel, living out the "escape from the domestic sphere" that Eric L. Tribunella identifies as typical of many conventional Anglo-American adventure novels (23), but with implications that are resistive rather than consolidating structures of gendered and imperial power. Gino's urban adventures pose varying degrees of actual danger to him, and this danger proves central to his subplot's political thrust. In one key scene, he finds himself in trouble with a policeman after stealing ice from a nearby railyard. In another, he runs away from the family's apartment after defying his mother, leaving a mess of broken dishes in his wake. Gino resembles any number of "mischievous boys" who "get . . . into scrapes in their own neighborhoods and towns" within the nineteenth-century US tradition of adventure tales epitomized by novels like "Twain's *Tom Sawyer*" (Tribunella 23). At the same time, the implications of his escapades distinguish *The Fortunate Pilgrim* from its earlier literary precedents, as when Gino's mother employs code-switching to articulate her fears for him: "You, *giovanetto*. From morning to night I don't see you. You could be run over. You could be kidnapped" (Puzo, *Fortunate* 59). Gino's mother emphasizes her son's immigrant identity as well as his youth while voicing a common objection among first-generation Italian American parents to US cultural expectations for their children. In general, the family is able to intervene enough to shepherd Gino into adulthood; in his confrontation with the policeman, he receives "a few pretty slaps" before his older brother

Lorenzo steps in, fighting the older man until he has obviously won although onlookers declare the outcome "a draw" to reestablish the peace (78). At other times Gino is alone but lucky, as when he is run over by a car after fleeing his mother but escapes with a "deep scrape" on his knee and a present of five dollars from the wealthier driver for his trouble (128). Yet these moments of peril are important: not only for the excitement they add to Gino's young life but for the more ambivalent feelings of "baffled rage and lost pride" that he feels at being beaten by the policeman or the "strange discontent" and worry that he senses in himself after fighting with his mother (75, 126). In exploring the both physical and emotional dangers of adventure, Puzo, like Baldwin, gets at issues such as police brutality, toxic masculinity, and socioeconomic inequality while confronting the liminal status of second-generation immigrant children who chafe at their parents' attempts to control them but who cannot help but feel relieved to have their sins "forgotten" in the end (129). Remove Gino's thirst for adventure from *The Fortunate Pilgrim*, and you would remove much of Puzo's most biting social commentary.

The fact that there are such clear precedents for Gino's story in US children's adventure narratives itself suggests a blurring of the boundaries between children's literature and its supposed alternatives. *The Fortunate Pilgrim*, despite being invested in the representation of children's identities and experiences, is not typically viewed as a book *for* children, yet the novel shares more with the children's books it recalls than such age-bound interpretations admit. Likewise, it proves edifying to consider *The Fortunate Pilgrim* in conjunction with *Davie Shaw*, which, despite its noticeable surface-level differences, proves equally adept at raising the sorts of sociopolitical issues that make its "adult" predecessor so interesting. In this short, episodic tale of a child's cross-country adventures, both the threat of danger and its ultimate failure to materialize offer provocative points of entry into discussions of US materialism and structural, deeply embedded forms of class stratification as well as entrenched architectures of ethnoracial and gendered injustice—all issues that connect with the web of ideas that pervades Puzo's earlier novel.

Relative to the rest of the books in this chapter, *Davie Shaw* feels almost strangely bereft of danger. Left without adult supervision when his parents take a vacation around the world and his relatives turn out to be too irresponsible to care for him, the novel's eponymous thirteen-year-old protagonist embarks on a journey from California to New York City. The trip seems as though it should be full of peril but turns out to be devoid of genuine risk. Familiarly episodic in nature, the short book traces Davie's adventures as he interacts with a quirky array of adult figures, from his grandparents and his uncle to the strangers he meets on the road. The vast majority of these adults turn out to be in some way ridiculous, foolish, or both. Davie shines by comparison, full of good sense and kindness as he navigates various adult worlds. We often get the sense that Puzo's young protagonist, as an unusually responsible child, is just treading the path that has been set for him by his careless parents; this is not an adventure that he has sought out: "But what am I going to do for the rest of my vacation?" he asks his uncle, nonplussed, when the older man decides to leave him to pursue a new job (*Runaway* 31–32). Still, an exciting aura of unpredictability permeates his trip across the nation as Davie meets a herpetologist who wears snakes around her body like clothing, races his uncle's horse Mustang, plays stickball for the first time, and is proclaimed "a Natural" (109), all while making his way to the bustling metropolis where his parents will end their whirlwind vacation.

Unlike in *The Fortunate Pilgrim*, the risks Davie braves seem most often hypothetical. He or his horse might be bitten by a snake, but they are not; he might somehow be endangered by one of the strange and irresponsible adults he interacts with, but he emerges from each interaction unscathed, if a bit wiser about the fallibility of the older people in his midst. In this respect, Puzo's children's adventure story is gentler to its younger characters than *The Fortunate Pilgrim* proves to be, with Gino's "pretty slaps" and "baffled rage." However, these possible perils, which again are socially constructed, create thematic avenues that are far more serious than their happy and often humorous resolution might suggest. In one episode, Davie visits his grandparents but decides not to stay with them because he realizes that his parents haven't warned them about his visit and he doesn't wish to impose. These grandparents are obsessed with their TV; Davie's uncle says that "they are really very busy watching all the television they can before they die. They are very old and they have to squeeze everything into their last few years" (32). As a kind of plot device, the "domestic issue" that triggers the remainder of his adventures, Davie's visit to his apathetic relatives jumpstarts his trip and becomes the reason he is exposed to all of the possible dangers that will follow. In the meantime, the irony here—that the elderly couple's looming mortality makes them more eager to watch TV than to spend time with their grandson—becomes a biting commentary on the obsession of the modern United States with passive entertainment at the expense of meaningful interpersonal connection.

Later escapades of Davie's marry suspense and satire. While a visit to a religious cult does not lead to any physical threat, it does give Puzo a chance to poke fun at false idols and their followers, like the seemingly old man who loses his devotees when he can no longer "hear the sound of one hand clapping" (59), and who ceases to be interesting even to Davie once he shaves off his beard and reveals his youthfulness. When Davie finds himself in New York City with no lodging—quite a precarious position for a thirteen-year-old boy—this becomes a chance for him to rub shoulders with an eccentric old woman, the sometimes-employer of his coachman host, who sends him into a shop to buy ten dollars' worth of pâté after defining the term as "French for expensive liverwurst" (101). With her choice of phrasing, the woman inadvertently emphasizes how ridiculous it is to spend such a sum on a food that Davie, when he tries it, finds just "O.K." (102). In the process, Puzo makes a critique of class elitism and inequality that echoes Gino's interaction with the car driver who hits him in *The Fortunate Pilgrim*. It seems that every hazard leads to a sociopolitical revelation for readers, and often for Davie himself. The lighthearted tone of the book is in this way deceptive; we are obliged to look beyond its superficial resemblances to the stereotype of the "frivolous" book for children that was indulged by many a twentieth-century critic (B. Clark 295) and that continues to proliferate today outside children's literature studies.

In a sense, as in *Little Man, Little Man*, the realest threat to Davie is his fear of something that may never come to pass, although this "something" is less poignant than TJ's nighttime worries. What Davie fears most is that his parents will be "angry because of his trip across the country," not grasping that their own irresponsibility and that of their family members have been the causes of Davie's adventure (94). Like every other possible risk to Davie's well-being, this one never materializes. Instead, the "irresponsible parents" are flattered when Davie tells them that he missed them too much to wait for them to return home, and the reunited trio spends "the happiest week in Davie's life" sightseeing and fraternizing with Davie's newfound friends, like the hotdog vendor to whom he has bequeathed his beloved Mustang (9, 118). Unspoken beneath the surface of this happy ending, however, are pressing questions about parenthood, childhood, economic justice, and materialism. Puzo's narrator describes Davie's parents as formerly affluent people who cannot get the hang of caring for their child now that they no longer have servants to wait on them:

> [B]oth Davie's parents had once been very, very rich and had lots of servants to do all the little things, and so they weren't used to bothering with all the little things. . . . That was why Mr and Mrs Shaw couldn't get used to taking care of everyday details. They forgot their plane tickets, but Davie reminded them. They forgot their overnight case, but Davie spotted it on the living room sofa. . . . They left it all to Davie. (11–12)

This description has disturbing implications given how Davie slips into the role previously held by his parents' servants, while his parents fail to mature beyond their former wealth. Davie's parents are not stunned or horrified at the perils their child might have faced in traveling thousands of miles across the country alone, and their response reads not just as Puzo's fantastical invention but as a parodic indictment of rich families who show far less care for their children than the working-class Lucia Santa shows for the rebellious Gino. In Puzo's hands, then, satirical renderings of childhood adventures become a subversive means of scrutinizing socioeconomic stratification along with wealth's incapacities and obsessions.

That Davie's parents seem to expect him to be emotionally unmoved by the adventure also speaks to how US cultural expectations for men's emotional invulnerability have historically extended to children, pushing "White boys... to be emotionless alphas" even as they are afforded the "grace and presumption of innocence" withheld from Black boys (Neitzel 11). Puzo captures both elements of this cultural approach to young white masculinity, since the fact that Davie hasn't been in any real danger becomes a tacit acknowledgement of his racial privilege as the nephew of a man who has changed his name from Bernard to Bernardo because he thought it "really sounded fine," with no thought given to the act of cultural appropriation that the change represents (Puzo, *Runaway* 22).[15] Matters of gender similarly assert themselves if we stop to consider how Davie's experience of cross-country travel might have shifted had he been a girl. Although *Davie Shaw* might not appear to explicitly critique the United States' culture of white supremacy or the gendered hierarchy that makes Davie's masculinity such an advantage, both Davie's racialized and gendered good luck and the association of white adult, masculine privilege with characters whom the novel paints as foolhardy and selfish bring it into the same activist universe that Baldwin engages. Though working from a different angle and in a satirical mode, *Davie Shaw* makes an intriguing contribution to the conversation occurring in contemporary "[r]ealistic adventure stories" that have addressed "racism, sex, and violence" (Butts 16).

Described in the novel's front matter as "a thoroughly satisfying adventure story for readers nine and over" (1), *Davie Shaw* exemplifies how fanciful childhood adventures and dangers either real or hypothetical can give way to sobering commentaries on US sociopolitical life. Considering both of these works of Puzo's makes it increasingly easy to recognize the parallel interventions that they make. Like Baldwin, Puzo engages in acts of cross-writing that help to disrupt facile notions of children's literature, in this case showing how the seemingly conventional or simplistic, when carefully interpreted, can reveal complex layers of meaning. If *The Fortunate Pilgrim* tells an engaging story of a young boy's neighborhood escapades, one that might appeal to children as much as any of Twain's fictional adventures, *Davie Shaw* likewise holds rich promise for adults.

Playful Youth, Vengeful Youth: Achebe Writing Children's Adventures

Baldwin and his writings are famed for the depth and intricacy of their transnationalism. As Rich Blint has commented, Baldwin

> lamented the fragile human impulse for categorization, that nagging will to "imprison ourselves in totems, taboos, crosses, blood sacrifices, steeples, mosques, races, armies, flags, nations." The dangerous and often violent need for "life neatly fitted into pegs" signaled for him the death of the imagination, a kind of indulgent innocence bent on refusing the demands and contradictions of history. The content of Baldwin's transnationalism is founded in his ethical resolve to pursue the human condition beyond all the concrete abstractions—race, religion, sexuality, and country, etc.—that we inherit.... Although he was among the first to make connections between the operations of power on populations across the world (between colonization on the continent and slavery and segregation in the Americas), the question of human connection remained for him an interior one ("love has never been a popular movement. And no one has ever really wanted to be free") concerning how one imagines oneself in a world which routinely misnames and divides us as a means of maintaining a particular order. (Blint and Jacobs)

In espousing this perspective, Baldwin both carried on and extended the tradition of transnationalist thought and writing that is so visible in Du Bois and Hughes, for example. This makes it fitting that we think across those same boundaries and "abstractions" in placing Baldwin and Puzo in dialogue with Achebe, whose cross-writing has tended to be similarly neglected, and whose works have expressed their own interest in "transnational cultures" (Uwakweh 35) despite the seeming distance of his oeuvre from the "'new' African literature" and its "[d]iasporic awareness" (Martin and Shaffer 5).

The transition from *Davie Shaw* to a short story like Achebe's "Vengeful Creditor" may feel jarring. Despite being centered on childhood, Achebe's story is perhaps not recognizable as an adventure narrative even to the degree that Puzo's Gino subplot is. Rather, "Vengeful Creditor" unspools a child's frustrated search for adventure, excitement, and discovery, a quest that instead ends in violence and grief. Unapologetically gloomy in its aesthetic and its thematics, the story confronts the callous responses of socioeconomic power to asymmetries in access to education, taking as its subject the "abortive introduction" (Innes 129) of "non-paying primary education" (Balogun 489) in the Eastern Region of the Federation of Nigeria during the mid-1950s. As Alain Séverac notes, this compact piece "demonstrates how the educational system serves only to entrench the privileges of the moneyed classes," so that "European-style education . . . has merely exported the Western class struggle" (249). Critics tend to be united in this general understanding, with F. Odun Balogun noting Achebe's investment in unearthing "the deceit and callousness . . . of contemporary Nigerian educated elites towards the poor" (487) in this historical moment when Nigeria remained a British protectorate and its national anthem remained "God Save the Queen."[16] Catherine Lynette Innes makes a similar point, arguing that the story demonstrates the willingness of the Mercedes-driving upper class "to sacrifice the poor and relatively helpless so that their own lives may not be discomforted" (128), though her short commentary does not necessarily recognize that this social tension has its roots in British colonialism. In their linguistically focused analysis, Adaoma Igwedibia, Christian Anieke, and Kelechi Virginia Ezeaku are much more direct, commenting on how "Vengeful Creditor," like Achebe's other short stories, captures "Igbo culture" in its "complete transformation due to . . . traumatic contact with the West" (80).

For Séverac, "Vengeful Creditor" is "the only text where Achebe lays blame for the disruption of social homogeneity on education" (249). Yet there are moving and painful thematic echoes that reverberate across the story and a range of works by both Achebe and our other cross-writing authors. Just as Balogun has suggested that we examine Achebe's story side by side with Chekhov's "Sleepy," arguing that the two works are bound together by a similar "crusading fervor" (Hingley, qtd. in Balogun 484), I would like to advocate for a transnational reading of Achebe, Puzo, and Baldwin that recognizes their shared commitment to socially engaged writing across the putative boundaries between adult and child readerships, where adventure—both as a genre category and as an elusive ideal of childhood—again becomes a unifying touchstone.

Veronica, the child at the center of "Vengeful Creditor," wants to go to school but is unable to bring her plans to fruition when the government's offer of free primary education is suspended. For her, the promise of the new and unknown is tantalizing and quickly evaporates. Vero envisions school as an adventure: "an escape from the drabness and arduous demands of home," where she must negotiate "the burden of caring for the younger children" (Achebe, "Vengeful" 58–59). Her mindset reflects that classic conception of adventure as an "escape from the domestic sphere," though the implications of her escape would of course be differently gendered: a flight to school would allow her to evade social expectations, rather than simply letting her flee a household space that boys are expected to view as foreign and unappealing. Obliged to withdraw from her school at the government's behest, Vero tries to see the childcare work that her mother accepts for her as an alternative means of escape into the exciting unknown. Though she is ten years old, she will be a caretaker for the children in a wealthy household, and while her mother knows that her new employer's vague promise to someday send her to school is "only a manner of speaking," Vero is filled with hope (62). She anticipates her transplantation into a new home as another opportunity, savoring "the joy of the big going away from the village, from her mother's drab hut, from eating palm-kernels that twisted the intestines at midday, from bitter-leaf soup without fish" (63).

As this "drabness" repeats within the story's narration, it becomes clearer that what adventure means in Vero's life is freedom from both gendered responsibilities and economic marginalization; school "promises the only avenue of escape from the poverty that looms menacingly in her future" (Balogun 488), but it also represents a form of anti-domestic self-actualization that evaporates once she can no longer attend. When Vero again finds herself trapped in a dull routine of caretaking without the promise of school being fulfilled, the loss of adventure means the failure of that multifaceted dream. The real danger of her departure from home emerges when she is provoked to poison the baby she is caring for by giving it red ink to drink "so that [she] can go to school" (Achebe, "Vengeful" 67). Vero's employer attacks her and, to make her confess, "beat her in a mad frenzy with both hands. Then she got a whip and broke it all on her until her face and arms ran with blood" (66). As before, it is not really the adventure itself—the experimentation with a new way of living, whether at school or in a bustling urban household—that threatens Vero's survival. The stifling of adventure by economic and gendered constraints has a chilling effect on Vero's life and her ethical relationship to the world around her, making the pursuit of something life-affirming—knowledge—into a catalyst for violence.

Here it becomes important to remember "the infiltration of Western influences" within Nigerian society under and in the wake of colonialism "as transformative to Nigerian political, economic, and social institutions, marking a transition from the cohesion of the past to the fragmentation of the present" by disrupting "structures of trade, inter-regional cooperation, and intricately layered communal identities" (Falola and Heaton 4). By this time, "the imposition of colonial rule" had wholly disrupted the pluralism of precolonial Nigerian societies' governance "by a sophisticated and effective set of locally-appropriate values," instead imposing a set of "social characteristics . . . that misunderstood, misrepresented, and undermined pre-colonial institutions" (4). In precolonial Igbo society, for instance, "horizontal and vertical mobility" had "provided both men and women opportunities" to "rise to positions of political, economic, and social eminence from which they led both men and . . . women" (Aham-Okoro 10). Despite its pretense to freeing women "from constricting traditions," colonial rule often entailed "the abrogation of [women's] political rights" and disrupted systems of labor in ways that left women "subjected to ... the burden of maintaining the household" while enforcing a "doctrine of male superiority" (11–12) and creating the conditions that would make an escape to school so critical for Achebe's girl protagonist. The colonial enterprise in Nigeria would thus prove multiply responsible for the turns that adventure takes in "Vengeful Creditor," which critiques these manifold disruptions that extend beyond the imposition of "European-style" class inequality although they certainly do not exclude it.

There Was a Country might seem to present another perspective on the prospect of education, which figured prominently in what Achebe refers to as "The Magical Years" in his own life, when his formal educational experiences mingled with exposure to forms of religious and other knowledge that countered British cultural influences. Achebe recalls that he "still had access to a number of relatives who had not converted to Christianity and were called heathens by the new converts," describing how this "access" allowed him to "approach ... the issues of tradition, culture, literature, and language of [their] ancient civilization" so that "a treasure trove of discovery was opened up to" him even as "the Bible ... played an important role in [his] education" (*There Was* 10–11, 13).[17] Such descriptions cast the multicultural pursuit of knowledge as a childhood journey that for Achebe was filled with just as much unexpectedness and excitement as the physical departure from home that he undertook in going to school.

Even in *There Was a Country*, however, educational journeys and adventures take on a double-edged quality, as when the nephew of Achebe's headmaster goes abroad to the United States to earn his PhD but dies before he can return home. "Sadly, just before he returned to Nigeria, he became quite ill," Achebe recalls. "Okongwu [his uncle] was devastated" (17). In another traumatic episode, a classmate of Achebe's at Government College, Umuahia, whom he describes as "brilliant" and who becomes his godson when he converts to Christianity despite their being the same age, later becomes a doctor and then dies by suicide (24). Achebe does celebrate his adventurous encounters with knowledge, particularly the access that they provide to "the sophistication of Igbo phenomenological thought," which he learns, for instance, from "the local villagers" in the town where his primary school is located (18).[18] At the same time, Achebe points to painful instances when forays into western education spell danger and ruin for his peers, complicating the prospect of "receiving an education akin to the royals of England!" (20). Like so much of Achebe's writing about colonialism, then, these sections of his memoir assert an anticolonial impulse even as they acknowledge his complex childhood feelings about his education, including the intellectual curiosity that led him to express interest in foreign ideas as well as his "traditional Igbo history" (39).[19] The ambivalent tenor of this section of Achebe's memoir echoes both the spirit of excitement and the eventual disillusionment that propel the action of "Vengeful Creditor," although the social justice issue here is not so much the straightforward fact of educational access as the costs or consequences of attaining it.

Achebe evokes increasingly painful images of childhood as he takes on the history of the Biafran War. In a review for *The Guardian*, Noo Saro-Wiwa comments on this turn in the narrative, recalling how "at a market, Achebe's wife Christie saw a bomb split a pregnant woman in two. Achebe relays such horrors—including the deaths of his mother and friend Okigbo—with stoic brevity." Achebe's much earlier chapter book *Chike and the River* avoids such physically violent content,[20] and indeed, unlike Achebe's allegorical picture book *How the Leopard Got His Claws*, it was published before the outbreak of the war.[21] Nevertheless, the double-edged childhood adventures of "Vengeful Creditor" and *There Was a Country* are transmuted in *Chike* into a form that does not compromise where it matters, even when it appears superficially distinct. If, as Uzoma Esonwanne reminds us, Achebe has called himself "a protest writer, with restraint" (qtd. in 243), both of these elements—the restraint and especially the protest—are visible in Achebe's compact and subversive adventure story.

At its most elemental, *Chike* is a book about a young boy who wants to cross the "River Niger," and whose adventurousness in pursuing that goal cannot be stamped out despite the warnings of the adults around him ("In particular do not go near the River Niger; many people get drowned there every year," his mother says [5]). With an air of resistance to adult authority that rivals that of Puzo's Gino, the character of Chike has captivated at least a few scholars in recent decades, although the conversation about Chike's adventures has been limited relative to the attention commanded by Achebe's works that are purportedly for adults.[22] The catalyst for Chike's ambition is his journey from his small "bush village" to the "big city" of Onitsha, where he will live with his uncle while going to school, and where he first learns from another child "how easy it was to cross the River Niger and come back again" (3–4, 8). From the first page of the book, Achebe's narrator underlines the "joy" and liberation of these upcoming adventures, which, like Vero's journey to her new employer's household, seem to have the potential to "free" Chike from the "worries" of life in his village, allowing him to "live in a house with an iron roof instead of his mother's poor hut of mud and thatch" (3–4). Readers who are not careful might mistake *Chike* for a book that fulfills the stereotype of children's literature as shielding younger people from more troubling realities, since much of Chike's planning works out for him: he enjoys life with his uncle, makes friends, and spends a great deal of time dreaming of ways to cross the river and reach the city of Asaba. But the newness of his life in Onitsha presents Chike with difficulties as he pursues his goal, and Chike's escapades offer a resultant premise for exploring issues that appear in Achebe's other writings.

For Miriam Dow, the answer to the question of why Achebe's children's books matter politically lies partly in Frantz Fanon's reflections about imperialist representations of white and nonwhite childhood in children's literature. Dow cites Fanon's description of how in so many canonical western children's texts, including in books that were forced on the children of colonized societies within European-style education systems intended to make cultural assimilation and identity loss mandatory, "the Wolf, the Devil, the Evil Spirit, the Bad Man, the Savage are always symbolized by Negroes or Indians; since there is always identification with the victor, the little Negro [reader], quite as easily as the little white boy, becomes an explorer, an adventurer, a missionary who faces the danger of being eaten by the wicked Negroes" (qtd. in 160). In Nigeria, as in other colonial settings, this imperialist function of children's literature played a key role in supporting an "essentially Eurocentric, exploitative, assimilationist, discriminatory and hegemonic" colonial education system (Egbo 63). As Dow points out, books like *Chike* resist this impulse by offering up "African stories for African children" (160) in which the "victor" with whom child readers identify is a Black child rather than a white one. Ernest N. Emenyonu connects this perspective on the book to Achebe's own intentions, describing how Achebe "wrote *Chike and the River* to fulfill a personal family need" (431) after discovering the negative impact of the white-centric curriculum at his three-year-old daughter's school on what Achebe himself called her "notions about race and colour" (qtd. in Emenyonu 431).[23] What I am especially interested in is how *Chike* engages age-diverse audiences in this resistive work, not just by centering an African child as its adventurous protagonist but by confronting specific inequalities and injustices within its plot. In this way, *Chike* operates more similarly to stories like "Vengeful Creditor" than it might initially appear to, while maintaining a tone of joy—and eventually victory—that has its own political power given the imperialist legacy of white-centric children's books.

Dow suggests that Chike's "situation is utopianized to the extent that he is free of familial and economic pressures and so is able to construct himself," while recognizing that "he can only do so with the materials at hand" (165). In reality, the "materials at hand" are such that Chike does face socioeconomic tensions not unlike the forces Vero encounters in "Vengeful Creditor," although his ultimate triumph is key to Achebe's activist project. First there is the simple fact that Chike cannot afford to pay the fare needed to cross the river on a ferryboat, a reality that his friend suggests is "too shameful" for him to admit to others since he is "a big boy" (Achebe, *Chike* 8). Passage across the river costs a sixpence, and both the small size of the sum and the social implications of Chike's not having the money speak to the depth of the class issues in the narrative, where child characters see a lack of access to financial resources as a personal deficiency or even as infantilizing. Although we have the sense that Chike is in this position simply because his uncle refuses to give him the money, the judgment that his lack of access to financial resources provokes remains telling on a larger scale. Then, later on, there is the actual trip from Onitsha to Asaba, a quintessential adventurous journey that Chike manages to make after earning his boat fare washing cars. Although Chike's success brings him happiness, even this moment is suffused with awareness of the social stratification that now characterizes the city of Onitsha:

> Chike thought it would be better to go for a big [car] with a wealthy owner. Soon an enormously long car pulled up. Chike immediately approached it.
> The owner looked like a very important person. Perhaps he was a minister. Then Chike lost his boldness. He stood by the car wondering what to say. But while he hesitated one of the other boys marched up to the man and said, "May I wash your car, sir?"
> ....
> Then one small car arrived. Chike, no longer choosy, wasted no time at all. He went up to the owner and said in good English, "May I wash your car, sir? ... When he had finished he told the owner. But the man was busy talking to his friend and paid little attention to Chike.... Chike stood there, shifting from one foot to the other. Eventually the man looked at him again and put his hand into his pocket. Chike's heart beat faster. He brought out a handful of coins and gave one to Chike. (65)

Rich in detail, this passage records the linguistic consequences of a colonialist approach to African languages that entailed "total proscription of use" as well as "benign neglect" (Mustapha 64).[24] It also invokes the socioeconomic hierarchies imposed by the British under colonialism and vivifies their echoes in early post-independence Nigeria, in which, as Achebe points out, the new "masters" of the "chauffeurs, maids, cooks, gardeners, [and] stewards" became "their own brothers and sisters" (*There Was* 49). With enough wealth to own at least a small car, the driver who offers Chike one of the coins from his pocket can barely be bothered to look at or speak to him, his attitude spotlighting the social consequences of this economic inequality just as Chike's determination to speak "good English" highlights the lasting legacy of British "linguistic hegemony" (Mustafa 57). In framing Chike's story around his ambition for and pursuit of adventure, Achebe creates space for these issues while still underlining the resourcefulness and resilience of his child protagonist.

Many of Chike's adventures prove relatively tame, although as Dow points out, Chike's school "is also a dangerous place, where older and bigger boys have power over younger, weaker ones in a replication of the hierarchical, bullying atmosphere of English schools" (162). At first, even the escapades of Davie Shaw feel more perilous although they yield unfrightening results. Still, the culminating episode presents a very real threat when Chike exposes Mr. Peter Nwaba, a "rich but miserly trader" from Onitsha, in his plot to rob a store (88). In this episode, as Achebe's narrator affirms, Chike comes "close to danger" and is then "rewarded ... with good fortune" in the form of a scholarship funded by the grateful shopkeeper when he exposes the plot (*Chike* 88). Editing the pessimism of "Vengeful Creditor" into a form that affirms the possibility of educational access for young people from diverse socioeconomic backgrounds, *Chike* nonetheless persists in probing unjust and unequal class structures by locating the site of corruption—in the form of the "miserly trader"—at the feet of the wealthy. As such, the narrative asserts the same critique of British colonialism and its role in this "class struggle" that emerges in Achebe's short fiction. Significantly, also as in "Vengeful Creditor," the child hero in *Chike* is endangered by an adult figure who abuses his social power. Chike's challenge to Mr. Nwaba is literally dangerous, inviting an attack by one of the miser's accomplices, who "seized him by the throat" after hearing his story (87). The larger danger, however, resides not in a single adult but in the social framework of which Mr. Nwaba is a part, which is characterized not just by socioeconomic inequality but by religious hypocrisy and domestic violence; we learn that Mr. Nwaba beats his wife if she puts "much fish in the soup" (59). In addressing this constellation of issues, Achebe effectively encouraged and supported an audience of children through, rather than in spite of, *Chike*'s recognizable activist links to his other works.

Cross-Writing Adventurous Children

As Chike's escapades become more perilous and as we wait to see the results of his speaking truth to power, Achebe confronts intersectional legacies of imperialist pathology, appropriating the narrative of boys' adventures into foreign and unknown worlds toward anticolonial ends. There are resounding parallels with both Baldwin's and Puzo's cross-writing, including their critiques of structures of white supremacy, class inequality, and gendered forms of injustice. We can see, then, how *Chike* might be worth teaching in a course on postcolonial literatures, for instance, and not just in a course on children's fiction. Likewise, *Chike* invites us to keep on reinterrogating narrow notions of child readerships as requiring the sort of tender handling that might have led Achebe to omit these manifestations of violence from a book intended for his own young family members. Like so many other contemporary activist writers who have been active in this genre, Achebe refuses this approach. Baldwin does the same, as does Puzo when he entrusts us with a dark, satirical rendering of a family's emotional life.

Bringing together contexts that are as linked in their themes as they are distinct in other ways, these postwar US and postcolonial writings help us to identify patterns in children's literature that emerge with special clarity when they are examined across expected boundaries of audience. From Puzo's explorations of immigrant life in early twentieth-century New York City to Baldwin's evocations of a postwar US culture that is obsessed with antiqueerness, the ostensibly adult narratives rely on representations of childhood adventures and explorations, the perils that they present, and the forces that arrest them. Meanwhile, writing of villages and cities an ocean away, Achebe presents a skewering look at the legacies of British colonialism and their influence on educational equity. That these three writers' children's books go just as deep in addressing these injustices will not surprise anyone who is well-acquainted with children's literature or with contemporary trends in the writing of children's adventure stories. What Baldwin, Puzo, and Achebe uniquely illustrate, however, is the power of cross-written adventure stories to intervene in discourses of social resistance as well as in limiting conceptions of what it means to write for kids.

CHAPTER 3

REDEFINING TERMS, RETHINKING CONCEPTS
Anticolonialism for All Ages from Erdrich to Santiago

Look at the writing that US educators and educational theorists have been doing for generations, and you will find an unsurprisingly substantial amount of space dedicated to the practice of learning the meanings of words. Writing in 1890 in the *Journal of Pedagogy*, a superintendent of schools in Brooklyn, New York, suggested that "the leading of children to grasp the meaning of words . . . is one of the most difficult problems set before the teacher," not least because "learning by rote" encourages students to ignore the multiplicity of meanings that a word may have (Maxwell 129). As an alternative to such acts of rote memorization that would still encourage correct word usage, the author suggested that "every child should be taught and habituated at the earliest possible moment in his school life to consult a dictionary whenever he is in doubt" about the meaning of a word, rather than risk using the term incorrectly. The persistence of this anxiety that children might fail to understand the vocabulary that they read or use remains visible in the inclusion of glossaries in some children's books, which allow child readers to absorb new words and assimilate their accepted meanings, though they may fail to provide the multilayered comprehension of each word that a full-fledged dictionary would offer. The availability of a glossary in a children's book has often been a factor in whether it is recommended for its potential pedagogical value; in their 1973 guide to "the best in children's books," for instance, the University of Chicago offers several recommendations for books that include a glossary, from memoirs to histories of art and US conservation efforts (Sutherland).

Interest in these types of resources may seem natural, although they position students as passive receivers of objectively true knowledge rather than as critical receivers and co-creators of that knowledge.

What happens to these already fraught pedagogical discourses when the very meaning of a word is contested—when its established definitions and typical usages have evolved from cultural bias and its redefinition proves politically necessary to the pursuit of justice? What happens when the words students are learning are ones like "civilization," or when their books take part in revisionist whitewashing that defines colonialism, whether implicitly or explicitly, in a way that excludes the "settling" of the United States? What happens when a book defines cultural belonging in exclusionary ways that marginalize or ignore bilingual and bicultural children? At times, the inclusion of a glossary of terms in a children's book can be a more resistive act that addresses one or more of these embedded biases. In her picture book *Bringing in the New Year*, Grace Lin provides an illustrated glossary that defines and concretizes terms like "qi pao" and "noisemaker," disrupting the western-centric assumption that there is a single "civilized" method of recording or celebrating the passage of time. Gary Soto has often included glossaries with Spanish and other non-English terms in both his picture books and his other "kidlit." This, too, is a resistive method, frustrating attempts to maintain the linguistic hegemony of English in the United States while asserting the legitimacy and cultural importance of code-switching and other linguistically diverse modes of expression. While the refusal to translate a culturally relevant term can send a strong activist message in a work of children's literature like Tagore's *The Crescent Moon*, these other examples illustrate the power that can reside in explicit textual acts of definition. Still, what I would like to take up in more detail in this chapter is the activist function of redefining, rather than defining, terms and concepts in cross-written works. This chapter scrutinizes a suite of contemporary authors ranging from Sandra Cisneros and Louise Erdrich to Joy Harjo, N. Scott Momaday, and Esmeralda Santiago, considering how they have encouraged child readers to resist and remake the definitions of terms and concepts that have played a key role in propping up US architectures of oppression.

Children's books that are engaged in these types of linguistic and pedagogical activism have long facilitated forms of intellectual invention by children that are often discouraged in school systems invested in preserving existing social structures and hierarchies.[1] This is equally true among authors who have not explicitly set out to cross-write separate works for age-diverse audiences. Lettycia Terrones recalls how in her picture book *Rice and Beans*, Muñoz Ryan "surrounds her selective use of Spanish with English to provide such a rich verbal context that translation would likely be unnecessary, even for a monolingual English reader" (231). *Rice and Beans* renders code-switching visible without the benefit of a glossary, normalizing this "linguistic flexibility" (Durán and Henderson 76) by asserting that it does not require extraordinary accommodations to be understood. In using this writing strategy, Muñoz Ryan redefines what it means to linguistically belong: to be understood as ordinary within the multitextured landscape of language use in the United States. A similar impulse appears in Deanna Himanga's *Boozhoo, Come Play with Us*, a board book published by the Fond du Lac Band of Lake Superior Chippewa, which is dedicated "to the many children of the Fond du Lac Reservation." The book's photographs of toddlers at play are pointed in their frustration of the pervasive notion, learned early by many schoolchildren, that Indigenous identities belong to the past of "a country that consistently pretends like they do not exist" (Nagle). Meanwhile, the book's bilingual text helps "teachers displace the erroneous and ubiquitous 'HOW' as the way Indians say hello" (Reese), undoing a stereotype that has long been tied to settler colonialist, othering depictions of Indigenous people. Then there are books like *Lowriders to the Center of the Earth*, which excavates the Indigenous history of Chicanx culture itself while redefining the concept of "civilization" by centering pre-Columbian forms of knowledge. I am interested in drawing attention to contemporary cross-writing authors who do similar redefinitional work, intervening in common understandings of sociopolitically central terms and concepts, ones that urgently require reworking. Reading these authors' children's books in conjunction with their other writings reveals their shared investment in these activist interventions across putative age-based borders of audience.

As a more specific point of entry, I want to begin with Cisneros's papers at Texas State University, San Marcos. There, among the "people" files featuring Cisneros's letters of recommendation for, newspaper clippings about, and other ephemera related to various US writers, is a file on Erdrich that contains a copy of her article "Where I Ought to Be: A Writer's Sense of Place." Cisneros took care in annotating this article, which describes, among other things, how the "mutability" of western culture contrasts with Indigenous patterns of "inhabit[ing] a place until it became deeply and particularly known in each detail" (Erdrich, "Where I Ought to Be"). Erdrich connects this concept of "mutability" to "a systemic policy of cultural extermination" through which "the population of Native North Americans shrank from an estimated 15 million in the mid-15th century to just over 200,000 by 1910." For Erdrich, the exploration of place and what it does or does not mean in literature cannot occur without reckoning with the deadly encroachment of settler colonialism on Indigenous life. At one level of interpretation, these types of archival connections between writers are simply a testament to the overlapping intellectual lives of the voices that have shaped so much of US literary culture in recent decades. At a deeper level, I read Cisneros's investment in Erdrich's thinking as an invitation to examine how cross-writing authors working within Latinx and Indigenous literary traditions have testified to the United States' colonialist history, resisted white-washed fictions of pioneer "settlers" encountering their divinely ordained destiny on uncharted and unpopulated land, and confronted the contemporary permutations of that colonizing impulse in Anglo-America.[2]

From Erdrich to Momaday and Harjo (who attended the University of Iowa with Cisneros), Indigenous authors have written works of children's literature that have redefined and reworked terms and concepts that been used to shore up structures of settler colonialism and institutional racism in the US and abroad. Children's books by Latina writers like Cisneros and stateside Puerto Rican author Esmeralda Santiago have similarly pushed for the deconstruction and redefinition of concepts like colonialism, "civilization," and cultural membership or belonging, drawing on the familiar definitional learning that children are so often asked to do in the classroom but turning it on its head. In the process, this multiethnic and transnational community of authors has made children into agents for rethinking, not just acquiring, definitional knowledge—which becomes revolutionary when used to reshape dominant narratives of identity and history from an actively anticolonial perspective. Examined side by side, Erdrich, Harjo, Cisneros, Momaday, and Santiago show the importance of recast and reconsidered terms, definitions, and concepts to a radical pedagogy of social justice. They also provide another site of generative overlap between texts with younger and older expected audiences, continuing to unsettle patronizing and othering notions of children's literature.

From Past to Future: Revisiting Colonialism and "Civilization" with Louise Erdrich

As the most overtly historical of these texts and a paradigmatic example of how a children's book can challenge received knowledge and the cultural bias from which it stems, Erdrich's *The Birchbark House* offers a good starting point. There is a telling moment early on in Erdrich's 1999 novel, which is set in what Erdrich refers to elsewhere as "Ojibwe country" (*Books and Islands*) during the mid-nineteenth century. The protagonist of the novel is a young girl named Omakayas, a girl who is adventurous and often unwilling to go where others—especially the adults in her life—expect her to be. This sense of authority over her own self leads her to secretly listen in on adult conversations like the one she overhears about the "chimookomanug," or white people, "who were traveling in larger numbers than ever to Ojibwa land and setting down their cabins, forts, barns, gardens, pastures, fences, fur-trading posts, churches, and mission schools," until "there was talk of sending the Anishinabeg to the west" (*Birchbark* 110, 76–77). This breathless accumulation of nouns captures the expanding stranglehold of white colonialists on Anishinabe land and across North America. In doing so, this short passage introduces a clear critique of settler colonialism and its supposedly "civilizing" impulse.

What is key is the way that this moment intervenes in centuries of historical denial of the colonialist history of the United States. In the dominant historical narrative in which the US is imagined as having been settled through the newly productive use of once-vacant lands, the reality that the United States since its founding has functioned as an oppressive colonial power becomes obscured, making colonialism a term that seems to refer to the acts of European powers in other spaces outside North America rather than to the acts of violent displacement of Indigenous people in what would become the United States. As Walter L. Hixson notes, "As the inheritors of a 'New World' and cultivators of a 'virgin land,' the settlers elided their actual historical role as invaders and conquerors of colonial space.... Denial and disavowal of the history of violent dispossession of the indigenes characterize settler societies" (11–12). In Erdrich's novel, however, no such denial is tolerated. The Anishinabeg are at the center of the text rather than being written out of it, so that it becomes easy to see the colonialists invading their land for what they are. Erdrich's novel, then, teaches readers to differently define and understand colonialism, perhaps in some cases before they have even heard the term. This reworked definition includes settler colonialist histories like that of the United States rather than rendering them as exceptional, thus rewriting mythologies of the genesis of the US. The description of the chimookomanug and their many encroachments is written in close-third narration that suggests that this is Omakayas's own knowledge—something that she has observed and come to comprehend. This, in turn, bespeaks the role of children not just in learning these redefinitions but in thinking critically to generate them.

At the same time, *The Birchbark House* invites readers to participate in redefining Eurocentric ideologies of civilization. It might be helpful to look at a passage from later in the novel, after Omakayas's baby brother has died of smallpox, a lasting reminder of the profound physical consequences of the white settlers' presence. In one scene, Omakayas watches an older woman named Old Tallow, a friend of her mother's who is vocal about these realities. Erdrich's narrator tells us, "She blamed them for the disease. She blamed them for the poor quality of game and the scarcity of food—naturally, when so many animals were hunted for sale to white traders for fur, there would be fewer left to eat for survival" (166–67). In addition to pointing out several historically grounded, intensely serious effects of the settlers' appearance, this passage destabilizes white-centric fictions of cultural superiority, which in the mid-nineteenth century tended to be phrased in what Anders Stephanson calls "destinarian language" (48). The destinarian myth of white people's fated and rightful expansion into Indigenous lands and displacement of existing communities both required and supported, in circular fashion, an exceptionalist belief in their supposed specialness. In Old Tallow's eyes and those of the novel, however, the chimookomanug are not special. They are merely shortsighted and destructive, a fact illustrated by their ever-expanding proliferation of "cabins, forts, barns, gardens, pastures" and more, which threaten the ecosystems of Anishinabe lands in a way that endangers everyone's survival and refutes their own exceptionalist logic. As Omakayas's father says at one point, the settlers "are like greedy children. Nothing will ever please them for long" (Erdrich, *Birchbark* 79). In other words, they are emphatically *un*civilized, and their architectural additions to the landscape, which in the Eurocentric imagination are seen as hallmarks of civilization, ironically show the depth of their ignorance. The novel offers up a new definition of the term, a new understanding of who is and is not civilized, that inverts these historical and persisting rationalizations. The act of revision has substantial implications both for readers who have been actively introduced to the term "civilization" and for those who will already have been exposed to and perhaps absorbed its cultural freight, even if their formal education has not yet included this word choice.

As it explores these big ideas, Erdrich's novel positions Omakayas as an authority on her own lived experience, modeling this conception of childhood. In the next scene, Omakayas's thoughts and observations seem to echo Old Tallow's: "The fish were biting only rarely," she worries. "They could fish all day and not even come up with a skinny lake trout" (168). Having learned from Old Tallow as a pedagogical authority within the community, Omakayas does her own conceptual work, thinking analytically in applying ideas that she has absorbed from her surroundings and using them in her own way. This is vital because it allows the novel to redefine terms and rework concepts while putting child readers in particular in a position not just to passively receive these ideas but to invent them and wield them in acts of social resistance, as Omakayas does when her adoptive parents and siblings become ill with smallpox. Having survived the disease as a baby, Omakayas is able to nurse almost all of her family back to health, and her actions become a tangible way of resisting both the physical consequences of the white settlers' presence and the overall project and logic of settler colonialism, which had once inspired John Winthrop to refer to smallpox as a divine miracle, saying in 1631 that "God hath consumed the natives with a miraculous plagey" (qtd. in Stephanson 11). Just over two hundred years later, Omakayas takes an active role in redefining colonialism and civilization in North America when she refutes this grotesque logic, showing that she and her family are survivors—that they are still there. What I am most hoping to stress is not only how Erdrich's novel redefines these concepts, but how it conceptualizes childhood as having an active part in those processes of redefinition and resistance. Erdrich's Anishinabe children are not passive victims of history; they are rebels and survivors whose rigorous thinking and strong actions support them as they refuse to disappear to make way for mainstream narratives of the founding of the United States.

Erdrich's consistent use of "Ojibwa [t]erms" (*Birchbark* 241) does something similar at the level of linguistic history, asserting and contributing to the survival of the language. *The Birchbark House*'s bilingual component encourages anyone who might not already know Ojibwa to acknowledge, value, and learn it, again with the help of a glossary at the back of the book. Meanwhile, readers who do speak or read Ojibwa can see their linguistic identities validated in *The Birchbark House*'s sentence-level style as well as its larger structure. Erdrich's approach recalls Terrones's comments about bilingualism in children's literature as a vital way to "achieve cultural specificity" (231), whether or not a glossary is provided. The novel also goes further in its linguistic activism by thematically redefining ideas of linguistic belonging to include subversive forms of bilingualism intended for projects of social resistance. In fact, this becomes a recurring theme throughout *The Birchbark House* as both children and adults undertake education in other languages than Ojibwa. One man, Fishtail, "went to the priest's school. To learn to read the chimookoman's tracks. That way they can't cheat us with the treaties" (Erdrich, *Birchbark* 112). In this reconfiguration of the white conceptions of language that would lead to the forced linguistic assimilation of Indigenous children, Erdrich's novel points to the importance of maintaining the Ojibwa language as well as the legitimacy of bilingualism as a strategy for resisting systems of power designed to disenfranchise Indigenous people based on language use. The novel asserts its membership within a multiethnic range of "radical" contemporary US children's books that includes texts like Sun Yung Shin and Kim Cogan's *Cooper's Lesson*, where "cultural and historical practices supersede issues of phenotype" (Chaudhri 28). In the afterword to the bilingual narrative, Shin writes in English about her own estrangement from the Korean language and the implications of this type of alienation for children "caught between two worlds," deploying English as a weapon against the forces that produce these feelings of marginalization for bicultural children. In a sense, Erdrich's characters do the same in that they strategically employ English for politically subversive purposes.

Redefining which languages matter by resisting the white racist belief that Indigenous "languages were inferior and had no value or place in a contemporary [school] curriculum" (King 119), Erdrich's novel dethrones English and French as the historical languages of choice among white settlers squatting on Anishinabe land while asserting that adults and children who embrace this subversive linguistic hybridity do not belong any less legitimately to the community of their birth. This same flexibility in defining cultural belonging extends to biracial identity in the novel, which features a protagonist with a French great-grandfather. Omakayas's father, when questioned about his racial identity, is assertive: "'Go ahead, cut off my arm,' offered Deydey, 'see if you can divide the white blood from the red blood'" (Erdrich, *Birchbark* 167). This reclamation of bilingual and biracial identities modifies cultural scripts that suggest that nonhybrid identities are the more legitimate, more "civilized," or otherwise superior ones, while identifying the original sources of this hybridity in colonialist violence and bearing witness to the agency and resilience of colonized people in their responses to that trauma. As Erdrich suggests in "Where I Ought to Be," contemporary "Native American writers . . . must tell the stories of contemporary survivors while protecting and celebrating the cores of cultures left in the wake of the catastrophe" of settler colonialism. *The Birchbark House*, through its acts of redefinition and rethinking, does the same, proposing pressing contributions that stand to reconfigure the conceptual understanding of readers of all ages.

While Erdrich's writing outside the realm of the children's book routinely tells "the stories of contemporary survivors," it is exciting to see that even Erdrich's recent foray into a very different type of speculative, dystopian fiction echoes these ways of operating. In her 2017 novel *Future Home of the Living God*, which was alternately praised and nearly panned by critics, Erdrich breaks new ground while returning to this still-important terrain with an insistence that speaks not just to the significance of the ideas involved but to the sophistication of the children's fiction that expresses these same concepts. From the opening pages of *Future Home*, hybrid cultural identities and the complexities they invoke are on display. Erdrich's first-person narrator describes herself as "Cedar Hawk Songmaker . . . the adopted child of Minneapolis liberals" and the biological daughter of a woman named Mary Potts, explaining how she became ashamed when she went to college, met "other indigenes," and became, not an "Indian Princess!" but "ordinary," with "no clan, no culture, no language, no relatives" (*Future Home* 4–5). As the book progresses and Erdrich develops its strangely familiar world, a world in which evolution is happening in reverse and in which a repressive government is progressively revoking the rights of women, Erdrich's dystopian vision becomes a pointed critique of a contemporary US society built on "the colonization of this region" (6) and all the other regions affected by the North American sequence of genocides and displacements that accompanied the Europeans' arrival. Scenes that happen on the reservation where the narrator's birth mother still lives serve as a reminder that such denials of human rights as women are experiencing in the novel's futuristic present are nothing new because they have been happening to Indigenous women for centuries—even if the Potts are "bourgeois," owners of "the Superpumper franchise first stop before the casino" (5). Despite its differences in setting, genre, and expected audience, *The Birchbark House* serves as a kind of unexpected precursor to novels like *Future Home*, demonstrating how Erdrich encourages us all, regardless of age, to think in inventive and urgently needed ways.

Resisting Settler Colonialism in Cisneros and Harjo

Cisneros's work to date has proved to be intensely wide-ranging, spanning chapbook-length and full-length collections of poetry, novels, short stories, essays, children's fiction, and illustrated fiction written expressly for adults that has played its own role in complicating overdetermined distinctions between children's literature and its alternatives by asserting that adults need picture books, too. *Have You Seen Marie?*, published in 2012, is a fascinating meditation on loss and grief that Cisneros's personal website, under the heading "About My Life and Work," describes as "a picture book for grown-ups." Other writings of Cisneros's espouse a kind of egalitarian spirit, picturing children as just one of the diverse readerships that they might speak to. Cisneros thus became one of the cross-writing authors in this book who not only write "for both child and adult audiences ... in separate works" but also "address younger and older audiences with equal care and respect" in a single book. Cisneros has problematized limiting conceptions of children's literature by infusing her cross-writing with a consistent activism.

In 1978, Cisneros would finish her MFA in poetry at the University of Iowa, where she had been alienated by an approach to teaching creative writing that marginalized the voices of students of color, women, and working-class writers. For many years now, Cisneros has been vocal about the insularity of programs like Iowa's—listen to her speak during interviews, and you will learn that it is in spite of the Iowa Writers' Workshop, not because of it, that she became a writer. What her time in Iowa City did do for Cisneros was further crystallize her sense of determination to tell stories that so many of her classmates and professors not only failed to comprehend but failed to recognize as important.

It also led her to develop a powerful friendship and relationship of solidarity with Mvskoke writer Joy Harjo, who was at Iowa at the same time although she was slightly older—and who, in Cisneros's own words, "fortified and guided" her as she "found [her] voice as a writer, as an activist" (Letter to Thomas Wortham). In the 2001 letter that included these comments, in which she recommended Harjo for a teaching position at the University of California, Los Angeles, Cisneros insisted that her evaluators recognize Harjo as "a maverick" who modeled "a poetry that could be socially-minded and grounded in the language of working-class people." It was at once a simple statement and a supremely worded summary of Harjo's literary activism.

Within the universe of children's literature, this worldview shared between Cisneros and Harjo has translated into politically inflected approaches to picture books and longer-form texts like Cisneros's *The House on Mango Street*, which its author envisioned as "a cross between poetry and fiction" (qtd. in Olivares 233). Emphasizing contemporary settings, both Cisneros and Harjo infuse their children's books with an urgent awareness of contemporary manifestations and consequences of settler colonialism in the United States of the late twentieth and early twenty-first centuries, while continuing to reenvision how the concept of civilization ought to be defined and advancing ideas of belonging that resist false narratives of triumphant conquest and cultural supremacy. These literary strategies allow Cisneros and Harjo to model redefining terms and rethinking concepts as the task and the birthright of assertive, brilliant, protesting children with sophisticated and insistent voices. They remind us that such intricate intellectual ambitions are well within the scope of children's literature, which demands the respect of all readers—even skeptical adults.

Cisneros's praise of Harjo reflects values similar to the ones that she has voiced in talking about her own work. Speaking about the now-canonical *Mango Street*, Cisneros describes how she intended the book to be "for all people, whether they were educated or not, and whether they were children or adults. My idea," she has said,

> was to write it in a way that it would not make anyone feel intimidated, but welcome. I had in mind a book that would be understood and appreciated by all readers, whether a working-class person, a child, poet, literature student, writer, or bus driver. So I came from that angle of being inclusive. I kept a child in mind as I was writing it, but it wasn't just for children. I kept fellow poets in mind, but it wasn't just for poets. (Cisneros and Queirós)

Today, Cisneros herself will tell you that *Mango Street* "is required reading in middle schools, high schools, and universities across the country" ("About My

Life and Work"), yet teachers who assign it risk inviting intervention by school boards like the one in St. Helens, Oregon, whose "reconsideration committee" attempted to ban the teaching of the book for middle school students in 2012. Protestations are common among those who believe that *Mango Street* is not acceptable for children because of its references to sexual assault, which seem to be persuasive in making people forget that Cisneros was also writing for kids. The book has been banned for "anti-American" content as well (qtd. in Scales 136) and was cited in the court ruling declaring Tucson's Mexican American studies program illegal in 2011.[3] In the meantime, those of Cisneros's works that have been received as being more exclusively for children—sometimes despite her own protestations—are among her least known and most neglected works. These include a book written in Italian and published in Italy called *Bravo Bruno!*, which Cisneros describes on her website as being "for readers age 6 to 106" ("Books") but which has not achieved sufficient popularity to be translated into English or other languages. They also include *Hairs/Pelitos*, a bilingual illustrated version of one of the early vignettes from *Mango Street* that *Publishers Weekly* has labeled as being for ages four to eight.

As a multiply cross-written work, *Mango Street* makes varied interventions in the conversation about settler colonialism that this chapter has taken up. As Hixson notes, the US settler colonialist enterprise was not confined to white settlers' violent displacement of Indigenous people like the Anishinabeg; further south, it included the theft of almost half of Mexico's territory in the Mexican American War, when "Mexicans found themselves squarely in the path of a crusading nation committed to an almost boundless settler colonial expansion" (94). While *Mango Street* is set over a century later in Cisneros's hometown of Chicago, it engages with this history by exploring how it is echoed and extended in twinned experiences of gentrification and white flight within the city's urban landscape. The young Esperanza Cordero, who is the narrative voice and authority, calls out these patterns in housing inequality in a vignette titled "Cathy, Queen of Cats." Cathy tells Esperanza, "I am the great great grand cousin of the queen of France. . . . You want a friend, she says. Okay, I'll be your friend. But only till next Tuesday. That's when we move away. Got to. Then as if she forgot I just moved in, she says the neighborhood is getting bad" (Cisneros, *House* 13).

One of the more famous moments in Cisneros's book, this passage has attracted attention because it so trenchantly spotlights the socioeconomic and racial elitism of Esperanza's childhood neighbor. More particularly, however, its evocation of white flight extends the redefinition of colonialism to include these later actions of the descendants of white settlers who, having taken over Indigenous land across North America, have then refused to share it with the descendants of people from other places colonized by the US. White flight might seem to be the inverse of this pattern of appropriation of spaces and resources, as it involves fleeing difference rather than invading othered communities—yet this type of white behavior shares with settler colonialism its fundamental disregard for the worth of people of color and their right to take up space. Like Omakayas's critical thinking about whiteness and what it represents, Esperanza's critique of Cathy and her pretense to old-world elitism rejects this white logic. There is a distinctly satirical edge in Esperanza's voice as she recounts Cathy's bragging about her supposed royal roots, and the end of the vignette makes it clear that Esperanza will refuse to acquiesce to Cathy's implicit demand that she assume a self-effacing or deferential attitude: "In the meantime they'll just have to move a little farther north from Mango Street" because Esperanza and her family refuse to disappear (13). Esperanza's narration further redefines the concept of colonialism to include its subtler twentieth-century permutations while asserting her ability as a Chicana child narrator to call out and resist this species of white entitlement.

Mango Street also destabilizes Eurocentric ideas of civilization: ideas that are so pervasive that readers of any age are likely to have encountered them either implicitly or explicitly. In several vignettes, the family's return trips to Mexico revise the simplistic narrative of immigrant assimilation on which the mythology of the American Dream depends. Resisting the idea that the United States represents a superior homeland from which migrants should have no wish to depart, Esperanza's narration reframes the US-Mexico border as something to be crossed recursively to access an alternate civilization with distinct practices to be respected rather than denigrated, like a different manner of "send[ing] the dead away" (56). Other vignettes reference brujería, legitimating syncretic religious traditions that marry Christian and Indigenous beliefs, as when "Elenita, witch woman," gives Esperanza access to "los espíritus" and predicts that she will find "a home in the heart" before asking "the Virgin" to "bless" her (62–64). This is a strategic act of revision of xenophobic US fears and stereotypes of brujería that cast these practices as uncivilized and irrational. As Christina Garcia Lopez puts it, "the knowledge systems of curanderismo and brujería place the integration of mindbodyspirit at their center and represent durable, living forms of counterknowledge, even as Western culture casts them as superstition" (32). Cisneros models this form of syncretic cultural resistance grounded in the "counterknowledge" of a child protagonist.

Other scenes question the urban logic of US cities as the putative seat of American civilization, since Esperanza connects more with the small pockets of nature in the landscape of Chicago, like the "four skinny trees" who "are the only ones who understand" her (Cisneros, *House* 74). She revels in the way that a garden, left untended until it is overgrown, begins to swallow up the trappings of supposed civilization as it is conceived in the white imagination:

> Flowers stopped obeying the little bricks that kept them from growing beyond their paths. Weeds mixed in. Dead cars appeared overnight like mushrooms. First one and then another and then a pale blue pickup with the windshield missing.... Things had a way of disappearing in the garden, as if the garden itself ate them, or, as if with its old-man memory, it put them away and forgot them. Nenny found a dollar and a dead mouse between two rocks in the stone wall where the morning glories climbed.... This, I suppose, was the reason why we went there. (95)

In asserting the indomitability of this uncultivated space relative to the automobiles and dollar bills it swallows up, Esperanza rejects what A. A. den Otter describes as the perceived "civilizing mission" of the European colonizers in North America as they sought, in their view, "to transform the wild northern territories into productive, civilized lands" (xii). Instead, Esperanza's narration celebrates a defiantly different definition of civilization in which the desirable places to inhabit are the ones that feel like they "had been there before anything" and "could hide things for a thousand years" (Cisneros, *House* 96). Cisneros's sophisticated construction of childhood gives Esperanza the capacity to deconstruct these pillars of settler colonialist ideology in the United States, expressing a vision that is consonant with Erdrich's ideas about Indigenous cultures "establishing a historical background for the landscape" as a diachronic constant in the life of a community ("Where I Ought to Be").

Mango Street is a clear product of a cross-writing strategy targeted to both children and adults. However, because it has been suppressed by some who view it as unsuitable for anyone who is not yet a grown-up, *Mango Street* also presents us with a unique opportunity to consider it in tandem with other books of Cisneros's that have not been similarly provocative. Their divergent reception histories might seem to suggest that *Hairs/Pelitos* will be less challenging or sophisticated than its "mature" counterpart, which one adult reviewer on the website Common Sense Media responded to in a tone of panicked horror, exhorting fellow parents to "GET THIS BOOK OUT OF YOUR KIDS [sic] VIEW FAST!" ("The House on Mango Street"). However, Cisneros's picture book is in fact as subversive as its precursor, especially in its disruption of settler colonialist terms and concepts.

Taken from *Mango Street*'s second vignette, the text of *Hairs/Pelitos* records Esperanza's observations about the hair textures of the members of her family. "Todos en nuestra familia tenemos pelo diferente," the bilingual narration begins ("Everybody in our family has different hair") (Cisneros, *Hairs/Pelitos*). The narrator, who is unnamed in the picture book but whom we recognize as Esperanza from the original vignette, goes on to explain that her father's hair is "como una escoba" ("like a broom") and that her own hair "nunca obedece a broches o diademas"—it "never obeys barrettes or bands." Meanwhile, her sister's hair is "resbaloso" ("slippery"), and her brother's is "grueso y lacio," or "thick and straight." With these straightforward declarative statements, Esperanza resists the pressure on Latinx children to do what Margaret E. Montoya describes as "mask[ing] immutable characteristics of skin color, eye shape, or hair texture because they have historically been loathsome to the dominant culture" (195). Through Esperanza's voice, Cisneros also does something similar to what Erdrich does in redefining cultural belonging to include bilingualism and biracial identity. The diversity of hair textures in Esperanza's family speaks to the need to reconceptualize family and community belonging to celebrate the physical diversity of individual identities that might otherwise be stigmatized because they less closely approximate the racist Eurocentric beauty standards that Esperanza resists. Esperanza's narration redefines these ideals of beauty that have been central to the white supremacist goal of promoting western "civilization" and its sociopolitical dominance, while redefining the concept of belonging to make room for variation in identities among people who are intimately connected to each other. As Chaudhri says of Monica Brown and Sara Palacios's bilingual picture book *Marisol McDonald Doesn't Match*, such texts assert that while "being different," and specifically multiracial, can make "other people uncomfortable" due to their own internalized prejudices, attempts "to accommodate them [are] unjustifiable" and unnecessary (30).

Finally, the bilingual narration of *Hairs/Pelitos* is an emphatic challenge to the ideology of English-only education programs in the United States and to other cultural authorities that have attempted to linguistically disempower Latinx children by defining belonging in the United States in terms of compliance with expectations for monolingualism, generating "a form of institutional discrimination that is oppressive" (Smokowski and Bacallao 79). As in Erdrich, not only is linguistic belonging redefined, but Cisneros depicts her child narrator communicating in multiple languages and laying claim to multiple linguistic identities. While the legitimacy of bilingual and non-English-speaking identities and the injustice of linguistic prejudice are already potent refrains that extend throughout *Mango Street*, as when Mamacita's husband treats her as though she "does not belong" in the United States because she will not speak English (78), the equal space given to the Spanish text in *Hairs/Pelitos* means that the form of the book reinforces its thematic bent where language is concerned. We might think of another of Brown's picture books, her "Pura Belpré

Award-winning book *Tito Puente: Mambo King/Rey del Mambo*," in which "[a]ll textual elements appear in both English and Spanish, including the text of the story as well as the author note at the end of the book" (Terrones 231), so that the two languages are placed on the same plane and linguistic identities other than that of the monolingual English speaker are validated. Like *Tito Puente*, books like *Hairs/Pelitos* have an anticolonial bent that rejects and resists the use of narrow definitions of belonging to force assimilation on children in the US who otherwise might prove troublesome to the settler colonialist apparatus in its contemporary form. Cisneros invites readers of all ages with multiple linguistic identities not to acquiesce but instead to trouble—or even to make trouble for—those institutional structures. These shared impulses across *Hairs/Pelitos* and *Mango Street* offer compelling evidence that they are both worthy of adults' serious attention, that they are both important for children to read, and that the strict demarcations that segregate the two books from one another need to be broken down.

I continue to return to Erdrich's novel in view of its relentless confrontations with persisting ideas that retroactively rationalize the history of US settler colonialism, and because of how the narrative grapples with questions that arise from that history about what it means to belong or to maintain one's identity in interfacing with a settler colonialist state. Yet it is also vital that Indigenous children today see their identities mirrored in contemporary children's books filled with contemporary Indigenous characters. As Thomas King has commented, "to maintain the cult and sanctity of the Dead Indian, North America has decided that Live Indians living today cannot be genuine Indians.... Dead Indians are Garden of Eden-variety Indians. Pure, Noble, Innocent. Perfectly authentic. Jean-Jacques Rousseau Indians. Not a feather out of place" (64–65). As much as it resists these stereotypes, *The Birchbark House* is a historical novel and has resulting limitations in how directly it can intervene in these pathological discourses surrounding "Live Indians living today." More generally, just as poems of Hughes's like "Negro Dancers" show why African American children's literature cannot and should not be limited to depicting slavery and its legacies, the broader world of Indigenous children's literature teaches us that such books should not be limited to narrativizing histories of white settlers' encroachment on Indigenous lands. These are just a few reasons why it is essential to spotlight books set in the twentieth and twenty-first centuries, like Harjo's *For a Girl Becoming*, illustrated by Mercedes McDonald.

A colonizing impulse has emerged in some responses to Harjo, which interpret *For a Girl Becoming* as a universal story of coming of age with the potential to uplift, empower, and benefit all readers who identify as "girls," regardless of their ethnonational identity or any other facet of their individuality. *Midwest*

Book Review has called it "a beautiful experience waiting to be treasured by its lucky recipient, appropriate for celebrations of such joyous transitions as birth, graduation, or any other significant turning point in a young woman's life" ("Reviewer's Choice"). The blurb chosen by the publisher for the back of the book similarly identifies it as "a blessing to bestow on all of the young women in our lives," where "our" seems to refer to a kind of universal audience; the writer of the blurb is not Indigenous. Although Harjo's power to move any reader is unquestionable, such readings do threaten to efface the culturally, personally, and politically specific elements of the narrative and its illustrations, which trace the story of an Indigenous girl's growing up, from her birth to her leaving home and navigating the world outside it.

Working in contravention to these responses, Harjo chose to dedicate the book to her grandchildren, first listing her granddaughter Krista Rae, to whom the original text was dedicated when Harjo posted it on her blog in 2005 ("For a Girl"). Harjo commented in more detail in a 2012 interview that the book "is a blessing poem for [her] oldest grandchild, a granddaughter, who, at the time [Harjo] wrote the poem, was coming of age. She just graduated from college" (Harjo and Steele). And indeed, the book itself encourages this both more personal and more culturally specific interpretation, with its references to "medicine plants," "tobacco and cedar," "a cradleboard, hope, white shell, and turquoise . . . blankets to wrap you in and soft, beaded moccasins of deerskin," all in the first few pages (Harjo, *For a Girl*). Harjo has taken care to clarify that the book is multicultural in invoking "Mvskoke, Navajo predominantly, as well as Pueblo and Cherokee" elements because her "grandchildren are multicultural beings" (Harjo and Winder 64). As another critic asserts, then, this is a text "whose intended audience" is Indigenous (Dimmett and Hoffman).

Harjo's own words are the best guide to the ways in which *For a Girl Becoming* represents both a rewriting of received notions of colonialism and civilization and a reenvisioning of what belonging means for contemporary Indigenous children and adolescents. Discussing the role of "protocol," Harjo comments that it "is important that the child reading about and participating in the story understand that protocol means respect. It is respect for oneself, gifts, family, and everyone's place in the world" (Harjo and Winder 66).[4] We can see this emphasis on self-respect, not just respect for others, in the exhortations of the book's speaker—"Clean your room. . . . Bury what needs to be buried. . . . Praise and give thanks for each small and large thing"—which first and foremost emphasize self-care and kindness to oneself (Harjo, *For a Girl*).[5] While Harjo's description of "respect for oneself, gifts, family" might be read outside its sociohistorical context as a generalized hope for any child, cultivating self-respect within this context is a direct act of political resistance to a colonizing force that has sought to undermine the self-esteem and self-concept of Indigenous children while using children's forced assimilation as a tool for the domination and oppression of Indigenous communities more broadly.

Elaborating on this particularized strain of resistance, Harjo has commented, for instance, on how *For a Girl Becoming* reflects Mvskoke and other Indigenous experiences of home:

> A house can be a home. Houses may assume importance here because my tribe was uprooted from our homelands East of the Mississippi River and forced to Indian Territory in what is now known as Oklahoma. Our homes were burned behind us, or taken over by colonizers. We are still recovering. This is true for many tribal peoples in this hemisphere. This process of takeover is still ongoing, in more recent years with the U.S. government's relocation program. (Harjo and Winder 66)

Thus, when the speaker proclaims, "May you always have a home: a refuge from storm, a gathering-place for safety, for comfort," and when she tells the adolescent subject of the book's blessings that there are "wayward humans who will hurt you," the blessing and the warning it counterbalances rewrite the global history of colonialism to include both the actions of US settler colonialists, who have stolen those homes from so many, and the resilience and public and private expressions of agency of contemporary Indigenous children and adolescents who can make and remake their homes in defiance of the never-ending efforts to force their disappearance (Harjo, *For a Girl*). They can "fall . . . and get back up again," Harjo's speaker insists. What binds this aspect of Harjo's writing to that of her former classmate Cisneros is her efforts to bring the conversation about colonialism in the United States out of the space of history and into the contemporary world of young readers who must confront the continually existing echoes of that history.

At the same time, Harjo's reference to "protocol," or "particular codes of behavior" that encode Indigenous knowledge of what is upright, just, and good (McGlennen 167), is essential because it gestures toward a different rubric for use in defining and applying the term "civilization."[6] *For a Girl Becoming* is indeed a guide to protocol, setting out ethical principles for "the child reading about and participating in the story" to understand and follow: "Give a drink of water to all who ask, whether they be plant, creature, human, or helpful spirit. . . . Feed your neighbors. Give kind words and assistance / to all you meet along the way— / We are all related in this place."[7] With these precise imperative phrases, Harjo insists on defining what it means to be civilized based on a rubric that distinguishes the European settler colonialist and his present-day

US counterparts as a massive failure of civilization on a transnational scale. By reclaiming the cultural authority to determine what civilization is and asserting longstanding alternative systems of knowledge, Harjo models the process of defining a term in contravention to the fabulist beliefs of the dominant "majority culture." Harjo is able to accomplish this without ever using the term, depriving it of its cultural power even as she encourages her audience to rethink and rework its definition.

By its final pages, *For a Girl Becoming* has rewritten the concept of belonging. Turning on its head the hemisphere's legacy of "uprooted" Indigenous communities and the histories of Indigenous children who had a politics of assimilation violently forced on them, Harjo insists on presenting belonging not as a form of cultural disappearance into the monolithic whiteness of "settler" society but as a familial, community-based, and fundamentally Indigenous practice for young people to engage in: the creation of a space where their personhood will be safe from acts of cultural sabotage. The speaker reassures the book's young readers in the second person, saying, "There are treacherous places along the way, but you can come to us.... Always within you is that day your spirit came to us." This species of belonging has nothing to do with the racist stereotypes of Indigenous identity that are so often foisted on Indigenous communities by cultural outsiders. The heritage and inheritances of the "girl becoming" include "medicine makers, stubbornness, beauty, tribal leaders, and a yard filled with junked cars and the gift of knowing how to make them run," all from her mother's side of the family, while her father's side is filled with "educators, thinkers, dreamers, weavers, and mathematical genius." Harjo clarifies that these are references to "the two sets of grandparents" of the child in the book, "though most have been passed from one generation to another" (Harjo and Winder 65). The "girl becoming" also sets out on a journey into a wider world: a journey that is illustrated by her walking through a crowd of faceless shadows carrying two suitcases and wearing a bold red dress, on a page of the book that becomes a beautiful invocation of Krista Rae's leaving for college. Here we can recognize a by-now familiar refrain that connects our writers in this chapter, who emphasize the diversity of identities within individual families as well as their powerful togetherness in love and insistent cultural knowledge and pride. As before, this attitude resists the colonialist violence of forced assimilation, the denigration and stereotyping of Indigenous communities, and persisting myths of white western cultural supremacy.

While I have already suggested that we view Cisneros's *Hairs/Pelitos* as powerfully, politically consonant with *Mango Street*, I would also like to bring Cisneros's and Harjo's children's books alongside their other verse, which tends to be most universally received or interpreted as writing for adults.[8] In one poem, "Mexicans in France," Cisneros's travels abroad translate into incisive reflections on both racism in the United States and European responses to it. Her poem's speaker encounters a Frenchman who engages her in a conversation that begins with "U.S. racism" and then turns to stereotypes of Mexican identity that the presumably white male figure himself subscribes to. The man attempts to distinguish himself and the society he represents from the ongoing problem of white racism in the United States, yet his determination to turn racism into a topic of curiosity and his request that the speaker engage in the labor of educating him mark his positionality as a beneficiary of the same transnational Euro-American system of colonialism that he purports to criticize. Harjo's poem "It's Raining in Honolulu" takes a similarly expansive position as it witnesses the United States' neocolonialist incursions into Hawai'i, which remain a historical and contemporary reality despite the fact of its statehood. Harjo lived in Hawai'i for eleven years and has spoken of how Hawaiian culture demonstrated to her "the power of cultural expression to grow and hold a people together, no matter governance, or gunpowder" (Winder and Harjo 64). The speaker of "It's Raining" uses words that embody this combination of oppressive governance and cultural resilience: "The wetness saturates everything, including the perpetrators of the second overthrow. / We will plant songs where there were curses" (194).[9] Poems like these spotlight the realities of the United States' colonial history and national identity, breaking down the putative distinction between the government of the United States and its European counterparts where this culture of domination is concerned.

In other poems, both Cisneros and Harjo invoke figurations of cultural pride that integrate distinct concepts of civilization and belonging. Cisneros's "You Bring Out the Mexican in Me" is written in a lyrical mode that vivifies the process of rediscovering and celebrating one's cultural heritage in all its contradictions and complexities through a romantic partner.[10] As the poem's speaker clarifies, this "Mexican" identity encompasses "tequila *lágrimas* on Saturday all / through next weekend Sunday," "[t]he Aztec love of war," "the colonizer," and "[t]he stand-back-white-bitch," all of which she carries within her (Cisneros, "You Bring" 4–5). Both linguistic and other forms of cultural hybridity are on display here, where belonging to Chicanx culture means proudly claiming an Indigenous identity, standing up to white aggression, and facing one's "colonizer" ancestry; none of this mestizaje makes the identity of Cisneros's speaker less legitimate. In referencing Mexico's pre-Columbian past, "You Bring Out the Mexican in Me" again asserts the need to rethink what civilization is in light of a far longer history of the Americas than is convenient for narratives of European "discovery" to admit. There are resulting thematic linkages that connect this poem not only to Cisneros's *Hairs/Pelitos* but to a larger universe of activist children's books by writers and illustrators such as Cathy Camper and Raúl the Third.

Harjo's poem "3 A.M." does similar work when the speaker reconfigures "the center / of the world" to include "Old Oraibi, Third Mesa" as well as "New York / Chicago" (8), while her poem "The Woman Hanging from the Thirteenth Floor Window" resists the tendency of cultural outsiders to invalidate or erase the indigeneity of "urban Indian" experiences whose blending of identities frustrates tired stereotypes of Indigenous identity (210). As Harjo reminds us in her notes for that poem, "One of the U.S. programs to attempt to disappear native people was a program called *Relocation*. The goal was the disappearance of Indian people, the logic being that if Indian families moved to the cities for jobs, to live, that they would become acculturated, would forget their 'Indianness'" ("Notes" 210). In recording the intense emotional pain of this physical dislocation from home and asserting the tenacious "Indianness" of the subject of her poem, Harjo puts an obstacle in the path of this campaign to obliterate indigeneity. Poems like "The Woman Hanging" give a new resonance to children's books like *For a Girl Becoming*, one that becomes all the more obvious given these candid depictions of what settler colonialism means for contemporary Indigenous people, communities, and nations. The angle of approach is different—one text reads as an act of blessing and the other as an act of mourning—but a foundation of resistance remains visible across the two works, and that resistance has everything to do with how Harjo teaches readers young and old to think about what it means to belong and to thrive in the wake of displacement, disenfranchisement, and loss.

Hybrid Identities, Religion, and Acts of Redefinition in Momaday and Santiago

While the best-known book by Kiowa writer N. Scott Momaday is arguably his 1968 novel *House Made of Dawn*, which received the Pulitzer Prize for Fiction, it is his much less well-known play *The Indolent Boys* that I wish to turn to before introducing *Circle of Wonder*. First produced in 1992 and published in 2007 with two other plays, *The Indolent Boys* retells the story of three children who ran away from the Kiowa Boarding School in Anadarko, Oklahoma in 1891 and who subsequently died in a snowstorm as they attempted to return to their families. Irony is at its most profound and painful in the play, as white teachers and administrators at the school pontificate about "civilization" and savagery in the wake of the boys' disappearance, incapable of grasping that it is their own thoroughly uncivilized and "savage" acts of both physical and psychological violence toward Indigenous children that have brought about the boys' deaths (Momaday, *Indolent* 22, 47). I have written elsewhere about how the play's deployment of Gothic tropes facilitates its critique of settler colonialist mythologies and their lethal effects on Indigenous children. What changes, however, when we reread *The Indolent Boys* in light of Momaday's illustrated children's fiction? Might this act of cross-reading offer the same sorts of mutually constitutive meanings that we saw in Harjo?

A look at Momaday's own edits to the original draft of the script shows the importance of this vocabulary. In the first draft, a teacher proclaims that if "it weren't for" the "fear and craziness" of the eldest of the three runaways, "those poor boys would be alive today" (39). In Momaday's handwritten annotations, he inserts the phrase "his . . . his *savagery*," and the eventual published version maintains that diction, though in a different permutation:

> WHERRITT: (with rhetoric) Well, look here, Carrie. If you think about it, it was bound to happen.
> CARRIE: What are you saying?
> WHERRITT: Why, you know as well as I do that Sailor was to blame. If it weren't for his fear and craziness, his . . . well, those poor boys would have been alive today.
> CARRIE: His fear and craziness, his . . .
> WHERRITT: Let's be honest, he is an Indian, a savage. (47)

What the play makes clear is that it is Wherritt and his compatriots who are the "savages" without whom "those poor boys would have" lived, although Carrie plays a more ambiguous role as a teacher who attempts to validate Indigenous cultural knowledge in small ways while still ultimately participating in an oppressive system. The play unfolds a history of abuse that will be familiar to those who know the history of the "Indian boarding schools" but that its white perpetrators refuse to acknowledge. Describing the response that he received after running away from the school himself, the older student John Pai is clear about the multiple valances of the system of punishment enacted at the school:

> JOHN PAI: I was disciplined.
> CARRIE: You were . . . whipped?
> JOHN PAI: That was the least of it. Physical pain was not inflicted upon me. It was symbolic, it was merely the pain of humiliation. Shame. I was made to do what I had to do when I first came to the school, as a little boy. They cut my hair, which was already cut short. They left cuts and little tufts of hair on my scalp. That is how we *Gaigwu* look when

we are grieving. It was as if I was mourning my own death. Then I had to stand naked with the new students, who were much younger than I and terribly frightened, who thought that they were being put to death, while we were deloused with poisonous powder; it got into our eyes and nostrils and mouth. And then I had to choose again my Christian name from a list on the blackboard, pointing with a stick. It was like counting coup. My name was my enemy. How is it you say?—I was made an example. (33)

In exposing these details through the character of John Pai, Momaday underscores the extremity of the lie of the compassionate white savior.[11]

The idea is reiterated even more explicitly in the play's final scene, when the oldest boy, Seta, is envisioned saying to his oppressors before he dies, "I am ashamed for you. You killed my brothers so easily, without sorrow, without asking their forgiveness, and now you would kill me without honor or dignity or sorrow. Shame! You do not beg my forgiveness. But, *haw*! I forgive you and make you ashamed. You are forgiven!" (63). *The Indolent Boys* thus redefines our key terms through the story of three real children, cutting off the received narratives of hardy pioneers "settling" unpopulated land and benevolent white people educating unschooled Indigenous children. What's more, Momaday resists the responses of readers who, as Amelia V. Katanski puts it, "have found it easy to discount or erase student agency" in the history of the boarding schools by viewing students "solely as victims" (14–15). When the play reveals that the oldest boy, Seta, has sacrificed himself to stay with the younger students although he "is twice as strong" and "could be far ahead, out of danger," this element of agency becomes apparent. The same current of resistance is visible when "Koi-khan-hodle, without words, moves on, for his whole strength is now in the taking of his last steps" before death; the movement with which he walks, "bends and dies" becomes a physical embodiment of his individual volition (Momaday, *Indolent* 62). While this is not precisely the "public form . . . of agency" in which a child is able to perform a triumphant, outward-facing type of political activism, that does not make it any less legitimate or valid.

For Katanski, the misunderstanding of some critics regarding the power, resilience, and resourcefulness of boarding school students seems to stem from their inability to recognize the tenuous balance between accommodating and rejecting the encroachments of white culture on Indigenous life. Katanski writes,

> The years around the beginning of the twentieth century for many American Indians were extremely painful and necessitated complex responses in order to survive. Too often in today's discourse on turn-of-the-century American Indian

literature, scholars focus on obvious statements of resistance and view the slightest sign of accommodation as "selling out." ... In a desire to make sense of this difficult period, scholars replicate the tenets of social evolutionary theory, reproducing the savage/civilized binary by proclaiming "no longer Indians" those who seem to have mastered their European American education. Or, worse, scholars proclaim them "trapped between two worlds" if they fail to fall easily into either side of the binary, thus stripping writers of personal or rhetorical power. (14–15)

This observation, though grounded in early twentieth-century US history, proves key to Momaday's children's book *Circle of Wonder: A Native American Christmas Story*, which was published in 1994. This becomes obvious from the book's jacket description, which bills it as "a rare view of the blending of Christian and Native American spiritual traditions"—this "blending" being precisely the sort of "accommodation" that sometimes draws the ire of critics (Momaday, *Circle*). Other children's books of Momaday's have perhaps been more unambiguous in their political impact; his picture book *Four Arrows & Magpie*, for instance, presents a precolonial vision of Indigenous history in what would become Oklahoma, narratively undoing the presence of the settler colonialists by beginning before their arrival and contradicting the mythology of the European discovery of a "New World." However, *Circle of Wonder* and its syncretic approach to religion offer up anticolonial resistance on several levels as Momaday recognizes the legitimacy and the political significance of culturally hybrid identities among Indigenous children like the young person he himself once was.[12]

The story told in this illustrated book had appeared earlier in Momaday's 1976 memoir *The Names*, where it was introduced in clear terms: "Later, in a recollection of my Christmases at Jemez," Momaday explains, "I wrote a story in which I could see almost everything of that special time, that special place" (137).[13] What follows is not autobiographical in the strictest sense, yet it captures the "specialness" of Momaday's own childhood experience. Much of the book is occupied with the Christmas celebration in which the child protagonist's parents are "the patrons of the Christ child," meaning that they "prepar[e] a feast for the people of the village, for after the first mass on Christmas morning they would come in procession to pay their respects and to kneel in adoration before the statue of the Holy Infant" (*Circle* 12). A description of the village church includes "paintings and prayer plumes, ribbons and wreaths" as well as "a crêche, in which the statue of the Christ child lay in a bed of straw" (17). The tenderness with which Tolo's mother "went to the manger and took the Christ child in her arms," then "sat with it cradled in her lap" with Tolo's father "beside her," bespeaks the sincerity of the family's investment in this Christian ritual (22). The second half of the book shifts its focus to a description of Tolo's own private spiritual adventure, in which he departs in search of his deceased grandfather, whose face he repeatedly sees among the worshipers, and who guides him to a "crackling" fire far from the village (28). There, he encounters an elk, a wolf, and an eagle who together make "a circle of wonder and good will around the real gift of the fire" that echoed "other, wider circles, made of the meadow, the mountains, and the starry sky, all the fires and processions, all the voices and silences of all the world," so that Tolo knows he has "been led to the center of the Holy Season" (36).

The syncretic blending of beliefs that Momaday's narrator unfolds runs parallel to Momaday's reflections about his own religious upbringing: "I grew up with both the Christian and Kiowa religious views. . . . At Jemez, I didn't have to work any of that out because the Christian and American Indian elements have existed side-by-side for years. . . . It's an inspiring thing because it shows it can be done" (qtd. in Fauntleroy 30–31). Momaday's take on this syncretic arrangement speaks to the resilience and the powerfully private, introspective form of agency that are visible in his child protagonist's response to Euro-American colonization, which in this case encompasses both Spanish colonialism and the US settler colonial violence that made New Mexico part of the United States at the conclusion of the Mexican American War. *Circle of Wonder* uses the religious belief and experience of a child as a prism through which to engage with this set of histories, again broadening the scope of colonial history while legitimizing Indigenous knowledge and turning ideas of civilization and "savagery" on their heads. In the process, Momaday resists ways of understanding Indigenous cultural belonging that do not allow for this sort of accommodation of hybrid identities, and *Circle of Wonder* extends the conversation about forms of agency and resistance that *The Indolent Boys* begins.

Esmeralda Santiago's *A Doll for Navidades*, illustrated by Enrique O. Sánchez, features writing about herself and her sister Delsa that also was first published in a different form, as part of an essay in *Sí Magazine* in 1996. In a process that recalled the publication history of Hughes's *The Dream Keeper* and its component parts, Santiago would take material that had once reached a more adult audience and repurpose it in a form that would be targeted to children, yet without making substantial alterations to it.[14] The final product has the potential to surprise adults who might expect a picture book with an elementary-school-aged protagonist to be less frank with children.

A Doll for Navidades is brutally honest about the idolization of blond-haired, blue-eyed dolls by Puerto Rican children of Santiago's generation who believed that this was what children's playthings should look like. The opening page is explicit about this: "I was seven and had never had a doll," Santiago reports. "I wanted a baby doll like my cousin Jenny's, with pink skin and blue eyes that shut when she lay her down. Jenny's doll was the size of a small baby, its chubby arms and legs slightly bent, its tiny fingers open to reveal a hand with deep furrows and mounds" (*Doll*). The doll is realistic in its details, yet the element of realism that is missing is any semblance of ethnoracial representativeness, as it is clear that the only dolls available in the world of the story look "like ... Jenny's." And while the young Esmeralda asks for her sister Delsa to receive a doll that is not "like [hers]," suggesting the possibility of a doll that does resemble her and her family, the one that Delsa eventually receives is just as blonde and just as pale-skinned, while Esmeralda does not receive a doll at all. Santiago demands sophistication of child readers who must recognize that this idolization of dolls with white features is not something to emulate: that the book documents an existing, unjust state of affairs rather than depicting what should be. This is the sort of difficulty that brings *A Doll for Navidades* into the same realm as books like Tagore's *The Crescent Moon*, Baldwin's *Little Man, Little Man,* and Cisneros's *Mango Street*, which so many have had trouble accepting as being "really" for children.

However, as in Momaday, part of what is exciting about Santiago's book is how it reclaims hybrid religious and other cultural identities and proclaims their legitimacy in the face of ongoing colonialist oppression—not just the European imperial impulse that led to the colonization of Borinquen by the Spanish government before its annexation by the United States, but the neocolonialism on the part of the US that has led Puerto Rico to remain a territory rather than being granted statehood or independence. Despite the appearance of their toys, Santiago's child protagonists have a cultural identity that cannot be effaced and that the specter of the blue-eyed doll functions to bring into relief through contrast. This becomes visible in the family's way of celebrating Christmas, beginning with the book's linguistic code-switching in its title and continuing with portions that depict the preparations for the family's private celebration as well as the religious holiday itself. In the time leading up to Christmas Day, we learn, the "smells of Christmas floated from Mami's kitchen: ginger and cloves, cinnamon and coconut, oregano, rosemary, garlic. Thick, gray smoke curled from other yards where pigs roasted, their skin crackling and sizzling to the strumming of *cuatros*, the scratching of *güiros*, the *aguinaldos* about *Nochebuena* and about the Three Magi." On Christmas Eve, like Tolo's family, Esmeralda's goes to church: "On *Nochebuena*, we went to the *Misa de Gallo*. We walked to church holding candles because the mass began at midnight.... Mami and Papi had to carry us home, asleep on their shoulders, as the roosters were beginning to sing to the rising sun of Christmas morning." In light of the United States' invasion, occupation, and annexation of Puerto Rico in the late nineteenth century, the continuation of religious practices that are not Anglo-American in origin is an act of resistance on the part of Esmeralda's family, even if those practices are originally a product of European colonialism. By testifying to the complexity of contemporary Puerto Rican religious identities and their origins, Santiago's book witnesses the realities of Puerto Rico's both colonial and neocolonial history, again reconfiguring the definition of colonialism to include the relationship of the United States to a "territory" that the US government has treated and treats as second-class. The definition of belonging, meanwhile, as it does from Erdrich through Cisneros and beyond, becomes flexible to emphatically include those with hybrid identities. In *A Doll for Navidades*, hybridity is cast as a fully legitimate type of cultural belonging rather than being painted as inferior in its political or personal import.

Just as we saw in Harjo, real civilization in this context becomes not the political domination or economic greed of the colonizer but the powerful family love and kindness expressed within colonized spaces. When the desired gift does not materialize on Christmas, Esmeralda's sister agrees to share the blonde baby doll, now named Rosita, and to make Esmeralda her "*madrina*," or godmother. Esmeralda learns to empathize with her father in his sadness at not being able to provide a doll for her: "Papi looked at me, his face as sad as I felt. He looked so unhappy that I knew he was disappointed, too. 'Maybe next year,' he said. 'I hope so.' '*Sí*, maybe next year.' I hugged him, and kissed his smooth cheek." The cultural subtext of this passage includes the hegemonic Eurocentrism that has long been visible in the politics of toy manufacturing; it also includes nationalist and neocolonial histories and accompanying forms of socioeconomic stratification, all of which are intersectionally embodied in the problem of the Christmas doll. The intersectional dilemma adds complexity to a gesture of kindness extended from child to parent that in a different book might read as a straightforward example of "cultural scripts" in western societies "telling girls that they have a duty to make others (often men) happy" (K. Alexander 126). As in *For a Girl Becoming*, this is a family of individuals who "belong to" each other and who are determined to buoy each other up. In holding up this method of being for all to see, Santiago yet again redefines what it means to be civilized through the figure of a child and casts the power of family love as a potent antidote to the brutality of the US colonial machine.

Santiago's other writings, like *A Doll for Navidades*, have often used memoir as the format for their unfolding. In her much more well-known autobiography *When I Was Puerto Rican*, Santiago recalls the shock of her childhood displacement from Puerto Rico to the United States—an experience that she would refer to as "probably the most traumatic thing that ever happened" to her (Grillot, Hurd, and Santiago). The transition involved not just moving from a "rural" home with "no electricity or running water," where Santiago "had never seen television," but also joining a public school system in New York City that was engineered to invalidate her intellectual gifts because of her lack of proficiency in English. In rendering her childhood for an ostensibly more adult audience, Santiago makes palpable the anger and sense of alienation that she felt on discovering this inherent failure of equity in the institutional structures governing the city's immigrant childhoods. While Santiago's novel *Conquistadora* directly grapples with the history of European colonialism in Borinquen, including its effects on the lives of enslaved Africans and Indigenous people, moments like these in *When I Was Puerto Rican* clarify the sociopolitically subordinate status of Puerto Ricans in the United States and the ramifications of US neoimperialist thought and neocolonial governance within the individual lives of Puerto Rican children growing up stateside in the second half of the twentieth century. To see these themes spun out across Santiago's cross-writing reinforces the potency of challenging narratives like her illustrated Christmas story. Whereas some reviewers have taken reductive, stereotyping approaches in recommending *A Doll for Navidades*, citing what they call "the brightly patterned fabrics worn by the island's inhabitants" and the "sprinkling of Spanish words and phrases" that they claim "*spice up the text*" (Jemtegaard, my italics), a cross-reading approach offers an antidote to these racist and colonizing interpretations, posing very different reasons for people of all ages to read and enjoy Santiago's picture book.

Terms and Concepts, Critical Thinking, and Cross-Written Texts

The most potent thread uniting this suite of cross-writing authors is their use of children's literature and its alternatives as sites for challenging dominant ways of understanding terms and concepts with an enormous impact on the sociopolitical architecture of injustice. These books challenge definitions and conceptualizations of colonialism, civilization, and belonging that are racist and culturally biased, and they show kids participating in this type of critical and resistive thinking, as well as acting in ways that put pressure on or even invalidate these convenient notions. This chapter's literary children and teenagers wield considerable power in choosing how they are going to live, the beliefs that they will uphold, and the ones that they will reject or expose as false. This power allows them to expose historical and contemporary realities of US settler colonialism and neocolonialism, to reconfigure the concept of civilization to unseat myths of white western cultural superiority, and to celebrate variations in belonging and make room for hybrid identities, whether linguistically, in terms of race or religious belief, or otherwise. In writing for age-diverse audiences, both in individual works and across their oeuvres more broadly, Erdrich, Cisneros, Harjo, Momaday, and Santiago offer tangible proof of what devoted readers of children's literature already know: that books "for kids" can be as subversive as writing that is envisioned as being for older people, and that often, not much changes or needs to change when a writer seeks to reach younger as well as older readers. These authors collectively challenge adults who would seek to take books like *Mango Street* out of the hands of children, suggesting that this sort of resistive writing is in fact what young readerships need as they face their own challenging and often painful quotidian worlds.

CHAPTER 4

EMBRACING AMBIVALENCE
Cross-Reading the Children of Desai, Danticat, and Morrison

Edwidge Danticat writes works of children's literature that are inflected with a very real sense of what childhood experiences of migration are like, a knowledge rooted in her own family's movements across national, linguistic, and other cultural borders. Danticat was born in Haiti, and when her parents immigrated to the United States, she and they underwent a period of living apart that she has returned to as a writer of stories of "immigration and separation" for kids as well as adults (*Mama's*). In the author's note for her 2015 picture book *Mama's Nightingale*, which she composed with illustrator Leslie Staub and which is recommended for readers ages five to eight, Danticat clarifies that she "grew up in a family that was separated, in part, by immigration. For most of my childhood," she says, "my parents were living in the United States while my brother Bob and I were living with my aunt and uncle in Haiti. I knew that my parents wanted to send for us, but we were always told that they couldn't because they didn't have the right papers." This snippet of direct communication between Danticat and her readers highlights the bittersweetly generative nature of Danticat's childhood migration stories: Danticat tells us that as a child, she converted this information about the reason for her separation from her parents into a source of inspiration for imaginative play. As she explains, "This idea of having the right papers has always fascinated" her, and so, while they were growing up in Haiti, she and her brother "sometimes played writing games, making up passports, visas, and other documents that might one day reunite" their family.

An ambivalent impulse is locatable in Danticat's memory of her childhood playtime. Separation from one parent or both, a source of grief and anxiety, becomes simultaneously a source of creative entertainment and learning and even a source of energy for writing. This contradictory mix of significations is visible throughout *Mama's Nightingale*, in which "good" and "bad" mingle in ways that make it seem impossible to characterize an experience, a place, or a person as wholly one or the other. In this way, there is an affinity between Danticat and authors like Anita Desai, a similarly global writer in the sense that she was born abroad and often writes about India, the nation of her birth, although today she lives in the United States. There are also intriguing connections between these postcolonial literary artists and Black US writers like Toni Morrison, who was born just a few years before Desai and more than thirty years before Danticat but who was their contemporary as a twenty-first-century novelist before her death in 2019. Together, these three writers represent a diversity of national and cultural identities that exemplifies the transnationally shared methods of our cross-writing authors at the end of one century and the start of another. The texts included in this chapter address ethical ambiguities head-on, feature contradictory characters, and trace the mixed emotional impacts of these tensions, running counter to stereotypes of children's literature and children themselves as simplistic creations and creatures uncomfortable with ambivalence. Just as Danticat and her brother embraced the contradictory ramifications of the concept of "having the right papers," experiencing it both as a barrier to happiness and as a childhood inspiration, these three writers' literary children and their textual worlds confront and even embrace ambivalent perspectives. As before, this approach to the writing of children's literature is far from exclusive to cross-writing authors, yet these projects of cross-writing are unique in that they serve to deconstruct assumptions about how an author's "adult" writings might differ—or might need to differ—from their efforts to write for kids. For an adult who still has doubts about the wider value of children's literature, the act of cross-reading Desai's, Danticat's, and Morrison's children's books may prove multiply edifying.

Desai's *The Village by the Sea* was first published in 1982 and was recommended for readers between the ages of ten and fourteen when the *New York Review of Books* republished it in 2019, offering new access to the ambivalent currents of industrialization and so-called development that Desai traces in a rural village outside Mumbai. In Danticat's picture book, the United States' criminal justice system and its intersections with the immigration system become the main targets of Danticat's skewering vision. Meanwhile, in *Remember: The Journey to School Integration*, a book illustrated with photographs from that portion of the campaign for civil rights and against US anti-Blackness at mid-century, Morrison engages the historical tension between the brilliant power of

Black children protesting and the ugly racism of the white children and adults in their midst, while pointing out the contemporary persistence of these issues.

One intriguing facet of the three works is their diverse methods of participation in the tradition of socially engaged nonfiction writing for children. Desai takes care to clarify that *The Village by the Sea* "is based entirely on fact": she notes at the start that its setting "is a real village on the western coast of India," explaining that "all the characters in this book are based on people who live in this village; only their names have been altered." This will be critical to the narrative's ambition of working through the ethics of "development" efforts in a decolonized space. *Remember*, too, tends to be treated as nonfiction and has the principal aim of illuminating a pivotal moment in US history, although Morrison has emphasized the imaginative quality of the places where she invented more specific examples of the thoughts and feelings that might have confronted the Black and white children pictured in its documentary photographs. Then there is Danticat's picture book, which tends to be classified as fiction by education retailers but which is deeply informed by the facts of Danticat's own childhood.[1] This semiautobiographical mode is not new within this book; it has appeared to varying degrees in our discussions of writers like Baldwin, Harjo, and Santiago, whose picture books have drawn on personal and family experiences in ways that recall Danticat's explanatory note. In this chapter, however, these various negotiations of the boundary between fictional and nonfictional storytelling modes will become even more vital. By grounding the stories they tell to varying degrees in nonfictional elements, these texts assert that their ambiguities, contradictions, and other difficulties are not authorial inventions: that when aspects of a book seem inconsistent or conflicting, this is not a flaw of the work but is rather the fault of the world that it reflects, which refuses to consistently make sense or to behave according to typical wishes and expectations.

In deploying this literary strategy, Desai, Danticat, and Morrison find themselves united across ethnonational boundaries as contemporary authors whose activist cross-writing unearths persistent injustices traceable to white racism, from United States histories of slavery and segregation to imperialist mythologies and their afterlives in India and elsewhere. The echoes of Tagore and Hughes's transnational ties are palpable here, though *The Crescent Moon* predates *Mama's Nightingale*, the most recent children's book included in this chapter, by more than a century. Importantly, these writers also join a community of other authors with similar methods and priorities who are not known as writing "for adults." Like Ruby Bridges's *Through My Eyes*, Morrison's *Remember* frustrates attempts to suppress knowledge about Jim Crow that could prove damaging to mythologies of whiteness and thus could threaten "the simplified moral or ethical codes within which childhood innocence is perceived to exist" (Hopkins 181) for white children in particular.[2] Like DACA recipient Areli Morales's *Areli Is a Dreamer: A True Story*, illustrated by Luisa Uribe, *Mama's Nightingale* troubles binaristic fables of "good" and "bad" immigration while drawing attention to the ethical fissures that adherence to unjust laws creates in the fantastical narrative of US equality. In the process, Desai, Danticat, and Morrison embrace various types of ambivalence, contradiction, and complexity, from the conflicting roles played by white people in the desegregation of public schools to the double-edged function of the United States government in both persecuting and securing justice for undocumented immigrants. By encouraging us to read for this writing strategy across the often-expected borders between children's and "adult" literature, their cross-writing helps to legitimate and deconstruct othering conceptions of and expectations for all of these books.

Desai's "Factual" Protest Narrative

In *The Village by the Sea*, the figure of the sea itself functions as an immediate exhortation to readers: to understand this text, they will have to accept that two seemingly contradictory ideas can be true at the same time. The opening scene finds one of its two child protagonists, Lila, making a pilgrimage to the shallows by the shore so that she can "offer flowers at the sacred rock" (Desai, *Village* 2). The seaside, it is clear, is a beautiful place where, at least for a little while, this child whose mother is ill and whose father is an alcoholic can enjoy a moment of peace and joy. The narrator describes Lila's time at the shore as "the only perfectly happy and peaceful" time in her everyday life (3). And yet the sea, we learn, betrays the local fishermen regularly—not just when there are not enough fish to be caught for sale to the wealthier inhabitants of the nearby towns and cities, leaving the villagers to cry "not enough left, so little left" in a kind of haunting chorus (24), but also when boys and men disappear into the sea in storms, never to return home. The physicality of the setting encodes this species of contradiction, which inspires ambivalent feelings in the children of the village and their parents, who both love the sea for its beauty and hate it for the danger it can represent. While Richard Cronin argues that Desai writes from the perspective of someone vacationing in the village, it would be problematic to suggest that Desai's descriptions of the setting's natural beauty can only be understood as originating from that viewpoint. Cronin argues that "the cock-pheasant and the pigeon"—and presumably the sea—"are being looked at by a writer on holiday, not by a peasant girl in debt" (46), but this interpretation presupposes that the poor children who live in the village are incapable of seeing the world around them through an aesthetic as well as a pragmatic lens. I would argue instead that Desai's vision of ambivalence allows her child characters to be complexly shaded in their worldview, aware of these contradictory currents in their environment: its beauty as well as its treachery.

The opposing set of implications and emotions that the sea represents and evokes will be mirrored in the "development" project that either promises or threatens to divert the village and its residents from fishing and subsistence agriculture to a life that they are told will now revolve around factory work. The government has determined that the village will become the site of a fertilizer-producing plant and that its lands will be taken over not just by the plant itself but by "[f]actories, housing colonies, shopping centres, bus depots, railway heads, engineers and workers" (Desai, *Village* 61). The narrative's other protagonist, Lila's brother Hari, wants to believe that this news is positive, as he has struggled to find enough work to support his sisters while their mother lies ill. The promise of future social change gives Hari the ability to hope that his circumstances might shift—whereas without this unfamiliar influence, it seems unclear where a change in his situation might actually come from. However, Desai avoids posing this set of circumstances as a straightforward problem and solution. As Hari wonders whether he should support the men working on the factory development project or the protestors mobilizing "for the right of the farmers and fishermen to earn their living by the traditional ways" (99), *The Village by the Sea* models the process of grappling and sitting with ambiguity for a child who is on the verge of adolescence and is coming to terms with the often confusing nature of his larger world.

This line of thinking allows Desai to take up more expansive questions that trouble the expectation of conceptual or ethical simplicity in children's literature. For instance, there is a clearly anticolonialist bent to the parts of the narrative where the binaristic western conceptions of modernity and tradition are deconstructed. In suggesting that it is not at all clear that the "progress" represented by the factory is a good thing for the village, especially since the higher-paying factory jobs will go to former residents of the surrounding cities rather than to the villagers themselves, Desai upends imperialist, Eurocentric assumptions about the benefits of industrialization that persist in the wake of decolonization movements. This makes *The Village by the Sea* feel like an extension of earlier writings like Tagore's and Achebe's. At the same time, Desai does not embrace the almost fetishistic vision of the fishing village's local culture that some of the urban antidevelopment activists espouse in proclaiming that they "believe" in the villagers' "way of life": "[Y]our green fields and the sea are valuable to all of us as they are to you," they say. "Our trees, our fish, our cattle and birds have to be protected" (120). Some of the villagers, including children like Hari, are indeed starving because of the inadequacy of the "traditional" ways for their individual circumstances, and *The Village by the Sea* suggests that it is paternalistic and problematic for outsiders to idealize these socioeconomic practices as evidence of the villagers' supposedly precious difference or otherness. This critique of Desai's becomes clear when it emerges that the activists wish to avoid the villagers' migrating from "their village and com[ing] to Bombay to find work" (121). The resulting confrontation with ambiguity and the ambivalent feelings it inspires in Hari allow Desai to intervene in discourses of postcolonial economic development, clearing a path for nuances that reflect the exploitation and othering of rural communities by parties on both sides of a heated political debate—while underscoring the agency and capability of rural children who can think, reason, protest, and advocate for themselves.

Hari's adventures in the city reinforce this feeling of ambiguity or contradictoriness. In one episode, Hari becomes ill and the restaurant owner who has hired him, Jagu, invites him back to his small, crowded home, where Hari discovers that his wife is justifiably anxious about the prospect of having to provide food for yet another young person. Desai's narrator addresses the problem head-on and indicates that Hari himself understands it better and sooner than the restaurant owner does: "Hari told him, 'I will go back to the shop, Jagu. There is no room for me here. I will go back.' . . . He nodded, and Hari could see that he realized he had made a mistake in bringing Hari home. He had done it out of kindness and a wish to help, Hari knew, and he wanted to thank Jagu but could not" (192). In another episode, Hari is turned away from a rich man's house by servants who do not want to compete with him for work, only to realize later that he "did not really wish to live in a rich man's house as a servant. He felt he would only make a fool of himself, break the glass and china, leave dirty finger and foot prints on shining surfaces, show his ignorance over such things as lifts, doorbells, telephones and cars. He was not a city boy and he did not want to become one" (212). Passages like this exemplify the multilayered characterization of Desai's fictional children. Hari is both intimidated by these trappings of postcolonial urban life and rebellious against them; he models a kind of stubborn nonconformity that rejects the values these objects represent, yet he is also insecure and self-denigrating in a way that shows the negative impacts of socioeconomic stratification and urban materialism on his consciousness and sense of self. *The Village by the Sea*, then, presents what is and not just what should be, and much of the tension and ambiguity in the book resides in its unwillingness to focus on one over the other.

The text's ultimate conclusion reinforces this sense of its unwillingness to simplify ethical or political questions to suit stereotypes of children's—or children's literature's—simplicity of thought. Hari and his fellow protestors lose the battle over the development project, and one of the activists does not mince words in saying why this has occurred: "The politicians won—so they can make plenty of money from the sale of land and licenses in the name of progress" (254). Hari's response to this event is resilient: he plans to start a chicken farm and open a watch shop, catering to the engineers and other outsiders who will benefit more directly from the opening of the factory. *The Village by the Sea* is far from celebrating this as a victory. It is painted as a necessary way to "adapt" and "survive" the march of so-called development and the greed and cultural bias at its root (257). But the narrative records these injustices without, again, stripping Desai's child protagonists of their power, much as poems like "Negro" and illustrated books like *For a Girl Becoming* record and respond to histories of white supremacist violence without occluding the power of diasporic communities or of Black and Indigenous children in particular. Like the task of redefining terms, the aim of embracing ambivalence becomes central to this vision of talented, resilient children engaging in activism and self-advocacy.

The Village by the Sea is far from being the only book of Desai's that operates like this, and the novella-length works contained in the more recent "adult" text *The Artist of Disappearance* offer some moving examples. In "Translator Translated," also set in post-independence India, a translator named Prema claims to be advocating for or amplifying the voice of a marginalized woman writer by translating her work into English, but she ultimately takes on a role whose ethics are far more problematic than she is willing to admit, suffused as they are with the "colonizing brutality" of Britain's history in India (Henitiuk 5). Beginning with the stated goal of discerning "what was right, what was wrong" and of being "only the conduit, the medium between that language and this," the translator begins instead to "be inventive" and "create a style" for the writer that does not correspond to her original one (Desai, "Translator" 60, 82). Comparing herself to "the Impressionist painters," Prema is motivated by concerns for her own reputation (she wonders what will happen to her "newly created career as a translator" if the book is not well received) as well as perhaps by an unearned sense of her own talent and a desire to compensate for her earlier failed attempts to have her own writing published (80–82). As the translator's ego begins to overtake her sense of professional ethics and responsibility, it becomes clear that Prema is exploiting the original author for her own gain, though in the end she gains little. After first being lambasted by postcolonial thinkers for her devotion to English-language translation, she is later exposed by the writer's nephew for taking these liberties with the novel's style. The nephew decries her "cavalier attitude" (88) toward the translation project, she never attempts another translation, and her renewed attempts to pursue her own writing are perennially frustrated.

Prema's character is by turns condescending, presumptuous, officious, and naïve, all of which may fail to endear her to us and which marks her as distinct from Desai's child protagonists in *The Village by the Sea*. Somehow Desai's translator protagonist never becomes loathsome, though, her weaknesses humanized in ways that mark her story as shaped by some broader human tendency toward frailty as well as by more specific, localized political dynamics. When we learn how Prema "had struggled to write stories herself when she was young—younger," her more problematic inclinations as a translator begin to become predictable, and we see how Desai is "translating" Prema's character for us (63). In another, when Prema mourns how she has "lost" her own "voice" in "adopting" that of the writer she was translating (91), it is difficult not to mourn along with her.

The imprint of injustice on the novella is likewise complex in its shading, with the woman translator battling her own sense of linguistic and cultural disenfranchisement in a post-independence landscape that presents substantial emotional challenges. The novella moves seamlessly between first- and third-person narration, and in one intimate-feeling passage written in Prema's own voice, she reflects that she is "not asked a single question about [her] involvement with this language" (59), which she identifies as belonging more to her mother than to herself. She muses, "I had been given no opportunity to explain how I came about it, what it meant to me and why, while teaching the usual, accepted course of English literature in a women's college, I had maintained my commitment to it" (59). Prema has accommodated the persisting cultural architecture of British colonialism by teaching canonical English literature from *The Mill on the Floss* to *Persuasion*, operating with an enthusiasm that makes the critiques she receives feel more earned when it is pointed out that she is translating into "a colonial language that was responsible for destroying the original language" (77). Yet it is clear that Prema's own linguistic inheritances have been unjustly suppressed in an environment still struggling against this ideological legacy, where those around her do not manage to do much better in the final calculus. The substitute teacher who replaces her when she goes on leave plans to introduce her students to "contemporary American authors not yet admitted to the academic pantheon" (81), which may sound progressive but threatens to replace British colonialist norms with the neoimperialist cultural hegemony of the United States, especially since it is unclear whether this new syllabus will include writers of color. Even the author Prema is translating has her own relationship of condescension with the "tribal children" for whom she has opened a school (92). In an atmosphere in which no one appears blameless in their responses to the lasting imperial specter, it becomes difficult to single Prema out for condemnation as opposed to understanding or "translation."

Desai has commented that she feels drawn to isolated and alienated characters, and "Translator Translated" develops Prema's character in that same direction. In an interview, Desai once remarked,

> I've often written about people who don't go along with the mainstream, who go against the current, who live outside of the current, or are stranded whilst everyone else just flows along. I think I'm drawn to such characters. Even in the last three novellas that I wrote [including "Translator Translated"], that same type of character surfaces again and again. I'm interested in people who live in a kind of exile; it may not be political exile, but in some sense it's exile from the rest of society. (Desai and Barnes)

There are also ways in which these aspects of Prema's identity recall Desai's own; Desai, like Prema, "was influenced by the British classics" and, of course, writes in English. All of this contributes to a sometimes uncomfortable but generative ambiguity that extends across Desai's writing, showing how little she is inclined to simplify questions or their answers according to age-based categorizations. Desai's children's fiction tends to locate its more ethically ambiguous and complicated characters at its periphery rather than its center, and perhaps this is one way of softening some of the more troublesome ambiguities that reside in "Translator Translated," allowing for fuller feelings of sympathy for her fictional child protagonists and a stronger sense of their goodness. Nevertheless, there is a shared ethics of ambivalence here that demonstrates how willing Desai is to make these sorts of challenges to child readers as well as adults. What this suggests is not that Desai is exceptional among writers of children's literature but that children's literature itself is exceptional relative to what some adults anticipate when they picture it as "very simplistic" in its "language" or themes (Naylor and Wood 95).

Danticat's Semiautobiographical Picture Book

As writers of "kidlit" who have complex relationships to both the formerly colonized countries of their birth and their adopted home of the United States, Desai and Danticat turn a multilayered gaze on these environments and their imprint on the lives of children.[3] Danticat's *Mama's Nightingale* is no exception, following a family fractured by their immigration to the US and by the lack of "papers" that one of them has. In this immigration story that recalls

Danticat's own even if the details have changed, what is most straightforward is the pain that the child protagonist feels at being separated from her mother, who is undocumented. The only thing that can fully alleviate this pain for Saya is being reunited with the parent she misses so much, something that fails to happen until the final few pages. In the meantime, seeing and hearing temporary snippets of her mother, whether at an immigration detention center or on the audio tapes her mother sends to her with recorded bedtime stories, is a bittersweet experience that lifts Saya's spirits while it lasts. Listening to one of the tapes, the child narrator tells us, "I close my eyes and imagine Mama lying next to me as she leans in to whisper the nightingale's story in my ear. I imagine Mama tucking me in, kissing me good night, then going to sleep in the next room with Papa" (Danticat, *Mama's*). Saya lets us know that "[s]ometimes the stories are as sad as melted ice cream," communicating the pain that she feels at her mother's absence even as she finds herself comforted by her mother's voice.

The ambivalent feelings that the visits and tapes inspire become a microcosm of the larger contradictions in the nature of the criminal justice system that separates and then reunites Saya's family. Early on in the book, the officers at the detention center reveal the depth of their callousness, telegraphing the inhumanity of the system that undocumented immigrants enter when they are found to be without papers. Saya tells us of a time when she has to leave her mother behind at the detention center called Sunshine Correctional, whose name is Orwellian in its irony. "I kick and I scream and beg to stay with her," Saya relates. "Tears run down Mama's face as she is led away. The two guards on either side of her give me very stern looks. One of them tells Papa not to bring me again *until I can behave myself*" (my italics).

This moment vivifies the unjust, pitiless, and self-righteous rhetoric of the immigration system in its approach to the children injured by it. It also illustrates the problem of respectability politics at work in the system and its intersections with US criminal justice architectures, which Danticat highlights when Saya rightly calls the detention center a "jail." Saya is not supposed to show her feelings about being separated from her mother because this might inconvenience or discomfit the officers watching; she is supposed to remain well "behaved" even after this denial of her fundamental human right to remain in the care of both of her parents. Indeed, this is specifically a human right articulated in international accords like the United Nations' Convention on the Rights of the Child, where it is stipulated that "a child shall not be separated from his or her parents against their will" except in cases involving "abuse or neglect of the child by the parents." The expectation that Saya not give loud, discomfiting voice to the pain she feels at this blatant violation of her rights is the epitome of respectability politics, showing how this insidious doctrine can become the yardstick for measuring children's behavior as well as that of adults within a system whose broken ethics are the real problem. Danticat confronts the intersectional ramifications of this sort of "emotion work" when it is demanded of girls whose exposure to these "age- and gender-based expectations and hierarchies" (K. Alexander 126) is intensified by their families' ethnoracial and immigrant identities. But the book does not end with Saya's mother covertly escaping from the detention center or finding that she will be forced to remain there; she goes before a judge, herself a Black woman, who liberates her so that she can "come home with Papa" and Saya (Danticat, *Mama's*). Through this turn in the narrative, Danticat suggests that there are pockets of fairness in a criminal justice system that so often proves ethically bankrupt in its dealings with immigrants, especially those who are women of color migrating from non-western spaces. What could have been a wholesale condemnation of the system instead becomes a record of its ambivalent nature.

This change in her mother's fortunes occurs after Saya embarks on a letter-writing campaign whose positive results underscore her own activist political power in advocating for her family and mobilizing for change. Saya remembers,

> I take Papa's advice, sit down, and write my own story. When I am done, Papa sends what I have written to one of the newspaper reporters he's been writing to.
>
> A few days later, there is a message on our answering machine. The message is from a lady reporter saying that she wants to print my story in the newspaper for everyone to read!
>
> The next day, another reporter comes to our apartment to interview Papa and me for the television news.
>
> With a big lump in my throat, I tell her how much I miss Mama and how I wish she could be with us again.

The ultimate takeaway is not that the US treats immigrants fairly but that one small child can be effective in speaking truth to power: that she can fight injustice and win. After all, the back cover of the book doesn't say, "A little girl discovers how kind journalists are" or "A little girl discovers that the United States is a just country after all"—it says, "A little girl discovers her words can change the world." This wrinkle also suggests one more strain of ambivalence that the book embraces: the way that injustice can carve out a space for a child to recognize or learn her own power. As in Desai, ambivalence serves as a means to resist disempowering, paternalistic or condescending constructions of marginalized communities and children. By stressing not just the injustice of the system but the power of individuals, including younger ones, to effect change, Danticat rejects the possibility of a fetishistic or essentialist interpretation of her protagonist as a victim, while still exposing the fissures in the social structures that surround her. Danticat thus joins a community of authors writing children's books about incarceration where such endings are not uncommon and, despite their hopeful tenor, "illustrate . . . profound cracks in the American criminal justice system," as *Booklist* said of Janae Marks's *From the Desk of Zoe Washington*. While Eugene Yelchin refers to the ending of *Mama's Nightingale* as demonstrating "the inherent power of words to pull off the near impossible," Danticat makes it clear that the potency of the words at play is far from "inherent"; Saya herself, the real heroine, infuses them with it.

The bittersweet quality of Danticat's book deepens its resemblance to her writing on explicit, purportedly "adult" subjects that have earned Danticat some measure of resistance in the past. One of Danticat's most acclaimed books, *Breath, Eyes, Memory*, has an ambivalent reception history on which Danticat has commented at some length. She writes,

> The virginity testing element of the book led to a backlash in some Haitian American circles. "You are a liar," a woman wrote to me. . . . Maligned as we were in the media at the time, as disaster-prone refugees and boat people and AIDS carriers, many of us had become overly sensitive and were eager to censor anyone who did not project a "positive image" of Haiti and Haitians. . . . But isn't that what the word *fiction* or *novel* on the book jacket had implied? Isn't even the most elementary piece of fiction about a singularly exceptional fictional person, so that even if that fictional person is presented as an everyman or everywoman, he or she is bound to be the most exceptional everyman or everywoman fictional person of the lot? . . . Furthermore, though I was not saying that "testing" happened in every Haitian household, to every Haitian girl, I knew many women and girls who had been "tested" in that way. (Danticat, "Create" 184)

In short, the ambivalence of the text—its less than fully "positive image" of Haitian culture—proved discomfiting and provocative in an urgent moment of anti-Haitian xenophobia within the "mainstream" United States. Nevertheless, despite these protestations, Danticat has remained firm in asserting her right to tell the stories of women like her characters. Like the United States in *Mama's Nightingale*, then, Haiti in *Breath, Eyes, Memory* is complexly rendered, and Danticat's writing from her earliest days as a novelist sets a precedent for her manner of approaching children's literature. This also suggests new affinities between Desai and Danticat, who, like so many of the writers in this book, have tended not to be read in tandem.[4] Desai and Danticat share these cross-writing strategies just as they share a complicated relationship to their postcolonial homelands, neither of which has escaped their criticism.

Short stories like "The Funeral Singer," from Danticat's 2004 collection *The Dew Breaker*, are similarly inflected, permitting her characters to feel emotions about both Haiti and the United States that recall *Mama's Nightingale*'s multifaceted portrait of the US government. In "The Funeral Singer," three women emigrants from Haiti under the Duvalier regime are united in the task of passing the exam that will allow them to earn their GEDs in New York City. The women are candid in describing what has made them leave their country or how they have been "expelled from" it ("Funeral" 167). One woman's husband has been shot for painting "an unflattering portrait of the president" (172), while another woman's father has been brutally attacked by a paramilitary soldier and has had his business taken over, and a third is sexually assaulted by a Tonton Macoute during her girlhood. The narrator describes her family's suffering in unflinching detail: "When my father returned, he didn't have a tooth left in his mouth. In one night, they'd turned him into an old, ugly man. The next night he took his boat out to sea and, with a mouth full of blood, vanished forever" (172). The narrator still wishes to go back to Haiti, to "join a militia and return to fight," although her compatriots warn her that she will die (180). The narrator cannot let go of her diasporic love of her homeland, a fact that is embodied both in her desire for return and in the community she has created with her fellow Haitians in a fictionalized New York. As Nadège T. Clitandre suggests, "Danticat calls for a reconsideration of truth beyond ethical absolutes of good and evil, right and wrong," and *The Dew Breaker*'s "defiance of ahistorical, oversimplified representation of Haitian people" is central to that "call" (173, 165). Such ambivalence is typical of diaspora in its many permutations and the singular pain that it provokes in Danticat's textual world.[5]

Meanwhile, the white teacher who promises that the three women will "all be considered high school graduates in no time" is not an effective pedagogue; two of the three women become "used to the idea that [they] may never get diplomas out of the class," and we never learn whether the women have passed the exam (Danticat, "Funeral" 167, 174). The teacher's absence from the bulk of the story and the ambiguous results of her efforts become a way for Danticat to resist the specious concept of the white savior in a history in which the United States played a pivotal role in supporting a brutal dictatorship, with even the ostensibly more progressive John F. Kennedy, whom Danticat's characters refer to at times, providing only "lukewarm support to Duvalier's opponents" (Dubois). As an alternative to the tired and racist trope of the white woman teacher-savior, Danticat centers the women students in their independent efforts to create new lives in the wake of trauma and to memorialize their dead in meaningful ways. The painter's widow, for instance, secures a job at an art gallery where she will be able to sell her husband's paintings. New York provides at least a temporary shelter for the three women, yet its power and importance are small in comparison with their emotional reserves and sheer determination, which will be echoed in the character of Saya in *Mama's Nightingale*.

Danticat's essays have been critical of both Haiti and the United States, and family tragedy in her inner circle has confirmed the need for these critiques. In 2004, the same year that saw the publication of *The Dew Breaker*, Danticat wrote a piece for *The New York Times* titled "New York Was Our City on the Hill." Personally reflective as well as broadly political, the essay opened with denouncements of both "the brutal regimes of François and Jean-Claude Duvalier in the early 1970s" and the "United States immigration red tape" that created a "family separation last[ing] eight years" for the Danticats, as well as the financial struggles that they continued to experience on their arrival in New York (Danticat, "New York"). After the article was submitted for publication, Danticat's uncle died in the custody of immigration officials, as a note appended to the bottom of the published essay reveals. Danticat writes, "On Nov. 3, after this essay was submitted, my Uncle Joseph died at age 81. More formally known as the Rev. Joseph N. Dantica, he died in Miami after fleeing gang violence and death threats in Haiti. He was detained by Department of Homeland Security officials after requesting asylum in the United States and died in their custody. The department said the cause was pancreatitis." What Danticat did not have to say was that this tragic event was yet another example of the many ways that the United States had failed to live up to her family's "utopian" vision of what their adopted country might mean to them. Across her work, Danticat refuses to ignore the ambiguities in the proposition that the United States makes to immigrants—a proposition that is extraordinarily flawed although it has given Danticat one of the "two places" that she "call[s] home" (Danticat and Adisa 345). I would like to argue for a method of reading and teaching Danticat that not only positions her "adult" fiction alongside these types of essays but also centers books like *Mama's Nightingale*, keeping in mind these vital continuities and their implications for our understanding of where children's literature belongs.

Morrison's Documentary Imaginings

As Andrea Davis Pinkney wrote in a letter to Morrison before *Remember* was published, the children's division at Houghton Mifflin saw the book as something that would "profoundly affect the lives of children" (2 Oct. 2003). In May of 2004, Houghton Mifflin representative Lori Glazer corresponded via email with Morrison's assistant Rene Boatman to celebrate a "nice column" about *Remember* in *Newsweek* that described it as a tool for parents "struggling to explain Jim Crow to [their] kids." This prevailing view painted *Remember* as important because it promised to simplify a difficult part of United States history, making life easier for "adults reading over" their children's shoulders. Yet what is equally essential is how Morrison's children's book grapples with the complexity and ambiguity of its historical moment and the more subversive work that it does as a result. There are powerful connections between the various exponents of Morrison's cross-writing, which tie together books ranging from *Beloved* to *Remember* within a clear activist project.

In her remarks prepared for the book's launch, Morrison described *Remember* as an effort to redress the wrong that is created when the story of *Brown v. Board of Education* and its aftermath is told with insufficient attention to "one segment of the population whose future was the center of the cause"—the children "who walked into those schools in the fifties" as well as "the ones who walk into schools now, fifty years later" ("*Remember* Luncheon"). Morrison expressed that her aim was for the book to "relate those days in a manner that spoke directly" to children, "not preaching, not patronizing, *not burdensome*" (my italics). Still, the book had to be frank about the difficulty of what this earlier generation of children had faced: "Imagine it. You are eight, twelve, fifteen. You are entering a street, a neighborhood, a building where you believe you are hated, know you are, because grown ups are screaming at you, calling you names. You are so not wanted, soldiers with guns are needed to protect you. And if they have guns, maybe your life is in danger; maybe someone in the crowd has a gun too, and will use it." Much of the ambiguity in *Remember* is traceable to this tension between wanting not to "burden" children and wanting to communicate the truth of this history—which the "children who walked into those schools" responded to with a "non-militant" courage, as Morrison emphasized in her handwritten notes on a printed draft of the speech.

Remember brings the realities of Jim Crow to life in passages that describe its injustice in the first person ("The law says I can't go to school with white children. Are they afraid of my socks, my braids? I am seven years old. Why are they afraid of me?" [8]) as well as in third-person interludes that present the historical facts of the protest movement: "When the new school year began in the autumn of 1954, some students went to school together who never had before. But in many places, people resisted the Supreme Court ruling" (19). While Morrison takes care to point out that "black citizens, *with white supporters*, became part of a movement to demand equality and civil rights" (52, my italics), she never minces words about the cruel white children and adults "trying to scare" Black children (45). *Remember* does counterbalance its depictions of white racism and white hatred with these references to allyship, perhaps making its content less "burdensome" for white children and certainly testifying to the contradictory roles of whiteness in this story of courageous protest. Yet whiteness is never allowed to feign the kind of fabricated innocence that we are so familiar with from other narratives of US history. While the details are different, here we might think of Desai's depictions of the city residents who assist the rural protestors in advocating for their village by the sea.

There is also a strain of ambivalence in *Remember* that has to do with the broader reach and range of United States history. When the book won the Coretta Scott King Award from the American Library Association, Pinkney accepted the award on behalf of Morrison with remarks that she had cobbled together from various other sources in which Morrison had discussed the book. One bit of text that was inserted into the 2005 ALA remarks was the assertion that "the struggle is not over" (Pinkney, Letter, 28 Apr. 2005). This is a critical statement given the way that the civil rights movement in the United States is often treated as a signal of the nation's own exceptional commitment to justice rather than as one moment of triumph on the part of protesters and renegades in a series of historical and contemporary failures on the part of the nation. These complexities emerge not only in the book jacket's description, which suggests that the "effects" of the clash over civil rights "still linger," but in the pages that follow as well (Morrison, *Remember*). The end, too, sounds an ambiguous note, dedicating the book to the four Black girls who died in the Birmingham, Alabama church bombing in 1963, then declaring that "[t]hings are better now. Much, much better," but implying that they are far from wholly resolved (72).

To some ears, this declaration of improvement might almost sound too gentle given the reality that Morrison had described just a few years earlier in a 2001 speech titled "What Is a Good School?":

> What I am emphasizing is this: in the absence or scale back of government interest, clarity or guidance or support of the public school system and the devastation being or about to be visited on that system; in this time of outrageous, deceitful re-distribution of wealth under the rubric of economic 'stimulus'; when, in this atmosphere of heightened dread, independent thinking (on the part of students and adults) is understood to be 'unpatriotic,' virtually treasonable; where accurate information leading to credible knowledge and humane public policy is a casualty in the media and the corridors of power; where censorship disguises ignorance; where serious debates are being held about the value of surgical assassination, of nuclear pre-emptive strikes, of domestic surveillance, volunteer spying, the necessity for the suspension of civil rights; where we face the danger of becoming the enemy whose despotic regime we say we despise; where, in fact, we may be witnessing the Nazi-fication of our country; in that dangerous

atmosphere ... community organizing, intervention, parental participation, demanding the best for our children ... is more important than it ever has been.

Nevertheless, Morrison's narration in her "first historical work for young people" has an implicit contemporary resonance when she asks readers to imagine what it might feel like to hear someone say, "You can't come in here. Get away from the door. This school is for white children. Only them" (*Remember* 32). This demand for perspective-taking remains urgent in a contemporary context in which the de facto segregation of schools means that many of the best-funded public educational institutions in the United States remain overwhelmingly white. By taking this approach to the fiftieth anniversary of *Brown v. Board of Education*, the book not only emphasizes the ambiguity inherent in this tension between Jim Crow and the powerful, inspiring children who helped bring it to an end; it also suggests that readers of all ages should have ambivalent feelings about a nation that oversaw the ending of de jure but not de facto segregation in education, housing, and other areas of public life.

One final element of ambiguity in *Remember* is its treatment of the difficulty of remaining "non-militant" in protesting and attempting to dismantle the institutional structures of white racism within US public education. Morrison's children's book does not go so far as to suggest that physical self-defense might be a necessary recourse for communities of color threatened by white supremacy, although as writers like Amiri Baraka and Nikki Giovanni have shown us, such forms of self-defense are absolutely a justifiable response to white people's acts of anti-Black terrorist violence. What Morrison does do, however, is acknowledge just how understandable it is to respond at least with emotional violence to such attacks. The first-person voice of the child narrator says, "Walking through a crowd of people who hate what we are—not what we do—can make us hate them back for what they are and what they do. A lot of courage and determination are needed not to. We try ... but sometimes ..." (35–36). The images that accompany these words and ellipses fill in the resulting gaps, showing white children and adolescents jeering at and chasing after Black ones. *Remember* witnesses the full range of emotional responses to racial injustice, taking care not to stigmatize child protestors' anger or to conform to the socioemotional code of respectability politics even as it does celebrate "non-militant" strategies for creating social change. Morrison allows child protestors their own complexity and their own feelings of ambivalence, just as she does in suggesting that they are "scared but not afraid" (60), and she removes the burden of "emotion work" that suggests that it is the responsibility of children of color to moderate or disguise their feelings in order to avoid producing discomfort in white people. Like Desai's descriptions of Hari's conflicted feelings about the "development" project whose roots in western cultural hegemony threaten his community, this characterization of children grappling with sophisticated questions offers a model for readers of any age.[6]

Morrison's oeuvre could support any number of comparisons between her "adult" writings and those of her books that are marketed to young audiences and their parents as *Remember* has been. However, *Remember*'s emphasis on memory beginning with its title calls out for a reading of it alongside *Beloved*, which is so much about the insistent reach and significance of memory.[7] In a speech called "Novel Endings," Morrison offered this now-iconic account of her approach to the project:

> I began *Beloved* in 1983, and after following a number of trails found the single most uncontroversial thing one can say about the institution of slavery vis à vis contemporary times—is that it haunts us all. That in so many ways all our lives are entangled with the past: manipulations of it—and, fearful of its grasp, ignoring or dismissing, or distorting it to suit ourselves, but always unable to erase it. When, finally, I understood the nature of a haunting . . . how it is both what we yearn for and what we fear, I was able to see the traces of a ghostly presence, the residue of a repressed past in certain concrete but also allusive detail. (7)

Beloved "remembers" the source of this "haunting," which is always present but which remains too easy to deny or "distort." Among other antidotes, the novel offers the powerful elixir of Black love, especially self-love and self-care, in response to this weighty inheritance.[8] It is not insignificant that *Remember* similarly emphasizes the act of remembering racial injustice without the "distortions" that would frame it as a problem of the past alone, and that it celebrates the strength of Black children as *Beloved* celebrates Sethe's strength in self-love as her own "best thing" (322). In some ways, *Remember* exists in a world apart from the explicitly heartbreaking content of *Beloved*, which in no way holds back as it comes face to face with the brutal physical and emotional violence of American slavery, and whose concept of "rememory" gothically confronts the more abstract components of this ongoing trauma in a concrete and visible form.[9] Still, this shared perspective on the need to face the "repressed" past without denials or "manipulations" binds the two books together and shows what Morrison refuses to keep from children even as she seeks to avoid "burdening" them.

The distance between *Beloved* and *Remember* is most visible in the novel's approach to Sethe and her story of filicide. Morrison has said of Sethe that she is "the mother who sacrifices everything and who murders the children, because she has the best political solution to slavery that ever came, which is that we can't—no one can—put up with it" ("Love" 4).[10] In representing the agonizing ethics of motherhood under slavery, *Beloved* is far more frank about the depths of the complexity at play than *Remember* is in addressing the ethics of nonviolence and its alternatives within protest movements or as revolutionary strategies.[11] Still, *Remember* provides access to similarly complex ideas by engaging with the emotional violence of white hatred and the self-protective responses that it necessitates from Black children who defend and advocate for themselves, with no obligation to self-censor their emotional lives for the comfort of others.

Embracing Ambivalence for Age-Diverse Readerships

In chapter 3, we saw child protagonists from Erdrich to Santiago redefine terms with real political importance to their lives. Here, the literary children of Desai, Danticat, and Morrison grapple with the ambiguities and contradictions of their textual worlds and the real worlds they reflect, modeling a vital epistemological strategy that flies in the face of demeaning notions of "didactic" protest writing composed with kids in mind. While many things may change from *Beloved* to *Remember* or from *Breath, Eyes, Memory* to *Mama's Nightingale*, their authors' grappling with ambiguity does not end. Instead, these children's books do intricate activist work by underscoring the ambivalence of childhood experiences across global and US settings shaped by social justice issues ranging from economic "development" and undocumented immigration to de jure and de facto segregation. They also exert resistive pressure on social expectations for children that are othering or are otherwise burdensome, from obligations surrounding "emotion work" to assumptions about what child readers are capable of understanding. Neither *The Village by the Sea* nor *Mama's Nightingale* nor *Remember* is a well-known book in comparison with their authors' ostensibly adult works, and I hope that by shifting readers' focus to these texts that sometimes live in the shadows, we can continue to spread a more nuanced vision of what children's literature is and what it can do.

CHAPTER 5

KIDS BEYOND BORDERS
Soto, Alvarez, and Cross-Cultural Cross-Writing

In the introduction to their recent edited volume on Latinx literature, Suzanne Bost and Frances R. Aparicio clarify the stakes of efforts to delineate a canon of Latinx writers and texts. They write,

> The existence of a companion to Latino/a Literature as such seems to assume the existence of a canon of Latino/a literature. While there is something to be gained from the generalizing impulse of this assumption (including the greater recognition that comes with the publication of anthologies of Latino/a writers and the creation of Latino/a literature courses), this canon is a contested and political site, giving greater representation to Chicano/a writers, for instance, and favoring certain literary styles and political modes. Canons have a certain inertia that leads them to reproduce themselves, obscuring internal differences and excluding works that challenge familiar forms. In this sense, they wield culture-shaping power.... There is a need to approach this canon in its plural form rather than as a singular entity. (7)

In the context of these discussions, Latinx children's literature becomes a compelling site of inquiry, as it remains marginalized within K–12 classrooms and in the broader scholarly discourse that falls outside the realm of children's literature studies. We should all be aware of the institutional racism that has left Latinx identities underrepresented in the children's literature publishing industry; as Kim Hoyos notes, out "of the over 3,000 children's books published in 2018, Latinx characters accounted for just 5% of protagonists," while "white characters account ... for 50% of books, followed by animals / other (fantasy creatures)" at 27%. So one of the revolutionary qualities of Bost and Aparicio's approach is their pointed inclusion of a chapter on Latinx children's literature by Mary Pat Brady, which, after chapters on science fiction and comics, rounds out the book's effort to widen the Latinx canon by spotlighting marginalized "literary forms" (vii). Their methodology amplifies the diachronic voices of Latinx authors who have written with young audiences in mind over the course of more than a century, while pointing out how neglected these books still are.

The marginalization of Latinx children's literature in the US publishing industry has been formative in illustrating the need for the hashtag #OwnVoices, coined by YA writer Corinne Duyvis in 2015 and used to describe "kidlit about diverse characters written by authors from that same diverse group." Whereas white writers of children's literature have historically been praised for centering child protagonists and secondary characters with ethnocultural affiliations different from their own, #OwnVoices writers have seen their books passed over in favor of these culturally appropriative works. This problem has given rise to the demand that "crooked, cracked, and inferior stories" by white writers be set aside in favor of ones that better "mirror students who rarely see themselves" and that "act as windows for students that need to see the rest of the world," as Laura M. Jimenez so aptly phrases it in her article "The Overwhelmingly White, Straight, and Able Face of Children's Literature" (67). The privileging and centering of white authorial voices has also led to the problematic neglect of children's books by marginalized writers who reach across cultural milieus, since when white outsiders do read these authors, they tend to demand that their books operate as tokenized purveyors of cultural detail, letting white readerships "in on the secrets" of spaces that might otherwise be closed to them. As a result, in a blatant double standard that ignores how white writers have been allowed and even encouraged to write cross-culturally, "ethnic-minority writers" have tended to "receive much more attention when they write about their own ethnicity than about another ethnic group" (Black 29).

One telling example that I will take up in this chapter, Gary Soto's *Pacific Crossing*, has received almost no scholarly attention since it was first published in 1992 and has not attracted the same promotional support by educational organizations like Scholastic that books like Soto's novel *Jesse* or his *Chato* series of picture books have enjoyed.[1] Although such intercultural narratives may fall outside the canon of Latinx literature as "singularly" conceived and may run counter to outsiders' essentializing expectations for Latinx authors, they embody the same spirit of intercultural influence and dialogue that characterized the outgrowth of Latinx studies as a "[p]an-Latino" intellectual space (Aparicio and Aguilar 6), as well as the ongoing efforts to negotiate the place of multiple Latinx literatures and cultures within an even larger universe of multiethnic US literary production and activist work. These cross-cultural stories also call out for attention because of the sophisticated challenge that they make to received notions of "majority" culture in the United States and to ideas of US nationhood, which makes them urgently relevant for readers of all ages. This challenge becomes a new way of redefining terms and concepts and a new way of embracing ambiguity, since such texts acknowledge pockets of goodness in the sociopolitical fabric of the United States even as they expose and underline its pathologies.

Some of the most exciting producers of this strand of Latinx children's literature have been writers like Soto. Originally lauded for his 1977 book of poetry *The Elements of San Joaquin*, Soto developed a reputation that might seem to belie the rather poignant title of his recent essay collection, *Why I Don't Write Children's Literature*. As the number of Soto's poetry collections increased, the list of his picture books, middle-grade texts, and YA novels grew longer, too, although the scholarship on his children's books has far from kept pace with his creative output, and in recent years his novel *Marisol* has been the subject of controversy.[2] Over the longer arc of his career, what Soto is perhaps most famous for in the world of children's literature is his searing representations of Chicanx culture and his confrontations with peculiarly US forms of injustice, both historical and contemporary. *Jesse*, for instance, which Scholastic classifies as suitable for sixth through twelfth graders, takes up the intersecting arcs of anti-Chicanx sentiment and US neoimperialism in the shadow of the Vietnam War. When the novel won the Phoenix Award for children's literature, it was with a view toward its contributions in this vein, echoing earlier sentiments about Soto's poetry "for adults."[3] But what is even more interesting about Soto's children's fiction is how it declines to limit itself to a single cultural home. Instead, just as poems in Soto's books *The Elements of San Joaquin* and *Where Sparrows Work Hard* capture the complexly hybrid history of a California populated with diverse communities of immigrants and migrants engaged in multilayered forms of exchange, Soto's children's fiction betrays a strong interest in the proposition of cross-cultural encounter. *Pacific Crossing* is one compelling example whose very title speaks to this distinctiveness in Soto's work. Seemingly simple interactions between Japanese and Chicanx teenagers destabilize deep-seated cultural categories and associations, undermining patriotic fictions of US nationalism that have had—and continue to have—profound implications in the world of both children and adults.

Of course, Soto has not been the only Latinx author in recent years whose children's books have taken up this challenge to nationalist and exceptionalist

US thought. The formation of a pan-Latinx canon in which Dominican or Panamanian American texts by immigrant writers have an essential place alongside seminal Chicanx and Puerto Rican literary works has been accompanied by a similar expansion in the world of Latinx children's literature. Some have raised concerns about these newer entrants to the canon espousing depoliticized perspectives tied to "cultural capital," which "seems to dilute their capacity to be oppositional" relative to that of the Chicanx and Puerto Rican writers who were at the center of Latinx literary studies at its inception as an academic discipline in the US university system (Dalleo and Machado Saéz 74). However, children's fiction has emerged as a site of equally resistive thinking among Dominican American writers like Julia Alvarez, who have at some moments been the target of these suspicions but whose writing for age-diverse audiences has turned out to be resounding in its activism.[4] In one of her least widely read "adult" novels, *In the Name of Salomé*, which was published in 2000 and today is often difficult to find in bookstores, Alvarez engages nineteenth-century Dominican history within a narrative of cultural crossing that spans Cuba, the United States, and a host of other nations as it reimagines the private and public lives of Dominican national poet Salomé Ureña de Henríquez. When Alvarez's middle-grade novel *Return to Sender* appeared on the literary scene several years later, it offered up similar themes within a story that represented undocumented immigration from Mexico to the United States along with currents of economic insecurity and cross-cultural tensions in rural agricultural communities like the one she moved to as a student at Middlebury College in 1969 (and where she has since become a writer-in-residence). Like Soto's work, this cross-writing of Alvarez's draws on her own lived experience while functioning cross-culturally to make its own edits to cultural categories and binaries. In the process, her novels deconstruct common ideas on which the myths of US nationalism and exceptionalism rest—in this case by reinterrogating externally imposed renderings of Mexican, Caribbean, and Central American history and by rejecting typical politically conservative US fables of "illegal" immigration.

    In what follows, I will scrutinize *Pacific Crossing* and *Return to Sender* in tandem with some of Soto's and Alvarez's other works as a way of underscoring the sophisticated depth of their cross-cultural cross-writing. Despite intermittent resistance from stakeholders, including publishers and parents, Soto's and Alvarez's children's books have a great deal to offer both younger and older readers. Much like reading Baldwin and Puzo or Desai and Morrison together, reading Soto's and Alvarez's cross-writing side by side allows us to interrogate points of contact that cross ethnonational borders as well as boundaries of expected audience.

Pacific Crossing, Cultural Categories, and Mythologies of Nationalism

It is easy to see why initial readers of Soto's verse found their attention captured by his poems' confrontations with specifically Chicanx experiences. "Field Poem," one of the most evocative pieces included in *The Elements of San Joaquin*, is one example: a poem that comes to terms with not only the physical contours of agricultural labor in the San Joaquin Valley but its economic, linguistic, and familial ramifications and the systems of power on which it rests. In two short stanzas and a total of just thirteen lines, "Field Poem" manages to encompass all of this. The first line invokes the whistle of "the foreman," an auditory reminder of the control of workers' bodies exercised by the structures of Californian agribusiness: when the whistle sounds, the speaker is liberated to move through space, but only to the waiting bus with its "smashed . . . window" (Soto, "Field" 11). The speaker's pay does not stretch far enough to pay for "tickets to a dance"—seemingly a reference to the entertainments organized for migrant labor camps—and it cannot compensate for the hurt that the speaker feels in seeing "the leaves of cotton plants / Like small hands waving good-bye" (11). These lines recall the fracturing of families by California's agricultural industry, not just in the quotidian work of chopping cotton but in longer histories like that of the Bracero Program, which systematically "recruited and distributed a male working force" during decades of postwar US-Mexican migration (Gonzalez and Fernandez 98). As Julián Olivares notes, this linguistic fragmentation also bespeaks "a bicultural experience in which the Mexican American is marginalized from American society, yet is not really Mexican, either," so that in "whatever language they speak, they are 'broken' by the working conditions imposed by the institutions of the majority society" ("Streets" 38). In this context, the United States' mythologizing narrative of unfettered immigrant opportunity becomes a casualty of actual historical reality.

The poem's articulation of this theme made it a natural choice when it was included in a 1973 issue of *The Greenfield Review* that, in spotlighting the authors of the NCAE Writers Workshop, reaffirmed its commitment to "breaking through the cultural barriers imposed by a dominant white society" by "offer[ing] a desperately-needed opportunity for an exciting new generation of ethnic writers to be 'heard'" (Burrows 3).[5] This workshop that Soto had attended at the University of Wisconsin-Stevens Point had also offered "the chance for representatives of Chicano, Black, Native American, Puerto Rican, and Asian American communities, from coast to coast, to discover each other, to share their mutual concerns, [and] to explore differences as well as affinities" (3), with other attendees including Simon J. Ortiz and a young Leslie Marmon Silko. Like the workshop, Soto's poetry from this period reflects a panethnic consciousness that at times emerges implicitly and at times makes itself explicitly heard. In "Field Poem," that the speaker and his coworkers talk "[i]n broken English, in broken Spanish" speaks to the ethnocultural hybridity of farm laborers' history in California, where "Okies" and Filipinos, for instance, have labored alongside Chicanx workers. We can see a similar train of thought in "Braly Street," also from Soto's original 1977 collection, where the speaker remembers a litany of disappeared figures who recall the multivalent composition of a Fresno that is home to both farm and factory laborers. "The Molinas, Morenos, / The Japanese families / Are gone," the speaker says, "the Okies gone / Who moved out at night / Under a canopy of / Moving stars" (26). Braly Street is the street in Fresno where Soto was born, and these same last names populate other works of his, such as "Being Mean," the opening piece in his "strongly autobiographical" book of children's stories, *Living Up the Street* (Tatum 188). In "Being Mean," we learn how the "Molinas grew scared and ran home" in the face of trouble and how the unnamed Okies scorned "the Sotos" as "dirty Mexicans" (2–3). The references in "Braly Street" similarly evoke the multiethnic history of Fresno's midcentury working-class communities as well as the "economic chokehold that relegated them to a lifetime of punishing labor in the cotton field, the orchard and vineyard or the small factory" (Ganz 426). While Soto's poems flesh out a continuum of Chicanx experiences "both urban and rural" whose struggles are, at their root, "societal," the fact that this "class of workers" (Bruce-Novoa 185) forms the target of Soto's attention in essence guarantees that Soto's poetic commentary will span a diversity of ethnic identities.

Successive collections of Soto's poetry find these cross-cultural elements deepening in their complexity. In "Bulosan, 1935," a poem from *Where Sparrows Work Hard*, Soto invokes the figure of Filipino American writer and activist Carlos Bulosan as he traverses the "small towns" of the West Coast by train:

> You rocked past the small towns
> Where you might have married
> White and worked Mexican,
>
> Or become lost in the Chinatowns
> In yellow, the tongue,
> The brow, and the cocked finger—
> Yellow and Filipino
> Shuffle, the *carabao* walk....
>
> At the table,
> Your eyes two cinders in a fire,

You wrote, but nothing stopped
The black loaf of lung" (67–68)

Bulosan was a committed labor activist and socialist who was targeted and harassed by the FBI for his beliefs before he died from bronchopneumonia at the age of 42. By resurrecting the figure of Bulosan on the twenty-fifth anniversary of his death and yoking him with the more culturally visible figure of César Chávez, who is similarly referenced in his first book of poems, Soto effects an act of remembering that signals his own political commitments and illustrates how they extend across ethnic boundaries to counter the fictions of happy capitalism on which so much of the US nationalist endeavor rests. The poem also marries commentaries on racialized patterns of labor and geography: the backbreaking labor embedded in the concept of "working Mexican" and the diasporic fullness of the "Chinatowns" where Bulosan might have "become lost."

It is important to contextualize Soto's Chicanx literary activism within this cross-cultural framework, which would take up increasing space in Soto's poetry over time. "Saturday in Chinatown," for instance, which was published in 1995, fills out and concretizes imagery that in "Bulosan, 1935" remains fragmented, associative, and surreal: "It was Armenian men slapping tobacco / From their trousers. It was Japanese / And Mexican, Chinese with blue bundles / Under their arms. It was chickens / In a wire cage" (173). Other poems written in the mid-1980s and early 1990s reference Soto's wife, who is indeed "a Japanese Methodist," while still others luxuriate in quiet, understated images of "old Italian women hunched together / Like pigeons" and "Italians clicking dominos / At a picnic table—men / Of the old world, in suits big enough / For Europe" ("The Family in Spring" 149; "Some Mysteries" 131; "Finding a Lucky Number" 90). Even in lines like these, which may not have the overt political resonance of his other poems, Soto does something radical in staking claim to a project of cross-cultural representation. By populating his poems with an array of faces and bodies from different communities, some of which he emphatically does *not* belong to, Soto subverts externally imposed expectations for the content of writing by "brown" voices (Soto, qtd. in McFarland 10). Significantly, Soto flips the script by representing white immigrant communities in some of these poems as well, reversing the pervasive white gaze on communities of color.

In general, like his poems of Chicanx communities from Fresno to the rest of the San Joaquin Valley, Soto's poems of cross-cultural encounter play an important role in his literary reckonings with what is fiction and what is truth within familiar cultural narratives of the United States. In undoing much of the pleasant "dream" of US economic opportunity and the nationalist reverence that it tends to inspire, these poems rely on careful and nuanced cross-cultural references. They set a precedent for cross-cultural work in later writings of Soto's that would prioritize and center children.

When Soto's children's books have articulated these sorts of politics, this has sometimes been against the odds and against the advice of his publishers. The editorial correspondence regarding *Cesar Chavez: A Hero For Everyone* reveals that Julia Richardson, Soto's editor at the children's publishing division of Simon and Schuster, requested that he "bring down some of the political overtones" of the book's first draft. Richardson instructed Soto not to "single out specific groups such as Republicans," giving us a vivid window into the pressure on US children's book authors to self-censor in order to cater to certain adult demographics. Although they might not focus as overtly on questions of age-appropriateness, such comments are akin to the suspicious responses of adult reviewers and others to books like Baldwin's and Cisneros's, which have been deemed unsuitable because they ignored conventional ideas about the need to suppress or limit the political interventions of children's literature. Soto, too, has persisted in disrupting these expectations, in this case through a cross-cultural lens.

This current of resistance is central to *Pacific Crossing*, which lives in the shadow of more famous novels such as *Jesse*, the book that Soto has referred to in interviews as his "best YA novel" (Soto and TeachingBooks).[6] In its own way, *Jesse* takes very seriously its responsibilities beyond US borders. With the Vietnam War as a key piece of the novel's historical context, it explores sentiments ranging from the straightforward conviction that "Vietnam was wrong" (Soto, *Jesse* 43) to more involved notions of "regret... follow[ing]" or pursuing US soldiers forced to kill someone in the war (52). Still, *Jesse* mostly obeys the domestic boundaries of the United States. *Pacific Crossing*, in contrast, veers into less conventionally expected territory as a narrative designated by Scholastic for grades six through eight. On Japanese shores, Soto's fourteen-year-old Chicano protagonist finds himself doubly displaced from "majority" US culture as a "brown boy in a white *gi*"—the phrase used in marketing blurbs for the book (*Pacific*).[7] In a way, the short phrase perfectly captures the uniqueness of Soto's novel, which turns its attention to Japanese linguistic and other identities as well as to US constructions of race and ethnicity.

It is still vital that *Pacific Crossing* advance notions of Chicanx pride as well as expressions of Latinx pride more broadly. From the first page onward, both translated and untranslated Spanish terms speak to what is unique about protagonist Lincoln Mendoza's identity. On a plane to Japan, where he will be living with a host family while continuing "to study *shorinji kempō*" (5), Lincoln remembers that "he was thirty-seven thousand feet above the earth ... with his lifelong friend, his blood, his *carnal*, his neighbor from the *barrio*, his number-one man on the basketball floor at Franklin Junior High—Tony Contreras" (1). With practiced artistry, Soto inserts context clues into this sentence that make the terms "carnal" and "barrio" legible to children who do not speak Spanish. This is significant given that *Pacific Crossing* has been recommended for readers as young as eight years old, who, in most US educational settings, are unlikely to be learning Spanish yet in school if they do not already speak it at home. This is not a linguistically activist text in the specific manner of Luis Valdez's *Zoot Suit*, whose systemic use of Spanish vocabulary decenters and threatens to confound English-speaking audiences in a gesture that is essential to the play's political intervention. By including a glossary of Spanish words and phrases in addition to the one that is provided for Japanese vocabulary, Soto seeks to orient non-Spanish-speaking readers rather than purposefully discomfiting them. Yet as the novel progresses, these readers are asked to be more independent in recalling the meanings of words like "mole" and "frijoles," just as they are asked to puzzle over the meaning of the Japanese words "Ichi, ni, san, shi, go" ("One, two, three, four, five") (76–77, 109). Otherwise, they are obliged to take the initiative to flip to the glossary, taking a literally active interest in the linguistic intricacies of the second most commonly spoken language in the US. There is a very real way in which demanding this sort of linguistic effort says something political. For readers who do speak Spanish, the novel offers up a mirror that validates their linguistic identities. For those who do not speak Spanish, the novel says, *Pay attention. English isn't the only language that is important to the fabric of the United States.*

Pacific Crossing's representations of bilingualism become one of the ways in which it delegitimizes the received notions underpinning US nationalism. Embedded in the United States' exceptionalist ideology is a set of cultural beliefs about language, including the mistaken idea that immigrants to the United States should forsake the languages of their homelands in favor of an unofficial "national language" that is somehow superior to their own. This idea, in turn, rests on often unspoken assumptions about why English supposedly deserves this place of honor: for instance, the assumption that English is a natural choice for a "universal" language and that it has been adopted for this reason rather than due to the histories of white supremacy and oppression represented by British and US forms of colonialism. As Robert Phillipson reminds us, this is a dynamic in which the "top language benefits through . . . an ideology that glorifies the dominant language and serves to stigmatize others, this hierarchy being rationalized and internalized as normal and natural, rather than as [an] expression of hegemonic values and interests" (40). Soto resists these notions of the English language, however, by refusing to make his adolescent characters obey "English-only" agendas, not just undermining the default association of the United States with American English but refuting one of the core principles on which the mythology of US nationalism depends.

This point deepens when Lincoln discusses language with his new Japanese "brother," Mitsuo, code-switching as he exclaims that the hot water at a bathhouse is going to "burn *[sus] nalgas*" and then, when asked, coolly explaining that "nalgas" means "your butt," without stopping to explain that one of these terms is Spanish and the other is English (Soto, *Pacific* 31–32). By allowing Spanish and English to run together in his own speech and in his explanations of it, Lincoln mirrors the bilingualism of the novel's narrative voice and asserts that his uses of Spanish are just as natural and legitimate as his uses of English, without any self-editing or apology for these linguistic moves. Such moments are perhaps even more powerful than the narrator's own code-switching with its built-in context clues, since Lincoln's words do not anticipate a lack of comprehension or a need for translation on the part of his listener; he just lets the words flow until he is stopped and questioned about them.

The style of Lincoln's speech patterns is consistent with the orientation of the novel's larger cultural conversation, which, among other things, emphasizes the teenage boy's pride in everything "raza-style" (14). It is Lincoln's friend Tony who first introduces this quintessential phrase along with the Chicano Movement-era history that it invokes, shouting "Viva la Raza!" in the middle of the Tokyo airport and making politically inflected jokes about "being caught and frisked by *la migra*" (12). These comic interjections are powerful, telegraphing a subversive refusal to fear the threatening specter of the United States border patrol and instead turning their policing—as well as the political policies it represents—into the butt of a joke. Later, Lincoln turns out to be just as invested in the concept of "Mexican pride" (67), even if he hesitates at first to explain the ethnoracial dynamics of the United States to Mitsuo, wondering how he can possibly put such complicated realities into words on his "first day" (23). That Tony and Lincoln have different ways of navigating these political questions keeps the novel from presenting a monolithic vision of what it looks like to be aware of and invested in social justice issues as a young person, while the two boys' ultimate investment in questions of ethnic pride and justice sends a strong message about the urgency of these topics.

The cross-cultural element of *Pacific Crossing* is equally essential to its unfolding of this type of thinking. Part of what is so intriguing about the novel is how its premise—a study-abroad trip being offered to two young Chicano boys from San Francisco because of their interest in martial arts—provides a platform for exploring these issues as Tony and Lincoln both attempt to communicate their complex status within a nation that has long attempted to suppress their ethnolinguistic roots. In Japan, Soto's protagonists are cultural ambassadors of Chicanx nationalism as a specific challenge to mainstream US nationalism, as much as if not more than they are ambassadors of US culture at large.[8] And indeed, there is a kind of freshness in the relatively equal footing that these two cultural inheritances enjoy in the boys' interactions, as though Lincoln and Tony have been at least temporarily freed from the "struggle to mediate between two unequal cultures" that colors so much of the hybridity of Mexican American identity in works like Soto's *Living Up the Street* (Erben and Erben 43). At the same time, a sea-change that occurs during the boys' time in Japan is their rewriting of stereotypes of Japanese culture, which requires them to reinterrogate the neat cultural categories that they have brought with them in their minds. Ask Lincoln or Tony before their departure from the United States, and they will tell you that San Francisco is a modern city, while Tokyo is an ancient, storied one. They will tell you that Japanese companies make more reliable automobiles, that people from the US make better jokes, and that Japanese people's love of martial arts is matched only by the United States' love of baseball. Even when they don't seem to promote the argument that one nation is superior to another, these exaggerated cultural distinctions make up much of the foundation for US nationalism. After all, fictions of national superiority rest on the premise that one nation is substantively different from another. With these distinctions collapsed, the rationale for understanding one's own nation as superior disappears. So it is significant when *Pacific Crossing* begins to surprise its adolescent characters with revelations that rewrite all of these preconceived ideas of cultural difference.

It turns out, in fact, that Japan is not a monolithic landscape populated with ancient buildings and ancient peoples as Lincoln first predicts when he imagines himself in Japan. At that time, Lincoln pictures "a dojo and a *sensei* sitting in meditation before a bowl of incense" alongside "snowcapped mountains and cherry blossoms parachuting from black branches" (Soto, *Pacific* 8). His imaginings are replete with stereotypes, which are corrected when he arrives in Japan and learns that this new-to-him nation, like the United States, is filled with diverse settings. Soto draws attention to this in transporting Lincoln and Tony from the airport in Tokyo where they first land to the rural village where they will spend the bulk of their time abroad. Tokyo itself is "disappointingly modern" (18), with its assertive resemblance to downtown San Francisco, while the rural community of Atami is as different from Tokyo as "any small town outside Fresno" (*Elements* ix) is from San Francisco. There, Lincoln stays in "a small western-style house on a tiny farm," where "faint stinks of chickens and compost" fill the air and the "moon hung, silver and round as a nickel, between two trees" (*Pacific* 19). In sketching the twinned rural and urban communities of both nations, Soto deconstructs monolithic notions of Japanese culture and points out the commonality that resides in the geographic and cultural diversity of both Japan and the United States.

This diversity of geographic and cultural spaces is mirrored in how the Japanese people Lincoln meets during his travels frustrate his expectations and the cultural categories in which he is invested before his arrival in Japan. Mitsuo's father has a sense of humor that surprises Lincoln: "Lincoln laughed. Mr. Ono was a comedian, like Lincoln's uncle Slic Ric, who was a member of the Chicano comedy act Culture Clash. It was all jokes from that *vato*, and from Mr. Ono it was poker-faced humor, even after a hard day at the railroad. Lincoln had always thought of Japanese people as reserved and serious. Now he was having second thoughts" (33). As we follow Lincoln's mind on this meandering route, subtle reminders of the intercultural dynamics of Californian life intermingle with an explicit rewriting of Japanese and US cultural stereotypes. No longer are people from the US the jokers and Japanese people the "reserved" ones. "America's pastime" of baseball turns out to be a favorite in Japan as well—a revelation that feels less like a symptom of US hegemony than a signal that what is so often seen as essential to the culture of the United States is in fact simply human. After all, baseball's rituals have historically been enshrined in the US national consciousness, with religious undertones and a patriotic flavor bolstered by pregame rituals like the singing of the National Anthem. In the wake of 9/11, Michael L. Butterworth described how the game of baseball glowed with "an aura of national unity and a perception of a foreign threat that delegitimized dissenting opinions" (50). For "foreigners" to love baseball, conversely, as we see in *Pacific Crossing*, converts the sport from a unique "expression . . . of American nationalism" (50) to a universally loved pastime, one that neutralizes the appearance of the "foreign threat" by demystifying non-US identities and collapsing the differences between them all. The multi-faceted complexity of the baseball reference, then, becomes an evocative example of the rich cultural commentary embedded in Soto's children's books.

These revelations complement other moments that more directly undermine the tenets of nationalism as the boys express their admiration for each other's cultures and disavow the claims of superiority made on both sides. Mitsuo explains that learning English at his school is "required" because "America is number one, and Japan is number two, so we must learn your language" (Soto, *Pacific* 28). Lincoln protests that "it's the other way around," saying, "You people have got it together. I like your cars"—to which Mitsuo replies that "cars are nothing," unwilling to accept the compliment (28). Scenes like this one stand in stark contrast to US fictions of journeys abroad written in the previous century, like Henry James's *Daisy Miller*, whose opening pages feature a little boy and a young man engaged in vigorous conversation about the various ways in which the United States is "the best" (6–7). Later, when the trusty Nissan Maxima that has long been the property of Lincoln's mother gives out on her, Soto seems to make a tongue-in-cheek gesture back to the boys' initial interchange; clearly, Japanese cars are not so infallible after all. But rather than validating Mitsuo's argument about the superiority of the United States, this sidenote seems to cast doubt on the supposition that any nation can be "number one." Tokyo and San Francisco have both proved to be big, beautiful cities; the farmers of Atami recall Lincoln's own mother when she "used to work in the fields" (Soto, *Pacific* 24); there is no need for one city or one nation to assert itself as superior, and a key objective of nationalist rhetoric falls away. *Pacific Crossing* says and accomplishes all this without denying problematic global geopolitical realities like the proliferation of English at the expense of other languages.

Just as Chicanx culture is allowed its own proud distinctiveness within this discourse, so is Japanese culture: for instance, in small details like the Onos' preference for taking off their shoes indoors as well as in less mundane habits like a poetic quality of speech that Mr. Ono betrays in calling the United States "big as the sky," which Lincoln finds strange but admires (16). Soto's novel blurs cultural categories just enough to destabilize patriotic fictions of national superiority without collapsing those categories into a nondescript haze that unrealistically denies difference. The novel in this way accomplishes something essential from an activist perspective. It makes an urgent contribution to the conversation about nationalism without adopting the kind of hegemonic view that seeks to subsume a world rich with distinct cultures into a single western-dominated and generic "global village."

A careful reading of *Pacific Crossing* reveals that like his poetry, Soto's children's fiction is as interested in cross-cultural encounter as it is in localized and specified explorations of Chicanx identities. These cross-cultural representations have their own activist resonance, dissolving stereotypes and categorical distinctions on which the mythologies of nationalism rest. Although *Pacific Crossing* makes this political intervention without the sort of productive bleakness that inflects some of his "adult" poems, it is easy to see the pointedly political quality that unites them.

Undocumented Immigration and Undefined Borders in *Return to Sender*

We will see something similar in Alvarez's fiction, which, like Soto's writings, are unwilling to leave cultural categories or hierarchies uninterrogated. Although my primary focus will be Alvarez's children's fiction, I want to begin with her novel *In the Name of Salomé*, which lays claim to Alvarez's own multilayered cultural inheritances as a child of the Dominican Republic who was born in the United States and who, after the age of ten, was raised in the US as well. Alvarez's fictional retelling of the life of Salomé, the beloved Dominican national poet, is also an opportunity for her to examine other geographic and cultural contexts: histories of Cuba, of Central American nations, and of the hemisphere more broadly. In the process, the novel takes on the problem of US-Cuban relations and reenvisions Cuban history and identities apart from the United States' anticommunist rhetoric and its nationalist preoccupations, while casting a critical eye on the larger politics of US neocolonial hegemony throughout the Caribbean and beyond. From the beginning, there are striking echoes of Soto's poetry here, especially if we consider poems like "Bulosan, 1935," with their activist consciousness of US labor history and their resistance to demonizing depictions of socialist organizing. There are also prominent notes of protest that recall the redefinitional work of writers like Erdrich, Harjo, Cisneros, and Santiago in exposing the realities of US settler colonialism and its neocolonial, gentrifying afterlives from the continental United States to Hawaiʻi and Puerto Rico. The end result is a novel that anticipates rather than eclipses the revolutionary quality of Alvarez's later cross-cultural cross-writing.

The foundation of much of this discourse is Alvarez's pointed critiques of US history in general and the US involvement in the political affairs of the Dominican Republic in particular. Much like Soto's poetry collections, Alvarez's novel works close to home even as it extends its gaze outward toward other communities. With the novel as a multigenerational account of the lives of Salomé and her daughter Camila, US-Dominican relations become an object of attention across a century of United States history. The earlier chapters devoted to Salomé, which are set in the mid-to-late nineteenth century, explore the current of progressivism associated with Abraham Lincoln's presidency and ideology. As narrator, Salomé recalls the grief that she felt on learning of Lincoln's assassination, saying that the US president "had struggled for the freedom of people our color" (Alvarez, *In the Name* 49). The admiration that Salomé feels for Lincoln suggests a kind of kinship or allyship that stems from the president's antiracist activism. Echoing the ambivalent tenor of United States history itself, the novel also confronts the more sordid legacy of US political intervention in the Dominican Republic: it "was the American occupation that forced [her father] Pancho out" of office during his brief stint as the Dominican president (41). The fact that the United States has "invaded another country and forced its president to live in exile on a neighboring island" becomes a core component of the novel's transnational history (195), showing the US's political and military machinations in an altogether different light than the fable of US nationalism permits. Like the novel's critique of US capitalism, which recalls Soto's poetry in referencing Vanderbilt and his "three-hundred-thousand-dollar mausoleum" (184), this aspect of the novel draws on Alvarez's dual Dominican American identity to produce a censorious vision of the United States.

As the novel progresses, its critique of US meddling deepens and becomes more global. In a chapter that she narrates, Camila comments on the seriousness of the problem, though with a kind of comically rueful tone:

> Proper channels! We have to go through proper channels to protest this country's outlaw actions toward us! . . . The president is distraught and has scheduled a trip to Alaska to relax. "Why not encourage him to go to the Caribbean?" I asked curtly. "He practically owns all of it now . . ." I enumerated all the occupied or supervised islands: Cuba, Haiti, Puerto Rico, as well as the Dominican Republic. I am afraid I am becoming as shrill as Papancho. (196–97)

Later, Camila's brother makes similar comments about the United States' inroads into the rest of Latin America, protesting "what the Yanquis have done in Mexico, Panama, Nicaragua" (200).[9] Set in 1923, these conversations invoke a problem that is at once political and personal—the exile of Salomé's husband and Camila's father from the Dominican Republic—but they quickly abstract outward from this more local concern to a pattern of neocolonial interference and power-grabbing on the part of the US that had infected a large part of the Americas by the early 1920s. Just as a young Salomé recognizes the affinities between "Cuba and Puerto Rico about to fight for their independence, and . . . the United States just beginning to fight for the independence of its black people" (25), her daughter takes a transnational view of the many places where the influence of the United States has represented a threat to democracy and human rights. At stake is a core tenet of the nationalist ideology that has colored so much of US foreign policy and that continues to problematically assert itself today: the paradoxical belief that the United States' purportedly special commitment to democratic principles qualifies it to impose its political will abroad. Alvarez thus takes on issues that have a cross-cultural resonance, moving far beyond her own personal connections to the United States and the Dominican Republic. This is an essential component of the "hemispheric view" that the novel promotes in asking readers "to imagine themselves as part of the same ethical and political struggle broadly construed instead of as being separated by more superficially-drawn national and ethnic borders" (Hickman 114). The "ethical and political struggle" is one against the US and its hegemonic tendencies, and US readers are asked to recognize this, possibly rewriting their own patriotic assumptions.

From here, it is not too much of a leap for *In the Name of Salomé* to question typical US assumptions about Cuban history and particularly about the nature of the Cuban Revolution. Salomé's earlier comments are made in 1861 and refer to Cuba's impending fight for independence from imperial Spain, while later commentaries of Camila's introduce a fresh view of Castro's Cuba. Whereas the stereotypical US understanding of postrevolutionary Cuba is of a deprived and stifled country thirsting for democracy, Alvarez's Camila counters this stereotype as she recalls "the peasants . . . singing, 'With Fidel, with Fidel, always with Fidel' to the tune of Jingle Bells" (Alvarez, *In the Name* 38), prompting then-President Eisenhower to ask, "What kind of a revolution is this?" (33). This vivid auditory image recalls the United States' neocolonial presence in Cuba, which not only "spurred an exodus" of Cuban immigrants due to the resulting "economic and political conditions on the island" but created the conditions for revolution as Cubans sought to frustrate these US attempts at political and economic hegemony (Torres 42). The passage also paints a very different picture of working-class Cuban society in its enthusiastic response to Castro. In both ways, Alvarez disrupts the typical US response to Cuban history that, in pitting a fairytale account of US freedoms against bleak imaginings of Cuban repression, is so critical to the US nationalist project. This does not mean that *In the Name of Salomé* makes no critique of Cuba. Camila identifies herself as "Cuban," then backtracks: "Dominican, really, by birth. The family had fled to Cuba years ago, only to find a dictatorship there as well. But they stayed on. Someone else's dictator was never as difficult as their own" (Alvarez, *In the Name* 36). Still, this is an ambivalent and complicated response to Cuba's position in the twentieth-century history of the Caribbean, one that embraces historical contradictions rather than denying them in the service of the United States' patriotic narrative. Reaching across national and cultural boundaries rather than being limited to representing the countries of her own birth and childhood gives Alvarez the latitude to explore these complexities, while suggesting that anyone who might expect her to confine herself to Dominican history ought instead to examine their prejudices.[10]

Rounding out its critique of US exceptionalism, the novel makes transnational references to the African diaspora that implicate the United States and its slaveholding history along with the European colonial machine. Within this cross-cultural framework, the novel excavates essential details of Salomé's identity as Camila reveals how her mother has been literally whitewashed in historical myth: "Actually that pretty lady is my father's creation," Camila reveals, referring to a portrait commissioned after her mother's death. "He wanted my mother to look like the legend *he* was creating. . . . He wanted her to be prettier, whiter" (44). Camila's description invokes historical traumas alongside persisting legacies of anti-Blackness. Rather than stop there, Alvarez makes herself an authority on shadowy moments in the United States' racial history that began long before her family set foot on US shores. Teenage Salomé's descriptions of the Ku Klux Klan "burning crosses in front of . . . negro people's houses" accompany Camila's musings about "what rules apply to a foreign woman who goes mad in this country," giving rise to a systemic picture of US injustice that encompasses racism and xenophobia as well as sexism and the stigmatization of mental illness (61, 32).[11] Cast in this light, the hypocrisy of the United States' efforts to dominate the region and the absurdity of its obsession with its own purported exceptionalism become undeniable.

In *In the Name of Salomé*, Alvarez positions herself as the arbiter of these dark US histories, even when they reach beyond the borders of her own personal and family lives. If there is a kinship between Soto and Alvarez that resides in their interest in cross-culturally rewriting mainstream narratives of US capitalism, opportunity, and patriotic pride, there are strong echoes of these ideas in *Return to Sender*, a novel whose purportedly middle-grade audience does not stop it from engaging in these same debates. Despite expressions of displeasure from disapproving adults, *Return to Sender* is assertive in claiming its membership in an activist literary tradition that, from classic examples like *Roll of Thunder, Hear My Cry* to newer works like *We Are Water Protectors*, has taught readers of all ages to think differently about these insidious myths.

Others have written powerfully about the personal frame of reference that Alvarez often draws on in her children's fiction. In her analysis of renderings of trauma in *The Secret Footprints*, Tiffany Ana López considers how Alvarez "embraces and acknowledges [the] centrality in her life" of the mythical creatures called ciguapas who are the focus of the book, making use of "the history of the Dominican Republic and . . . the history of its violence which demands documentation and the bearing of witness" (224). In contrast, *Return to Sender* draws on Alvarez's teenage and adult life as a resident of New England—including her experiences living in rural Vermont—while examining pressing issues at the intersection of US domestic and foreign policy that are the business of everyone living within US borders or affected by what goes on there. Continuing to resist outsiders' assumptions about what novels by Latina writers should look like, *Return to Sender* chooses a white boy named Tyler and a Mexican-born girl named Mari as its child protagonists, charting the twists and turns of their cross-cultural confrontation, which begins with Tyler contemplating reporting Mari's family to the police but has changed dramatically by the time he finds himself writing a letter to her that he signs with the phrase "Your friend forever" (307). Latina-run collectives like the organization *Latinxs in Kid Lit* specifically classify Alvarez as an "#ownvoices creator" and recommend *Return to Sender* for middle-grade readers. In doing so, they endorse Alvarez's wide-ranging authorial gaze and cast her cross-cultural narrative as working symbiotically with the movement's goals.[12]

The hybrid form of *Return to Sender* literalizes its multiple perspectives on undocumented immigration through a bifurcated structure devoted alternately to Tyler's worldview, which is depicted through a sort of close-third narration, and Mari's, which is captured in a series of letters that she writes. Like its title, then, the structure of this semiepistolary novel recalls the infamous US government operation called "Return to Sender," which Alvarez comments on in an afterword to the novel, explaining how workers "without legal papers were taken away on the spot, leaving behind children who were cared for by friends, relatives and older siblings ... the casualties of their parents' decision to leave behind their homelands in order to survive" (*Return* 322). In this same commentary, Alvarez draws an explicit parallel between undocumented immigrants and rural US farmworkers left without ways of hiring "affordable help" and threatened with "the loss of their ancestral homes" (322). As the action of the novel unfolds, it becomes clear that these cross-cultural problems "transform the nation's local and regional spaces ... into spaces of cultural and/or agrarian transnationalism that displace geographic and political borders," posing their own challenge to logics of nationalism in an increasingly transnational, globalized era (Socolovsky 387). *Return to Sender* thus espouses the same resistance to "more superficially-drawn national and ethnic borders" that we see in *In the Name of Salomé*. The cross-cultural encounters that occasion this critique also generate an overt resistance to US exceptionalism, whose mythology of unfettered opportunity, progress, and freedom does not admit the realities of rural farmers' struggles any more than it acknowledges the ethical stickiness of condemning Mexican families for "illegally" crossing a border created largely through the United States' violent theft of half of Mexico's territory in the mid-nineteenth century. These ideas echo others that we have seen already in this chapter, and the echoes are productive: they reaffirm the power of cross-cultural storytelling by a diversity of contemporary Latinx writers to do "radical" activist work across putative age-bound demarcations.

In bringing to life the consciousness of a young white boy living on one of rural Vermont's family farms at the start of the twenty-first century, *Return to Sender* creates an occasion for scrutinizing white, conservative attitudes toward undocumented immigration. At the outset of the novel, sometimes-protagonist Tyler doesn't hesitate to air his uninformed opinions about the people he conceives of as foreign lawbreakers on US soil. Recalling Lincoln Mendoza's initial imaginings of Japanese culture in *Pacific Crossing*, Tyler's musings about the ethics of hiring undocumented workers to keep his family's farm from going under provide a vivid illustration of the sorts of faulty beliefs that the novel's action, and Tyler's eventual revelations, will contradict. When he suggests that his family "call the police" after realizing that Mari and her family are undocumented, his reasons are as clear as they are simplistic: "All his life his parents have taught him to obey the laws and respect *the United States of America*" (Alvarez, *Return* 56–57, my italics). Pointedly invoking the full name of the United States, Alvarez's narrator brings to life a child's vision of what it means to "respect" a country, with "patriots" and lawbreakers separated into clear categories with hard boundaries that Tyler will learn to reinterrogate (56). Socolovsky touches on this point as well in noting how the novel "teaches a new patriotism that advocates transnational exchange and movement" while obligating Tyler "to recognize the complexity of categories such as legal/illegal and patriot/traitor"—in other words, to embrace conceptual ambiguity and ambivalence (397).

Building on this reading, what I find most exciting in Alvarez's cross-writing is the way that Tyler's evolution echoes similar moments in Salomé's story. Beginning to search his prior knowledge of US history for ways to comprehend the actions and the moral argument of his parents, Tyler envisions himself as a modern-day abolitionist: "He can't believe he is the same boy who several months ago wanted this family deported. Now he's plotting how they can escape capture. But maybe it's like the Underground Railroad: helping slaves find freedom" (Alvarez, *Return* 117). This passage raises questions about Tyler's participation in illusive narratives of white saviorhood, but it also calls up Salomé's admiration of Abraham Lincoln, creating a tangible link between Alvarez's individual writings. Alvarez's other protagonist, Mari, plays an equally key role in developing this train of thought, using "the war of slavery in this country" and what she knows of Lincoln's own sentiments ("United we stand, divided we fall") to help explain how her family has been split down the middle by the citizenship status of her sisters, some of whom are US-born and some of whom, like her, are not (59). Together, these invocations of antebellum history and its applications recast patriotism not as unerring devotion to existing US laws—a more traditionally nationalist view—but as willingness to question and reshape the moral fabric of the United States through ethically informed modes of dissent. Here there are palpable parallels with Salomé's own poems, which her father calls "seditious" and which nonetheless are devoted to *la patria* (*In the Name* 61). This similarity highlights the sophistication of Alvarez's appeals to age-diverse audiences, which demand a nuanced understanding of history and patriotism. In this case, Alvarez's cross-cultural rendering of these two distinct child protagonists plays a decisive role in deconstructing overdetermined cultural categories.

At other times, more minute details of the novel's cross-cultural vision have substantive implications. Near the end of *Pacific Crossing*, Lincoln and Mitsuo take part in a playful scavenger hunt in a Tokyo office building at the behest of Mitsuo's father. The episode might feel somewhat tangential, yet it offers a pretense for Soto's literary portraits of Japanese spaces and people, which frustrate western stereotypes of serious, "ancient" Japan, creating layers of meaning that belie the zaniness of the boys' escapade. Something akin to this happens in *Return to Sender* during a town meeting where an older man named Mr. Rossetti, who is Italian American, suggests that "anyone who's not here legally needs to be rounded up" (189). Mari and Tyler's teacher speaks out against the elderly man's motion, not just because of its inhumanity but because of Mr. Rossetti's own ethnic history. He reminds listeners that "Rossetti is an Italian name" and asks what would have happened "if Vermonters had raised an outcry about these foreigners endangering our sovereign state and nation" when Mr. Rossetti's own family first immigrated to the United States in the 1880s (190). While this cameo by an older Italian man might seem tangential, it captures the dynamic of bad allyship on the part of Italian Americans who have historically betrayed people of color in joining white supremacist and nativist social movements rather than antiracist ones. Alvarez's deserved skewering of the Italian diasporic community in the United States reinforces the misguided character of the sort of nationalist rhetoric that so many in the community have been prey to.

Many in the United States did "raise an outcry" about the influx of Italian American immigrants to the United States around the turn of the twentieth century, and this "outcry" sometimes included deadly acts of violence. While this reality doesn't invalidate Mr. B's essential point about the hypocrisy of later generations of Italian Americans rejecting other immigrants, it is an example of one issue about which *Return to Sender* declines to be explicit when it comes to US histories of brutality. More urgent examples emerge in some of the novel's references to Indigenous history and settler colonialism, as when the family celebrates Thanksgiving without any real commentary about the disturbing origins of the holiday, or when Tyler's grandmother remembers her husband explaining how "[w]e Paquettes came down from Canada back in the 1800s. Nobody but nobody in America got here—excepting the Indians—without somebody giving them a chance" (87). At first, these references seem to rehearse the pleasant narrative of interethnic cooperation that so often serves to obscure the real history of US settler colonialism in "mainstream" US history curricula in K–12 schools. But the novel does not leave the views of Tyler's family unchallenged, instead mixing their imaginings with direct acknowledgments of historical events like the Trail of Tears, where "the Cherokee Indians had been forced from their land to become migrants and march a thousand miles to the frontier. So many of them had died" (6). Patriotism in *Return to Sender* means acknowledging these devastating chapters without attempting to justify or minimize them. The exceptionalist mythology of the United States' special commitment to justice for all buckles under the pressure of these cultural memories, which Alvarez imagines being acknowledged by white children who do not engage in fragile obfuscation or avoidance to minimize these legacies of US whiteness. Projecting a certain optimism about a new generation of white children like Tyler, who may prove themselves to have such capacities, Alvarez generates an affirmative vision of possibility from her cross-cultural acts of representation. We might think again of Hughes or of *Pacific Crossing*, although in Soto, the most optimistic instances of young people disavowing nationalist or exceptionalist thinking involve children of color rather than white children.

Mari's family's experiences in crossing the border between the US and Mexico also offer a critical window into the character of the United States. For an uninitiated reader, the story of how Mari's mother is brutally abused by the *coyotes* who have promised to help her reenter the US might seem just to reflect conditions in Mexico itself, as Mari comments in describing the protestors who have camped out in Mexico City "demanding that the government make their country a place they could live in" (311–12). With a bit of the historical context that both adults and children in the US often tend to lack, however, the United States' responsibility for creating these conditions becomes obvious in light of events beginning with the Mexican American War and its aftermath, in which the United States wielded its influence in ways that favored its own interests and drastically worsened socioeconomic conditions in Mexico.[13] These historical realities run counter to established myths of US exceptionalism and reveal the deleterious impacts of these mistaken beliefs, which have been used to justify such neocolonial incursions in the first place. The violation of Mari's mother's human rights, which leaves her terrorized and traumatized even after her return to the US, becomes difficult to separate from this pathological history of US influence.

Undoing fictions of US nationalism and exceptionalism in *Return to Sender* does not mean denying the existence of brighter moments in the history of the United States: moments of resistance to injustice within US borders and of allyship in forging that resistance. Like *In the Name of Salomé*'s references to US abolitionists or *Pacific Crossing*'s expressions of Chicanx pride, these elements of *Return to Sender* render US individual and collective identities complexly rather than one-dimensionally, intimating that Alvarez is comfortable with ambiguity in her cross-writing. However, this act of undoing does mean rewriting received narratives of United States history so that, rather than accepting without question exceptionalist notions of the US's special, unerring commitments to freedom and justice, readers can recognize where the United States has gone wrong and how badly it has done so. Alvarez achieves all this through an often difficult but rewarding relationship between two protagonists who in many ways are coming from perspectives different from her own as they navigate diverse worlds of childhood in the contemporary United States. As much as *In the Name of Salomé* does, *Return to Sender* works from a sophisticated cross-cultural premise.

Bold Child Readers and Cross-Cultural Cross-Writing

Latinx teachers who have taught *Return to Sender* in border communities in the southwestern United States have expressed that the novel reflects "their community's realities" (Zúñiga), echoing the praise expressed for the book when it won the 2010 Pura Belpré Award. Meanwhile, today's digital platforms give child readers an increasingly public voice in expressing varied and individual views; they include venues ranging from Amazon.com to Common Sense Media, whose stated mission is to help parents and other adults curate the media content that children are exposed to but which does offer children and adolescents an opportunity to express themselves about the books they read. On the Common Sense Media site, reviews of children's books by younger and older contributors share virtual space, displayed side by side along with both sets of contributors' recommended age ranges for each book. While the site features only a few reviews for *Return to Sender*, the child-authored comments about the book are illuminating. About the traumas Mari's mother faces during her trip from Mexico to the United States, one twelve-year-old reviewer writes, "I think all kids need to eventually be exposed to those kinds of dangers" ("Return to Sender"). In contrast, the website's own "expert reviewer" has given the novel just three of five stars for "positive messages" and "positive role models and representations," with the unsatisfying explanation that a "central worry for both main characters is breaking the law and getting caught. Enforcers are presented negatively." Websites like this one provide a unique window into the diverse reception of children's fiction with content that adult cultural outsiders and those outside the world of children's literature studies may cast as controversial. They illustrate that younger audiences can be more receptive than adult ones to such activist, countercultural content, and they gesture toward the importance of novels like Soto's and Alvarez's in advancing ideology-challenging viewpoints that many adults find too difficult to grasp or accept.

The act of bringing child protagonists to life is inherently an act of cross-representation for adult writers, one that demands an antiessentialist vision that resists the colonizing impulse to "other" child characters and readers.[14] Soto and Alvarez have multiply made and met this challenge, reaching across the boundaries of a number of identity categories in their cross-writing. They do not just write in ways that express this antiessentialist vision of childhood; while working as #OwnVoices creators, they also embrace projects of cultural encounter by bringing to life the cross-cultural adventures of diverse child protagonists and secondary characters with varied ethnic identities and citizenships. In taking this approach to deconstructing cultural stereotypes and categories, Soto and Alvarez make subversive political interventions in important conversations surrounding US nationalism and exceptionalism: conversations that require the participation of readers of all ages.

CONCLUSION

ADAPTATIONS AND REWRITINGS
Tan, Shange, and More

All of the writers in this book have composed texts for age-diverse audiences that share in the same activist ambitions and that engage in sophisticated ways with urgent concerns about the sociopolitical worlds they reflect. These authors' works of children's literature powerfully echo their other writings—and vice versa when the latter come later—in confronting injustice and channeling future potentialities. I would like to close by considering some of the most direct parallels of this type, in which writers have taken works that are ostensibly for adults and have adapted them into various forms that are explicitly tailored to child readers. In collaboration with talented illustrators, writers like Ntozake Shange and Amy Tan have used this strategy of adaptation to reframe their fiction and poetry so that it becomes more obviously intended for this purpose. While these sorts of cross-writing might at first seem to reinforce inflexible demarcations between adults and children by acknowledging the need or at least the market for age-differentiated texts, reading the original versions with their newer counterparts reveals that little of substance needs to change in these acts of reenvisioning. Instead, the adaptations continue to convey the power and the revolutionary ideas of their authors, rewriting faulty mythologies and raising questions about why these slim volumes tend to be relegated to single sentences or brief footnotes in the scholarship on Shange and Tan outside of children's literature studies. Like the larger tradition of activist children's literature of which they are a part, these books deserve to be read and taken seriously by audiences of all ages. The strategies that their authors employ serve as a testament to the ever-tenuous borders between readerships, encouraging us to persist in rethinking and troubling those boundaries.

Published in 1992, Amy Tan and Gretchen Schields's *The Moon Lady* is a captivating reworking of a portion of Tan's *The Joy Luck Club*. The text of *The Moon Lady* comes from a chapter with the same title and is narrated by Ying-ying St. Clair. What may be most immediately visible is what is omitted from Tan and Schields's illustrated version, like Ying-ying's biting commentary at the start of the chapter about her daughter, who "sits by her fancy swimming pool and hears only her Sony Walkman, her cordless phone, her big, important husband asking her why they have charcoal and no lighter fluid" (*Joy* 67). In the original, the daughter's inability to hear her mother becomes the pretext for the story that follows: Ying-ying insists on asserting that there was once "a time when [she] ran and shouted" and when, in this way, she demanded to be seen and heard (67). The story of the Moon Lady becomes evidence of this, its significance deepened by the way that Ying-ying's childhood noisemaking deconstructs intersectionally raced and gendered stereotypes of Asian women as docile and submissive.

Nevertheless, even while omitting Ying-ying's critique of her daughter, *The Moon Lady* retains much of this impetus for the telling of the story. In this version, it is the narrator's three young granddaughters who do not know or at first believe that their grandmother once "shouted," let alone that she "shouted very loud" (*Moon*). As in the original scene, Tan's narrator is motivated to tell a story of childhood to correct others'—especially girls' or other women's—misunderstanding of her "true nature" (*Joy* 67). The picture book's subtler rendering of intergenerational conflict has its own resistive implications, even as it puts the narrator in a role that might seem more universal and more depoliticized: that of the elderly woman whose grandchildren cannot imagine that she once was young. This universalizing impulse functions as its own brand of social commentary insofar as it frustrates white assumptions about cultural difference and asserts Tan's right to produce a story that is different from the one some white readers might expect of her. It also gives Ying-ying's character a subversive pedagogical function as she invites her Chinese American grandchildren to reject these othering mythologies.

Moving further into the narrative, we discover other subtle edits to individual details of the plot as well as some formal changes. The word "servants" (68) is omitted from the picture book, deemphasizing the narrator's socioeconomic status and the problem of class injustice that the original word choice invokes. Other changes in this vein, however, are double-edged. While both versions specify that the narrator has a nursemaid as a child, offering up an alternative marker of the narrator's class privilege, *The Moon Lady* describes the nursemaid as sleeping "on a cot in the same room" as the narrator rather than "on a cot in the little room next to" the narrator's (*Joy* 68). Does this edit obscure the nursemaid's subordinate position in the household, casting her as a child's affectionate companion more than an exploited domestic worker, or does it underline how little personal space the nursemaid is afforded: how the boundaries of her identity are threatened by the expectation that her every moment will be devoted to Ying-ying's needs, even while they are both asleep? Such questions illustrate that seemingly simple adjustments made in this process of adaptation are not always so straightforward in their possible ramifications, and that some changes may operate more subversively than they appear to. Then there are the references to class issues that did not change at all when the original was rewritten. In the scene where Ying-ying is separated from her family and strangers are attempting to determine whose family she belongs to, both versions emphasize the importance of the soles of her feet, which indicate that she has "worn shoes all her life," marking her in these strangers' eyes as a loved and wanted child from a wealthy household rather than a "beggar girl" (*Moon*). In both cases, this detail highlights the stacked socioeconomic odds that shape Ying-ying's childhood world as well as the ways that those odds might influence and define experiences of childhood. Ying-ying's experience is identifiably colored by the visibility of her socioeconomic status and the acts of recognition that it secures for her among strangers.

Later, when Ying-ying dirties the new clothes her mother has made for her, the original bilingual text—"'Syin yifu! Yidafadwo!'—'Your new clothes! Everything, all over the place!'" (*Joy* 72)—is shortened to read, "Ying-ying! . . . Look at your new clothes!" (*Moon*). While this change might seem to center English-speaking readers, placing the book in a different realm than Tagore's or Soto's, *The Moon Lady* is punctuated with shorter exclamations like "Anh! Don't you have eyes?" and "Ai-ya! . . . You're somebody's lost treasure." One of these phrases appears in the original as well, while the other, although it is not included in the chapter "The Moon Lady," appears elsewhere in *The Joy Luck Club*. Through these interjections, *The Moon Lady* retains the antihegemonic linguistic impulse of Tan's novel. Issues of linguistic identity, then, like ones of class, remain visible in this version that is billed by Simon & Schuster as being for readers ages six to nine, even if the picture book's engagement with these topics sometimes occurs in different forms.

Where *The Moon Lady* makes the fewest alterations to its "adult" companion text is in its intersectional manner of addressing gender issues both within and outside its textual world, especially ones that are inextricable from white racist views of Asian identities. In the original, Ying-ying recalls her mother's words: "A boy can run and chase dragonflies, because that is his nature. . . . But a girl should stand still" (*Joy* 72). This phrasing reappears verbatim in *The Moon Lady*. Ying-ying soon sees some boys on a raft and finds herself "envying their carefree ways" (76), expressing an idea that recurs in the illustrated scene where Ying-ying remembers how she "wished [she] could be one of those boys" (*Moon*). The message is clear: while Ying-ying might sometimes enjoy taking her mother's advice, it is as much in her "nature" to crave adventure as it is in any boy's. The illustrated version also reproduces an episode from the original in which the Moon Lady, after spouting platitudes about women as "the darkness within, where passions lie," is revealed to be a man. With this turn in the narrative, the apparent authority of his ideas disintegrates, and Ying-ying runs instead of saying what she wishes for as she is supposed to. Although the ending is brighter than the ending of Tan's chapter, featuring a happy grandmother and grandchildren making their own wish come true by dancing outside under the moon, both versions include the same foreboding, gendered pronouncement and the same subsequent revelation. The moment intervenes in racist western conceptions of Asian women as submissive and sensual while interrogating the intergenerational impact of those ideas when Ying-ying's grandchildren at first cannot picture her as an assertive, loud-speaking girl. Sau-Ling Cynthia Wong has excavated "inaccurate cultural details" from Tan's writings, including *The Moon Lady*, that problematize some critics' "anthropological" readings of her fiction as "faithful chronicles of things Chinese" (184). Tan's fiction, however, is undeniably "accurate" in its grappling with these Anglo-American issues: it reflects their deep embedding within white US culture and their ripple effects on a range of communities. They are quite visible in the two renderings of Ying-ying's story, even if many white people have glossed over them in looking to the characters in Tan's books as "a mirror and a differentiator" (177) designed to ensure their access to some "authentic" and representative cultural knowledge.

It is satisfying, I think, to read *The Moon Lady* in light of the texts that have come before it in this book, since so much of what was present there is visible in this one slim volume, too. *The Moon Lady* takes its child readers seriously, confronting them with complicated and unsettling obstacles to social justice in a United States that often pretends it has already achieved that goal. It is an adventure story that uses those adventures to get at these very issues, from linguistic hegemony to intersectional gender stereotypes. It redefines belonging to include bilingual and bicultural identities, like those of Ying-ying's grandchildren, who are named Maggie, Lily, and June. It is unafraid of ambiguity and ambivalence, problematizing elements of Ying-ying's "childhood in China" (Tan, *Moon*) while suggesting that the contemporary US context is not the exceptional haven it claims to be. That it does all this through an exercise of adaptation from Tan's purportedly adult novel only makes the case of *The Moon Lady* more interesting. It adds one more writing strategy to a compendium of approaches that help our authors who "also write for kids" to bring socially engaged literature to life.

Ntozake Shange's 2004 book *ellington was not a street*, which was illustrated by Kadir Nelson, is distinct from Tan's work in a variety of ways. Whereas *The Moon Lady* was published just three years after *The Joy Luck Club*, it took more than two decades for Shange's poem from her collection *A Daughter's Geography* to become a picture book. This difference parallels the telling disparity in the reception of *The Joy Luck Club* and *A Daughter's Geography*, which was welcomed with far less fanfare than Tan's novel and today is out of print. *The Moon Lady* was marketed as a book "spun off" from *The Joy Luck Club* and followed a "$4 million advance that Putnam reputedly paid" for Tan's second novel, *The Kitchen God's Wife* (Wong 174). Also unlike Tan's retelling, Shange's book represents the full text of her original poem "Mood Indigo" without alteration, so that the most visible adjustments become two additions: the illustrations themselves and a nonfictional section at the back of the book that offers brief biographies of Duke Ellington and the other Black artists and intellectuals referenced in the main text. Still, Tan and Shange have potent affinities that speak to the importance of this method of cross-writing.

Shange's original poem is an "elegiac autobiographical" work (von Merveldt 235) that centers and celebrates a wealth of cultural heritage viewed from the perspective of a powerful Black child, who is the youthful analogue of the poem's adult speaker. At a time when "ellington was not [yet] a street," the child at the center of the poem witnesses the greatness of intellectual, political, and artistic luminaries like Paul Robeson, Dizzy Gillespie, and Kwame Nkrumah alongside the more private forms of greatness of her own father, whose "arms held [his children] safe and loved" (Shange, "Mood" 13). The reminiscing adult speaker invokes a period of upheaval in which "politics [were] as necessary as collards" while celebrating how, in their diverse modes of resistance and protest, these luminous figures "changed the world" (13). The poem serves as the gateway to the rest of a section titled "It Hasn't Always Been This Way," which takes its title from the first line of "Mood Indigo." The two poems that follow and complete the section, "Improvisation" and "Take the A Train," are unflinching in their righteous anger at white racism. "Improvisation" takes up the figure of the speaker's baby daughter and envisions her childhood in a persistently racialized world: "she dont know where she is yet / she dont know alla black kid's gonna get / is a fist in her mouth or a white man / who says she's arrogant / cuz / she can look him in the eye" (16). Meanwhile, "Take the A Train" is mournful as it repeats the section title; the speaker laments, "but it hasnt always been this way / i swear / we were not always missing" (18).

In a way, the illustrated *ellington was not a street* makes its largest act of adaptation by removing the text of "Mood Indigo" from this surrounding context, although nothing changes about the poem itself in the process. The actual added material, including both the illustrations and the additional text, reinforces the resulting effect: the triumphal notes that Shange's poem reaches are allowed to reverberate without interruption by traumatic confrontations with white supremacy. This meaningful adjustment is not about sheltering child readers; instead, it allows the book to privilege Black love and joy, working in contravention to othering images of Black childhood while refusing to center the pathologies of whiteness. In one of Nelson's illustrations, which accompanies the lines "sleeping in the company of men / who changed the world," Du Bois and Robeson sit together drinking from teacups while the child sleeps on the sofa with Robeson's suit jacket as a blanket (*ellington*). The image reemphasizes the extent to which these gatherings of minds shape what childhood means for the speaker at the time. The same illustrations of Du Bois and Robeson accompany their biographies at the back of the book so that their faces can be easily recognized, and readers who peruse this final section will learn that Robeson was an "Actor. Singer. Athlete" as well as continually "speaking against racism and fascism," while Du Bois's "research helped bring social consciousness and was valuable in the development of the National Association for the Advancement of Colored People (better known as the NAACP)." Thus, the illustrated, annotated reenvisioning of the poem spotlights a vital period in African American intellectual and artistic history as well as offers a satisfying representation of a tranquil and protected Black childhood. *ellington was not a street* holds up a validating mirror for African American child readers and disrupts a host of racist stereotypes that outsiders continue to project onto Black families.

Shange's writing, like Tan's, is a fitting addition to this concluding section because it encapsulates so much of what this book has located in its array of previous texts. The child protagonist is immersed in the daring and necessary adventures of these famous individuals "who changed the world." Redefining Ghanaian president Nkrumah as "no foreigner" although he lived most of his life outside the United States, the speaker remembers herself as a child resisting and rethinking ideas of foreignness and ethnonational belonging; she also takes on a cross-cultural, transnational role in invoking the figure of this world leader. There is ambivalence, too, despite the triumphal tone of most of the book; it is bittersweet to realize that while Robeson was once "no mere memory," he has become so for the adult speaker who now recalls him after his death. Perhaps most importantly, while this illustrated version of "Mood Indigo" contains an explanatory final section saying "[m]ore about a few of the men 'who changed the world,'" it also calls for mutual acts of meaning-making. Poetic turns of phrase require readers to fill in both grammatical and informational gaps as well as to interpret potentially ambiguous and meaning-laden lines (at one point the speaker says, "our windows were not cement or steel"). For readers of any age, the payoff of all of this challenging work is the text's intervention in both historical and contemporary conversations about racial justice, as the book jacket suggests in describing the "lives and works" of the individuals spotlighted there as a "guide to how we approach the challenges *of tomorrow*" (my italics).

Variously addressing these challenges, the constellation of authors included in this book have shown us how consonant activist children's literature tends to be with texts received as speaking to adults. In their sophistication, these cross-written works are far from representing an exception within the broader world of children's poetry, fiction, and nonfiction that engages with these big questions. Yet they are uniquely valuable to us because of the distinctive proposition that they make to uninitiated or skeptical readers, whom they offer to show something that may not be as visible when readers are only dealing with writing targeted to younger audiences. Paired with their "adult" companion texts, these books make it easy to see that not much needs to change from one type of writing to the other: that contemporary adventure stories marketed to kids can as effectively disrupt imperialist ideologies, or that cross-cultural children's fiction can as fundamentally rewrite xenophobic notions of linguistic belonging. In unveiling these realities, our cross-writing authors invite people of all ages to envision both children and children's literature as more than capable of joining these conversations as well as shaping and shifting them in radical ways. They also ask readers to keep on rethinking the inflexible demarcations that have been used to categorize these works as being "for adults" or "for kids." Instead, they suggest, activist children's literature should—and does—belong to all of us.

ACKNOWLEDGMENTS

This book was made possible with support from the Children's Literature Association, which allowed me to do archival research on children's books by Sandra Cisneros, N. Scott Momaday, Toni Morrison, and Gary Soto. Thanks especially to the ChLA for being so open to supporting the work of an adjunct lecturer and for modeling what it looks like to carve out these possibilities for contingent faculty. It was more thrilling than I can say to correspond with Gary Soto about this project, and his generosity in allowing me to quote so widely from his poems is something I will never forget. I am also grateful to the editor of *Children's Literature Association Quarterly*, Sara K. Day, who shepherded an early draft of the first chapter of this book through the publication process at *ChLAQ*, and to the anonymous reviewers who provided invaluable feedback on that article. I am equally indebted to this book's peer reviewers, whose insights into what it was aiming to accomplish were as formative as they were perceptive.

As always, Katie Trumpener has my gratitude for what is now sixteen years of mentorship and for her generous and patient support of this research. Katie Keene at the University Press of Mississippi also encouraged me in this work when I was still a graduate student and then when I found myself balancing this research with adjunct teaching on an increasing number of college campuses. Katie, thank you so much for encouraging me to believe, six years ago, that *They Also Write for Kids* could actually become a book. Today I am so happy to be teaching at the University of Groningen, in a department that has given me the time I needed to complete this manuscript. Thanks to Ann Hoag, Ashley Maher, David Ashford, and John Flood for their unwaveringly warm and collegial support. The graduate students in my seminar on contemporary Gothic children's literature at the RUG also deserve special thanks for embodying the approach to reading children's books that this project has hoped to encourage outside the field.

They Also Write for Kids has its most distant roots in my own experiences of childhood and the books I read then, so I want to thank the lifelong friends who have encouraged me to stay connected to that space. To Myriah Pahl, Martha Tillson, Tara Kurland, and Kyle MacQueen Feldman—you are amazing women, and I will always love you. Special thanks are also due to Dana Murphy for writing with me through the descending dark of fall, to K. Adele Okoli for being so steadfastly present, to Lynn Wang and Kate Lieberman just for being their miraculous selves, to Jessica Teague for creating public forms of beauty in a painful and complicated time, and to Jaclyn Vásquez, whose own children's books I can't wait to see in print. I am grateful to my father, Bob Manizza, who believed that an eight-year-old could learn the word "prolific," and to my mother, Lucy, who passed away more than a decade ago now but who as an adult would have loved reading these books "for kids."

While Jonny Roszak already knows that I could not have written this book without him, I hope that our son Sander grows up to realize how much inspiration I've drawn from our bedtime stories. Thanks to my irrepressible toddler for always reminding me of what children, and children's literature, can do.

NOTES

Chapter 1. Sophisticated Children: Reading "Child-Poems" with Hughes and Tagore

1. Readers have been quicker to examine Tagore alongside writers like Pablo Neruda and Aimé Césaire. The three poets were the focus of an international forum sponsored by UNESCO on the 150th anniversary of Tagore's birth. Hughes is only briefly mentioned in the programming's background information on Césaire.
2. While some might hesitate to conceptualize Tagore as an activist due to his self-identification as a poet rather than a politician, I find these readings of Tagore to be overly literal.
3. See Goswami's *Colonial India in Children's Literature*.
4. See Bhattacharya.
5. Given that Tagore translated these poems from the original Bengali himself, this rhyming quality of the language is his own choice rather than an imposition by an outside translator.
6. Burnett was born in England but lived for much of her life in the US. While a number of anthologies, encyclopedias, and histories of American literature have classified her as a US writer, I join biographers and critics such as Gretchen Holbrook Gerzina and Adrienne E. Gavin in viewing Burnett as British and *A Little Princess* as a British imperialist novel, not just a US one, because of its London setting and colonial themes as well as Burnett's familial origins.
7. See Richman. Regarding Tagore's comments on Valmiki's text and its importance, see Sikdar Datta.
8. I am especially thinking of Chimamanda Ngozi Adichie's recollections of her childhood reading habits in Nigeria, where exposure to British stories filled with ginger beer and apples led her to populate her own early works with similar items.
9. See Mehta.
10. Goswami makes a similar observation about Tagore's allegorical children's play *The Land of Cards*, with its traditionally happy ending. Goswami also draws attention to an

early children's poem of Tagore's in which he recounts the violent death of a child during an early eighteenth-century conflict between the Sikhs and Mughals. It is interesting that this subject matter does not necessarily have the same activist tenor of much of Tagore's other verse, even if it does serve a tangentially activist function in recording an event in India's precolonial history. If anything, as Goswami notes, the poem signals Tagore's commitment to taking a balanced or "objective" view rather than working exclusively to glorify India's cultural past (107).

11. See Trivedi.
12. See Jeyathurai.
13. See Rampersad.
14. See Rampersad.
15. In a nod to the staying power of this poem, in 2013 it was adapted into a standalone picture book with illustrations by Sean Qualls.
16. See Glissant.
17. See Roberts; Washington; Collins.

Chapter 2. Subversive Adventures and Intrepid Kids: Cross-Written Activism in Baldwin, Puzo, and Achebe

1. See, for instance, *The Columbia Anthology of American Poetry*.
2. Since critics like Miriam Dow have already explored some of the most interesting connections between *Chike and the River* and *Things Fall Apart*, I am more engaged in unearthing these connections between less canonical works.
3. Notably, Bilan quotes Tagore in an epigraph at the start of the novel.
4. Regarding the "other modernism" of *Giovanni's Room*, see, for instance, Johnson-Roullier (932).
5. See Jacobson; Roediger; Guglielmo and Salerno.
6. In Italian American studies, it is just now becoming more common for the links and the overlap between African American and Italian American communities, writers, and other artists to be unearthed in literary and cultural criticism. See Gennari; Pardini.
7. Clarence E. Hardy III reads David's biblical reference as an acknowledgment of the innocence that David has lost in finally "fac[ing] the reality of Giovanni's death" (94). While I do not disagree, I also read David's use of the word "childish" as a paradoxical reference to his momentary lack of inhibition in his sexual self-disclosure with Joey. In David's worldview, to "put away childish things" means to give up the seeming self-indulgence of such resistance to performative heteronormative modes.
8. See Boggs, who comments in detail on Baldwin's characterization of Blinky.
9. Some reviewers, like Ann S. Haskell, suggested that the book floundered because of an insufficient awareness or "concept" of its audience (qtd. in Boggs and DeVere xx).
10. Karefa-Smart specifically uses the word "adventure" to describe her childhood with TJ, resisting critics' attempts to reduce her little brother's escapades to a "loose sketch" (Lester) with no significant plot or action.
11. This text was included in the jacket description of the original version of the book when it was published in 1976.
12. Regarding *Little Man, Little Man* and Dickens, see also Zaborowska.

13. This pronouncement is consonant with Puzo's own frustration about the relative lack of attention that books like *The Fortunate Pilgrim*—and, by extension, *Davie Shaw*—received relative to the *Godfather* series. Meanwhile, as Jonathan Karp recalls, "one literary critic described Mario Puzo's style as 'somewhere between pulp and Proust.'" That is to say, to call Puzo's work in some way "pulpy" is not to discount the very real artistry of Puzo's writing in much of the *Godfather* series; as Thomas J. Ferraro suggested in his 2000 article, "the time for esteeming Puzo" rather than "merely tolerating or outright reviling Puzo as a hack populist . . . is near at hand" (514).

14. See *Intersecting Diasporas*.

15. Indeed, this narrative detail perfectly captures the hallmarks of cultural appropriation: a white man is able to adopt cultural characteristics of a marginalized community without the negative consequences that members of that community themselves experience, whether those consequences manifest as microaggressions or overt acts of xenophobic violence.

16. See Musa and Oyeleye.

17. While Chimamanda Ngozi Adichie was lukewarm in her assessment of some other portions of Achebe's memoir, this portion of the text—the one that functions as "a celebration of the richness of Igbo philosophy and cosmology and its inclusive culture"—met with her more enthusiastic approval ("Things Left Unsaid").

18. It is worth noting that some readers, such as Aghogho Akpome in his recent article "Ways of Telling: (Re)Writing the Nation in the Novels and Memoir of Chinua Achebe," have objected to this phrasing as portraying "the Igbo as a homogenous, undifferentiated, and centrally organized political unit" in a way that he perceives as oversimplifying or "lack[ing] nuance" (44–45). Nevertheless, the tenor of Achebe's anticolonial gesture is important, as it illustrates a willingness to speak directly and explicitly against discourses of western cultural supremacy.

19. I will return to this species of ambivalence in chapter 4.

20. The recently reissued version of *Chike* contains illustrations by Edel Rodriguez, who also did the cover art for many recent editions of Achebe's other books.

21. The book is also predated by a story titled "Chike's School Days," which was first published in 1960 in the magazine *Rotarian*, a publication of Rotary International that in the same issue had published an article titled "Changing Africa." In an unsurprising display of racism that demonstrated the need for Achebe's voice, the article described African nations as being recently "catapulted out of the slumber of centuries" (J. Hughes 12).

22. See Miller; Dow; Emenyonu; Uko. The edited collection *Emerging Perspectives on Chinua Achebe*, published in 2004 by Africa World Press, has done a great deal to focus more attention on Achebe's children's books.

23. Emenyonu reminds us that Achebe dedicated the book to his nephews and nieces in addition to his daughter; the connection to Baldwin is worth remarking on.

24. In *There Was a Country*, Achebe grapples with the ambiguities of this issue, too, reflecting that while "African languages and writing should be developed, nurtured, and preserved, how else . . . would [he] have been able to communicate with so many boys from different parts of the country and ethnic groups, speaking different languages, had [they] not been taught one language?" (25). Passages like this one demonstrate how students like Achebe used the agency and resilience that they possessed to appropriate and redirect tools of colonialist domination and abuse.

Chapter 3. Redefining Terms, Rethinking Concepts: Anticolonialism for All Ages from Erdrich to Santiago

1. Schools whose textbooks frame the history of colonialism in the Americas as the "discovery of the New World" offer one example that will be germane to this chapter.

2. Comparatively little scholarship has put Cisneros and Erdrich into conversation with each other. In 1991, Wendy K. Kolmar wrote an essay on the presence of the supernatural in a multiethnic array of texts that included writing by both authors. Cursory references to Cisneros have also sometimes appeared in book-length works on Erdrich's writing, like Hertha D. Sweet Wong's *Love Medicine: A Casebook* or Frances Washburn's *Tracks on a Page*, as part of a scholarly effort to contextualize Erdrich's oeuvre within a larger history of literary production by writers of color who have "actively confounded" Eurocentric "expectations of narrativity" (Sweet Wong 101) and who have functioned as "wedge authors" in demanding attention for nonwhite literary, cultural, and political voices (Washburn 113).

3. Roque Planas's news coverage of this horrifying event included the eyewitness accounts of students like "Nicolás Domínguez, 18," who "watched as one of the former Mexican American Studies teachers came into his classroom at Tucson High to pack up the books and take them to storage. 'They did it in a very dirty way,' Domínguez said." In this case, *Mango Street* was banned even in high school classrooms where Mexican American studies had formerly been taught.

4. Harjo's interviewer had just defined protocol as "cultural etiquette" (66). Harjo's response, an alternative definition, seems intended to gently point out that protocol is far more than "good manners" or polite behavior—that it has a fundamental ethical heft that the word "etiquette" does not quite capture.

5. I use the term "speaker" rather than "narrator" in deference to the original form of the text as a poem rather than a work of prose.

6. McGlennon draws attention to similar strands of thought as they appear in Harjo's poem "Protocol."

7. This is one of the moments in the book when using the lineation from the original poem gives the text a more explicitly verse-like effect. At other times, lines in the book are simply broken at the edge of the page, especially when single lines in the original poem were too long to be presented that way when the book was printed.

8. Harjo at some points has indicated when a poem in one of her books is intended for children, as she did in the notes for "Naming" when it appeared in *How We Became Human*. There, Harjo explicitly called it "a children's poem" ("Notes" 233).

9. As Harjo clarifies in her notes for this poem, "The *second overthrow* refers to the *Cayetano v. Rice* decision in which the U.S. Supreme Court struck down Hawai'i's practice of allowing only the beneficiaries of the Office of Hawaiian Affairs (OHA), indigenous Hawaiians, to vote for OHA trustees" ("Notes" 235).

10. Regarding the significance of contemporary lyric poetry by Latinx writers in challenging stereotypes of Latinx literature, see R. Rodríguez.

11. Such events were commonplace not just at the Kiowa Boarding School but at the more famous Carlisle Indian School in Carlisle, Pennsylvania, the paradigmatic model for several such institutions.

12. In an author's note at the beginning of the book, Momaday tells of his own first Christmas in Jemez Pueblo, New Mexico in 1946 when he was twelve years old, which "was beyond [his] imagining" and from which the story of the book sprang.

13. Momaday also provided the illustrations for *Circle of Wonder*.

14. The original essay, for instance, more explicitly proclaims that the young Esmeralda does not receive the wished-for doll because her parents do not have enough money to purchase one for each of the girls—but the illustrated version, as we will see, is equally blunt in grappling with issues of race.

Chapter 4. Embracing Ambivalence: Cross-Reading the Children of Desai, Danticat, and Morrison

1. For example, *AKJ Education* classifies the book as fiction.

2. The 2000 winner of the NCTE Orbis Pictus Award for outstanding children's nonfiction, *Through My Eyes* has been praised for its "freshly riveting" account of the "threatening" atmosphere Bridges encountered as "the first black child to attend a New Orleans public elementary school" ("Through My Eyes").

3. Desai has sometimes shared that she is most comfortable writing about India, and this is reflected in her chosen settings for her children's books. In one interview, Desai commented, "I suppose I feel more sure of myself when I'm writing an Indian scene. I lived there, I know it, I know I'm getting it right" (Desai and Barnes). *The Village by the Sea* and *The Peacock Garden* reflect this preference.

4. The few critics who have drawn together Desai and Danticat in substantive ways include Maria DiBattista and Deborah Epstein Nord in their recent collaborative volume *At Home in the World*, where the two writers are the partial focus of a chapter on "multinationals" (197) that also includes Jhumpa Lahiri and Nadine Gordimer, among others.

5. See Safran; Clifford. In this way, Danticat's narrator is unlike some other diasporic Caribbean characters fleeing state-sponsored violence; here I am thinking of Lourdes in Cristina García's *Dreaming in Cuban*, who has a far more unambivalent view of her former homeland. There, the textual ambiguity and contradiction arise from the conflicting perspectives of García's quite different Cuban and Cuban American characters on their shared birthplace.

6. Readers who have seen commonalities in Desai and Morrison have tended to focus on their "heroines" and the "feminist" components of their purportedly adult works (Parikh 17; Chakravarty). Here we can see a potentially less gendered affinity between Desai and Morrison, although this idea is itself connected to the burgeoning discourse of "emotion work" and gender in children's literature.

7. *Beloved* has also been one of the points of entry into comparative work on Morrison and Danticat, as in Donna Aza Weir-Soley's book *Eroticism, Spirituality, and Resistance in Black Women's Writings*, which pairs the novel with Danticat's *The Farming of Bones*. Other books, like Maha Marouan's *Witches, Goddesses, and Angry Spirits*, pair *Breath, Eyes, Memory* with Morrison's *Paradise*. To my knowledge, Morrison's and Danticat's picture books have not been read in tandem by scholars as of the time of writing of these notes, though they have both been included in lists of children's books like Today.com's "Books to Help School-Aged Children Understand Racism" and one Goodreads.com user's "Books for Woke Kids: Part I," where *Mama's Nightingale* and *Remember* are twentieth and twenty-second, respectively, on a list of one hundred texts.

8. Morrison writes at length about this concept of self-love in the essay "Love and Pleasure as Political Liberation," in which she includes a passage from *Beloved* where "resistance to slavery" means "enshrining and developing love for oneself" (3–4).

9. See Henderson; Spaulding.

10. Of course, this is also the nonfictional story of Margaret Garner.

11. I use the term "revolutionary" purposefully here, as one of the hypocrisies of respectability politics is that it celebrates the violence of historical moments like the American Revolution yet demands meek, obedient forms of "protest" from marginalized communities even when they are violently attacked.

Chapter 5. Kids Beyond Borders:
Soto, Alvarez, and Cross-Cultural Cross-Writing

1. Like *Davie Shaw*, *Pacific Crossing* has not previously been the focus of a scholarly article.

2. *Marisol* ignited controversy with a storyline about a family's relocation from the Chicago neighborhood of Pilsen to the suburbs, which some community activists interpreted as racist. Soto has emphatically denied these claims, noting among other corrections that his protagonist's family moves to an equally Latinx suburb. As Karen Coats notes, Soto also "drew from his own and countless others' experiences of serial migration" in writing the book, using this "fidelity to his own experience" to ground the text. See Zaslow and Rudolph as well as Soto's *Why I Don't Write Children's Literature*.

3. Other awards for Soto's children's books have included the Pura Belpré Award for illustration, which *Chato's Kitchen* and *Chato and the Party Animals* both received.

4. In a nod to Alvarez's enduring interest in the perspectives and educational experiences of young readers, the tone and some of the unique features of Alvarez's website biography—including a link to another site with an audio recording of Alvarez "explain[ing] the pronunciation of her name"—seem geared especially toward students.

5. The NCAE is the National Center for Audio Experimentation, and the workshop was dedicated to "exploring the techniques, problems, and possibilities inherent in the use of radio and television," particularly in order to challenge the ways in which "electronic media . . . [are] rigidly controlled by business/government/white interests" (Burrows 3).

6. *Jesse* also features the Chicano Movement-era phrase "Viva la raza!" With direct ties to Soto's earliest poetry through the farm labor that his teenage protagonists do while enrolled in college, the book transmutes Soto's poetic evocations into a narrative format. In doing so, *Jesse* offers a great deal as both a potential "window text" and a potential "mirror text." See P. Alexander; Botelho and Kabakow Rudman.

7. This does seem to be at least one of the reasons that so little scholarly research has been done on *Pacific Crossing*. In contrast, books like *Living Up the Street* have drawn the attention of critics including Hector A. Torres, Bus Heiner, and Rudolf and Ute Erben. Notably, Erben and Erben's work in *MELUS* focuses on questions of Chicanx identity in *Living Up the Street*, reaffirming how Soto's more explicitly Chicanx-focused works have invited and attracted types of analysis to which *Pacific Crossing* may seem less obviously suited at first glance.

8. Unlike US nationalism more broadly, which has been connected with claims of US exceptionalism and superiority, Chicanx nationalism has historically promoted ethnic pride and has embodied resistance to the pressures of linguistic and other forms of assimilation.

9. See Brickhouse.

10. In a nod to the distance between her own personal identity and those of her characters, Alvarez has described in interviews how she had to extensively research both Dominican and Cuban history to write *In the Name of Salomé*.

11. Although "legally resident non-citizens [like Camila] possess . . . nearly equal status to citizens," de facto discrimination against those who are not US citizens is a reality within US borders (Rodríguez and Rubio-Marín 81). Mental illness can lead to deportation rather than to treatment and rehabilitation; affected individuals "bear a heavy burden of proof to show that they should be afforded a legal status in the United States and not deported" (S. Mehta).

12. For some of Alvarez's own reflections on how her lived experience intersects with the content of *Return to Sender*, see Bodette and Wertlieb.

13. See Gonzalez and Fernandez. One of the challenges that has influenced the mainstream US political response to undocumented immigration between Mexico and the United States has been a lack of awareness of the history of the Mexican American War and its aftermath, including not just the amount of Mexico's territory that was confiscated through US military aggression but also the negative economic influence of the US on Mexico in the wake of the war and into the twentieth century, which has dramatically complicated the ethics of subsequent border-crossings.

14. As Victoria Ford Smith puts it, "knowledge of real young people inevitably is obscured by adults' investment in children as idealized others" (240).

BIBLIOGRAPHY

Achebe, Chinua. *Chike and the River*. Illustrated by Edel Rodriguez, Anchor Books, 2011.
Achebe, Chinua. "Chike's School Days." *Girls at War and Other Stories*, Penguin, 2018.
Achebe, Chinua. *There Was a Country: A Personal History of Biafra*. Penguin, 2012.
Achebe, Chinua. "Vengeful Creditor." *Girls at War and Other Stories*, Penguin, 2018.
Achebe, Chinua, and John Iroaganachi. *How the Leopard Got His Claws*. Illustrated by Mary Grandpré, Candlewick, 2011.
Adichie, Chimamanda Ngozi. "The Danger of a Single Story." *TED*, Jul. 2009, https://www.ted.com/talks/chimamanda_ngozi_adichie_the_danger_of_a_single_story?language=en.
Adichie, Chimamanda Ngozi. "Things Left Unsaid." *London Review of Books*, 11 Oct. 2012, https://www.lrb.co.uk/v34/n19/chimamanda-adichie/things-left-unsaid.
Adisa, Opal Palmer, and Edwidge Danticat. "Up Close and Personal: Edwidge Danticat on Haitian Identity and the Writer's Life." *African American Review*, vol. 43, no. 2–3, 2009, pp. 345–55.
Aham-Okoro, Sussie U. *Igbo Women in the Diaspora and Community Development in Southeastern Nigeria*. Lexington Books, 2017.
Akpome, Aghogho. "Ways of Telling: (Re)Writing the Nation in the Novels and Memoir of Chinua Achebe." *Journal of Literary Studies*, vol. 30, no. 1, 2014, pp. 34–52.
Alexander, Kristine. "Agency and Emotion Work." *Jeunesse: Young People, Texts, Cultures*, vol. 7, no. 2, 2015, pp. 120–28.
Alexander, Patricia A. "Portrayal of the Culturally Diverse in Literature: A View of Exceptionalities." *Integrateducation*, vol. 21, no. 1–6, 1983, pp. 212–14.
Alter, Alexandra. "A James Baldwin Book, Forgotten and Overlooked for Four Decades, Gets Another Life." *The New York Times*, 20 Aug. 2018.
Alvarez, Julia. *In the Name of Salomé*. Plume, 2001.
Alvarez, Julia. *In the Time of the Butterflies*. Algonquin, 1994.
Alvarez, Julia. *Return to Sender*. Yearling, 2009.
Alvarez, Julia, and Jack Smith. "Julia Alvarez Interview: In the Time of Discovery." *The Writer*, 4 Aug. 2016, https://www.writermag.com/2016/08/04/julia-alvarez-time-discovery/.
Anderson, Paul Allen. *Deep River: Music and Memory in Harlem Renaissance Thought*. Duke UP, 2001.

Aparicio, Frances R., and Juan Zevallos Aguilar. "Latino Cultural Studies." *Critical Latin American and Latino Studies*, edited by Juan Poblete, U of Minnesota P, 2003, pp. 3–31.

Apol, Laura, and Janine L. Certo. "A Burgeoning Field or a Sorry State: U.S. Poetry for Children, 1800–Present." *Handbook of Research on Children's and Young Adult Literature*, edited by Shelby A. Wolf, Karen Coats, Patricia Enciso, and Christine A. Jenkins, Routledge, 2011, pp. 275–87.

Armengol, Josep M. "Black-White Relations, in Red: Whiteness as Class Privilege in Langston Hughes's *The Ways of White Folks*." *MELUS: Multi-Ethnic Literature of the United States*, vol. 43, no. 1, 2018, pp. 115–33.

"As the Crow Flies." *The Brownies' Book*, vol. 1, no. 1, Jan. 1920, pp. 23–25.

"As the Crow Flies." *The Brownies' Book*, vol. 1, no. 2, Feb. 1920, pp. 63–64.

"As the Crow Flies." *The Brownies' Book*, vol. 2, no. 10, Oct. 1921 pp. 296–97.

Athique, Adrian, and Douglas Hill. *The Multiplex in India: A Cultural Economy of Urban Leisure*. Routledge, 2010.

Atkinson, Yvonne, and Michelle Pagni Stewart, editors. *Ethnic Literary Traditions in American Children's Literature*. Palgrave Macmillan, 2009.

Ayyıldız, Nilay Erdem. *British Children's Adventure Novels in the Web of Colonialism*. Cambridge Scholars, 2018.

Balagopalan, Sarada. "Colonial Modernity and the 'Child Figure': Reconfiguring the Multiplicity in 'Multiple Childhoods.'" *Childhood in India: Traditions, Trends, and Transformations*, edited by T. S. Saraswathi, Shailaja Menon and Ankur Madan, Routledge, 2018, pp. 23–43.

Baldwin, James. *Giovanni's Room*. Vintage, 2013.

Baldwin, James. *Little Man, Little Man: A Story of Childhood*. Illustrated by Yoran Cazac, Duke UP, 2018.

Baldwin, James. "On Being White . . . and Other Lies." *Black on White: Black Writers on What It Means to Be White*, edited by David R. Roediger, Schocken, 1998, pp. 177–80.

Baldwin, Kate A. "The Russian Connection: Interracialism as Queer Alliance in Langston Hughes's *The Ways of White Folks*." *MFS: Modern Fiction Studies*, vol. 48, no. 4, 2002, pp. 795–824.

Balogun, F. Odun. "Russian and Nigerian Literatures." *Comparative Literature Studies*, vol. 21, no. 4, 1984, 483–96.

Bandyopadhyay, Asit. "Rabindranath Tagore: Poet and Dramatist." *Studies on Rabindranath Tagore, Volume 1*, edited by Mohit K. Ray, Atlantic, 2004, pp. 1–46.

Basu, Biman. "Figurations of 'India' and the Transnational W. E. B. Du Bois." *Diaspora: A Journal of Transnational Studies*, vol. 10, no. 2, 2001, pp. 221–41.

Beauvais, Clémentine. "Didactic." *Keywords for Children's Literature*, edited by Philip Nel, Lissa Paul, and Nina Christensen. New York UP, 2021, pp. 57–60.

Beckett, Sandra L. *Crossover Fiction: Global and Historical Perspectives*. Routledge, 2009.

Beckett, Sandra L. "Crossover Picturebooks." *The Routledge Companion to Picturebooks*, edited by Bettina Kümmerling-Meibauer, Routledge, 2018, pp. 209–19.

Beckett, Sandra L. "From Traditional Tales, Fairy Stories, and Cautionary Tales to Controversial Visual Texts: Do We Need to Be Fearful?" *Challenging and Controversial Picturebooks: Creative and Critical Responses to Visual Texts*, edited by Janet Evans, Routledge, 2015.

Beckett, Sandra L., ed. and introduction. *Transcending Boundaries: Writing for a Dual Audience of Children and Adults*. Routledge, 2012.

Bernstein, Robin. *Racial Innocence: Performing American Childhood from Slavery to Civil Rights*. New York UP, 2011.
Berry, Faith. *Langston Hughes: Before and Beyond Harlem*. Citadel, 1992.
Bhattacharya, Sabyasachi. *Rabindranath Tagore: An Interpretation*. New York: Penguin, 2011.
Bilan, Jasbinder. *Asha and the Spirit Bird*. Chicken House, 2019.
Bilan, Jasbinder, and Ian Eagleton. "*Asha and the Spirit Bird*: An Interview with Jasbinder Bilan." *The Reading Realm*, 24 Feb. 2019, https://thereadingrealm.co.uk/2019/02/24/asha-and-the-spirit-bird-an-interview-with-jasbinder-bilan/.
Bilan, Jasbinder, and Oran M. Doyle. "Book-Spoiled: *Asha and the Spirit Bird*." *Orandoyle.com*, 2 Mar. 2020, https://www.orandoyle.com/2020/03/02/book-spoiled-asha-the-spirit-bird/.
Black, Shameem. *Fiction Across Borders: Imagining the Lives of Others in Late-Twentieth-Century Novels*. Columbia UP, 2010.
Blint, Rich, and Sean Jacobs. "The Global Imagination of James Baldwin." *Africa Is a Country*. https://africasacountry.com/2011/06/the-global-imagination-of-james-baldwin.
Bodette, Melody, and Mitch Wertlieb. "Julia Alvarez Writes and Fights for Migrant Justice." *Vermont Public Radio*, 12 Nov. 2014, https://www.vpr.org/vpr-news/2014-11-12/julia-alvarez-writes-and-fights-for-migrant-justice.
Boggs, Nicholas. "Baldwin and Yoran Cazac's 'Child's Story for Adults.'" *The Cambridge Companion to James Baldwin*, edited by Michele Elam, Cambridge UP, 2015, pp. 118–32.
Boggs, Nicholas, and Jennifer Devere Brody. Introduction. *Little Man, Little Man: A Story of Childhood*. Duke UP, 2018.
"Books to Help School-Aged Children Understand Racism." *Today Parenting Team*, 5 December 2017, https://community.today.com/parentingteam/post/books-to-help-school-aged-children-understand-racism.
Borden, Anne. "Heroic 'Hussies' and 'Brilliant Queers': Genderracial Resistance in the Works of Langston Hughes." *African-American Review*, vol. 28, no. 3, 1994, pp. 333–45.
Bost, Suzanne, and Frances R. Aparicio, editors. *The Routledge Companion to Latino/a Literature*. Routledge, 2013.
Botelho, Maria José, and Masha Kabakow Rudman. *Critical Multicultural Analysis of Children's Literature: Mirrors, Windows, and Doors*. Routledge, 2009.
Brickhouse, Anna. *Transamerican Literary Relations and the Nineteenth-Century Public Sphere*. Cambridge UP, 2004.
Bridges, Ruby. *Through My Eyes*. Scholastic, 1999.
Brown, Jeffrey, and Esmeralda Santiago. "Conversation: Esmeralda Santiago, Author of *Conquistadora*." *PBS*, 12 Aug. 2011, https://www.pbs.org/newshour/arts/conversation-esmeralda-santiago-author-of-conquistadora.
Brown, Monica. *Marisol McDonald Doesn't Match*. Illustrated by Sara Palacios, Children's Book Press, 2011.
Bruce-Novoa, Juan. *Chicano Poetry: A Response to Chaos*. U of Texas P, 1982.
Burrows, Ed. "A View of the Mountaintop." *The Greenfield Review*, 1973, p. 3.
Bus, Heiner. "Sophisticated Spontaneity: The Art of Life in Gary Soto's *Living Up the Street*." *The Americas Review: A Review of Hispanic Literature and Art of the USA*, vol. 16, no. 3–4, 1988, pp. 188–97.
Butterworth, Michael L. *Baseball and Rhetorics of Purity: The National Pastime and American Identity During the War on Terror*. U of Alabama P, 2010.

Butts, Dennis. "Adventure Books." *The Oxford Encyclopedia of Children's Literature*, edited by Jack Zipes, Oxford UP, 2006, pp. 12–16.
Camper, Cathy. *Lowriders to the Center of the Earth*. Illustrated by Raúl the Third, Chronicle Books, 2016.
Chakravarty, Radha. *Feminism and Contemporary Women Writers: Rethinking Subjectivity*. Routledge, 2008.
Charles, John C. *Abandoning the Black Hero: Sympathy and Privacy in the Postwar African American White-Life Novel*. Rutgers UP, 2013.
Chaudhri, Amina. *Multiracial Identity in Children's Literature*. Routledge, 2017.
Chaudhuri, Amit. "The English Writings of Rabindranath Tagore." *A History of English Literature in English*, edited by Arvind Krishna Mehrotra, Columbia UP, 2003, pp. 103–15.
Chaudhuri, Supriya. "Domestic Space in Tagore's Fiction." *Tagore's Ideas of the New Woman: The Making and Unmaking of Female Subjectivity*, edited by Chandrava Chakravarty and Sneha Kar Chaudhuri, Sage, 2017, pp. 54–73.
Cisneros, Sandra. "About My Life and Work." *Sandra Cisneros*, https://www.sandracisneros.com/mylifeandwork.
Cisneros, Sandra. "Books." *Sandra Cisneros*, https://www.sandracisneros.com/books.
Cisneros, Sandra. *Bravo Bruno!* La Nuova Frontiera, 2011.
Cisneros, Sandra. *Hairs/Pelitos*. Illustrated by Terry Ybáñez, Knopf, 1994.
Cisneros, Sandra. *Have You Seen Marie?* Illustrated by Ester Hernández, Knopf, 2012.
Cisneros, Sandra. *The House on Mango Street*. Vintage, 2009.
Cisneros, Sandra. Letter to Thomas Wortham. 20 Sept. 2001. Sandra Cisneros Papers, The Wittliff Collections, Texas State U Library, Box 277, Folder 12.
Cisneros, Sandra. "Mexicans in France." *Loose Woman*, Vintage, 1995.
Cisneros, Sandra. "You Bring Out the Mexican in Me." *Loose Woman*, Vintage, 1995.
Cisneros, Sandra, and Carlos J. Queirós. "Sandra Cisneros: Facing Backwards." *AARP*, 1 Apr. 2009, https://www.aarp.org/entertainment/books/info-04-2009/sandra_cisneros_house_on_mango_street_25th_anniversary.html
Clark, Beverly Lyon. "*Tom Sawyer*, Audience, and American Indians." *The Oxford Handbook of Children's Literature*, edited by Julia Mickenberg and Lynne Vallone, Oxford UP, 2011, pp. 293–311.
Clark, Keith. *The Radical Fiction of Ann Petry*. Louisiana State UP, 2013.
Clifford, James. "Diasporas." *Cultural Anthropology*, vol. 9, no. 3, 1994, pp. 302–38.
Clitandre, Nadège T. *Edwidge Danticat: The Haitian Diasporic Imaginary*. U of Virginia P, 2018.
Coats, Karen. "Teaching the Conflicts: Diverse Responses to Diverse Children's Books." *The Edinburgh Companion to Children's Literature*, edited by Clémentine Beauvais and Maria Nikolajeva, Edinburgh UP, 2018.
Collins, Patricia Hill. *Black Sexual Politics: African Americans, Gender, and the New Racism*. Routledge, 2004.
Crenshaw, Kimberlé. "Demarginalizing the Intersection of Race and Sex: A Black Feminist Critique of Antidiscrimination Doctrine, Feminist Theory and Antiracist Politics." *Feminist Legal Theory: Foundations*, edited by D. Kelly Weisberg, Temple UP, 1993, pp. 383–395.
Cronin, Richard. *Imagining India*. Palgrave Macmillan, 1989.
Csapo, Marg. "Universal Primary Education in Nigeria: Its Problems and Implications." *African Studies Review*, vol. 26, no. 1, 1983, p. 91–106.
Dalleo, Raphael, and Elena Machado Sáez. *The Latino/a Canon and the Emergence of Post-Sixties Literature*. Palgrave Macmillan, 2007.

Danticat, Edwidge. *Behind the Mountains*. Scholastic, 2002.
Danticat, Edwidge. *Breath, Eyes, Memory*. Soho Press, 2014.
Danticat, Edwidge. "Create Dangerously." *Black Ink: Literary Legends on the Peril, Power, and Pleasure of Reading and Writing*, edited by Stephanie Stokes Oliver, Atria, 2018, pp. 173–86.
Danticat, Edwidge. *The Farming of Bones*. Soho Press, 1998.
Danticat, Edwidge. "The Funeral Singer." *The Dew Breaker*, Vintage, 2005.
Danticat, Edwidge. *Mama's Nightingale*. Illustrated by Leslie Staub, Dial Books, 2015.
Danticat, Edwidge. "New York Was Our City on the Hill." *The New York Times*. 21 Nov. 2004.
de la Peña, Matt. *The Hunted*. Delacorte Press, 2015.
de la Peña, Matt. *The Living*. Embre, 2013.
de la Peña, Matt, and Scott Simon. "Even on the Water, Class Remains in Session." *NPR*, 23 Nov. 2013, https://www.npr.org/transcripts/246380621.
Den Otter, A. A. *Civilizing the Wilderness: Culture and Nature in Pre-Confederation Canada and Rupert's Land*. U of Alberta P, 2012.
Desai, Anita. *The Peacock Garden*. Mammoth, 1991.
Desai, Anita. "Translator Translated." *The Artist of Disappearance*, Mariner, 2011.
Desai, Anita. *The Village by the Sea*. Heinemann, 1982.
Desai, Anita, and Joshua Barnes. "You Turn Yourself into an Outsider: An Interview with Anita Desai." *Sampsonia Way*, 14 Jan. 2014, https://www.sampsoniaway.org/interviews/2014/01/14/you-turn-yourself-into-an-outsider-an-interview-with-anita-desai/.
DiBattista, Maria, and Deborah Epstein Nord. *At Home in the World: Women Writers and Public Life, from Austen to the Present*. Princeton UP, 2017.
Dimmett, Deborah, and Angie Hoffman. "MTYT: *For a Girl Becoming*." *World of Words*, 10 Oct. 2018, https://wowlit.org/blog/2018/10/10/mtyt-for-a-girl-becoming/
Dow, Miriam. "A Postcolonial Child: Achebe's *Chike* at the Crossroads." *Children's Literature Association Quarterly*, vol. 22, no. 4, 1997, pp. 160–65.
Du Bois, W.E.B. *Dark Princess*. UP of Mississippi, 1955.
Dubois, Laurent. "How Will Haiti Reckon with the Duvalier Years?" *The New Yorker*, 6 Oct. 2014, https://www.newyorker.com/news/news-desk/will-haiti-reckon-duvalier-years.
Durán, Leah, and Kathryn I. Henderson. "Pockets of Hope: Cases of Linguistic Flexibility in the Classroom." *EuroAmerican Journal of Applied Linguistics and Languages*, vol. 5, no. 2, 2018, pp. 76–90.
Duyvis, Corinne. "#ownvoices, to recommend kidlit about diverse characters written by authors from that same diverse group." *Twitter*, 6 Sept. 2015, https://mobile.twitter.com/corinneduyvis/status/640584099208503296.
Edwards, Brent Hayes. *The Practice of Diaspora: Literature, Translation, and the Rise of Black Internationalism*. Harvard UP, 2003.
Egbo, Benedicta. *Gender, Literacy and Life Chances in Sub-Saharan Africa*. Multilingual Matters, 2000.
Ehrenhaft, George. *AP English Language and Composition: With 5 Practice Tests*. Kaplan, 2020.
Emenyonu, Ernest N. "Selection and Validation of Oral Materials for Children's Literature: Artistic Resources in Chinua Achebe's Fiction for Children." *Emerging Perspectives on Chinua Achebe*, edited by Ernest N. Emenyonu, Africa World Press, 2004.
Erben, Rudolf, and Ute Erben. "Popular Culture, Mass Media, and Chicano Identity in Gary Soto's *Living Up the Street* and *Small Faces*." *MELUS: Multi-Ethnic Literature of the United States*, vol. 17, no. 3, 1991–1992, pp. 43–52.

Erdrich, Louise. *The Birchbark House*. Hyperion, 1999.
Erdrich, Louise. *Books and Islands in Ojibwe Country: Traveling Through the Land of My Ancestors*. Harper Perennial, 2014.
Erdrich, Louise. *Future Home of the Living God*. Harper Perennial, 2017.
Erdrich, Louise. "Where I Ought to Be: A Writer's Sense of Place." Sandra Cisneros Papers, The Wittliff Collections, Texas State U Library, Box 276, Folder 24.
Esonwanne, Uzoma. "'Restraint . . . My Style': Deliberative and Mournful." *PMLA*, vol. 129, no. 2, 2014, pp. 243–45.
Falconer, Rachel. *The Crossover Novel: Contemporary Children's Fiction and Its Adult Readership*. Routledge, 2009.
Falola, Toyin, and Matthew Heaton. Introduction. *Nigerian History, Politics and Affairs: The Collected Essays of Adiele Afigbo*, edited by Toyin Falola, Africa World Press, 2005, pp. 1–14.
Fauntleroy, Gussie. "Vivid Memories of Christmas Form Momaday's Pueblo Tale." *Pasatiempo*, vol. 60, 1993, pp. 30–31. N. Scott Momaday Papers, Yale U Library, MS 807, Box 23.
Fell McDermott, Rachel, Leonard A. Gordon, et al, editors. *Sources of Indian Traditions: Modern India, Pakistan, and Bangladesh*. Columbia UP, 2014.
Ferraro, Thomas J. "Ethnicity and the Marketplace." *The Columbia History of the American Novel*, edited by Emory Elliott, et al., Columbia UP, 1991.
Ferraro, Thomas J. "'My Way' in 'Our America': Art, Ethnicity, Profession." *American Literary History*, vol. 12, no. 3, 2000, pp. 499–522.
Flynn, Richard. "'Affirmative Acts': Language, Childhood, and Power in June Jordan's Cross-Writing." *Still Seeking an Attitude: Critical Reflections on the Work of June Jordan*, edited by Valerie Kinloch and Margret Grebowicz, Lexington Books, 2004, pp. 159–85.
Flynn, Richard. "Introduction: Disputing the Role of Agency in Children's Literature and Culture." *Jeunesse: Young People, Texts, Cultures*, vol. 8, no. 1, 2016, pp. 248–53.
Ford Smith, Victoria. *Between Generations: Collaborative Authorship in the Golden Age of Children's Literature*. UP of Mississippi, 2017.
Galindo, Delma Letticia, and María Dolores Gonzales, editors. *Speaking Chicana: Voice, Power, and Identity*. U of Arizona P, 1999.
Ganz, Robin. "Gary Soto." *Updating the Literary West*. Texas Christian UP, 1997.
García, Cristina. *Dreaming in Cuban*. Ballantine, 1992.
Garcia Lopez, Christina. *Calling the Soul Back: Embodied Spirituality and Chicanx Narrative*. U of Arizona P, 2019.
Gardaphé, Fred L. *From Wise Guys to Wise Men: The Gangster and Italian American Masculinities*. Routledge, 2006.
Gargano, Elizabeth. "Oral Narrative and Ojibwa Story Cycles in Louise Erdrich's *Birchbark House* and *Game of Silence*." *Ethnic Literary Traditions in American Children's Literature*, edited by Yvonne Atkinson and Michelle Pagni Stewart, Palgrave Macmillan, 2009, pp. 29–43.
Gennari, John. *Flavor and Soul: Italian America and Its African American Edge*. U of Chicago P, 2017.
Ghosh, Ranjan. "Caught in the Cross Traffic: Rabindranath Tagore and the Trials of Child Education." *Comparative Education Review*, vol. 59, no. 3, 2015, pp. 399–419.
Gibson, Ernest L. *Salvific Manhood: James Baldwin's Novelization of Male Intimacy*. U of Nebraska P, 2019.
Glazer, Lori. Email to Rene Boatman. 17 May 2004. Toni Morrison Papers, Princeton U Library, Box 128, Folder 11.

Glazer, Lori. Letter to Toni Morrison. Toni Morrison Papers, Princeton U Library, Box 128, Folder 11.
Glissant, Edouard. *Caribbean Discourse: Selected Essays*. Translated by J. Michael Dash, U of Virginia P, 1989.
Gonzalez, Gilbert G., and Raul A. Fernandez. *A Century of Chicano History: Empire, Nations, and Migration*. Routledge, 2003.
Goswami, Supriya. "The British Empire and Indian Nationalism in Rabindranath Tagore's Historical Poems and *The Land of Cards*." *The Routledge Companion to International Children's Literature*, edited by John Stephens, Routledge, 2017, pp. 105–13.
Goswami, Supriya. *Colonial India in Children's Literature*. Routledge, 2012.
Graff, Jennifer M. "Children's Literature as Tools of and for Activism: Reflections of JoLLE's Inaugural *Activist Literacies* Conference." *Journal of Language and Literacy Education*, vol. 9, no. 1, 2013, pp. 136–43.
Graves, Lucia. "A is for Activist: Why Children's Books are Getting Political." *The Guardian*, 2 May 2019, https//:www.theguardian.com/books/2019/may/02/childrens-books-political-diversity-shift.
Grillot, Suzette, Sarah Hurd, and Esmeralda Santiago. "Author Esmeralda Santiago Finds Identity Through Art." *KGOU.org*, 11 Sept. 2014, https://www.kgou.org/post/author-esmeralda-santiago-finds-identity-through-art.
Gubar, Marah. *Artful Dodgers: Reconceiving the Golden Age of Children's Literature*. Oxford UP, 2009.
Guglielmo, Jennifer, and Salvatore Salerno. *Are Italians White?: How Race Is Made in America*. Routledge, 2003.
"Hairs/Pelitos." *Publishers Weekly*, https://www.publishersweekly.com/978-0-679-86171-3.
Hall, Anthony J. *The American Empire and the Fourth World*. McGill-Queen's UP, 2003.
Hall, Stuart. "Cultural Identity and Diaspora." *Identity: Community, Culture, Difference*, edited by Jonathan Rutherford, Lawrence & Wishart, 1990, pp. 222–37.
Hardy III, Clarence E. *James Baldwin's God: Sex, Hope, and Crisis in Black Holiness Culture*. U of Tennessee P, 2003.
Harjo, Joy. "3 A.M." *How We Became Human: New and Selected Poems, 1975–2001*. W. W. Norton, 2002.
Harjo, Joy. "For a Girl Becoming." *Joy Harjo's Poetic Adventures in the Last World* Blog, 18 Nov. 2005, http://joyharjo.blogspot.com/2005/11/for-girl-becoming-by-request-for.html.
Harjo, Joy. *For a Girl Becoming*. Illustrated by Mercedes McDonald, U of Arizona P, 2009.
Harjo, Joy. "It's Raining in Honolulu." *How We Became Human: New and Selected Poems, 1975–2001*, W. W. Norton, 2002.
Harjo, Joy. "Naming." *How We Became Human: New and Selected Poems, 1975–2001*, W. W. Norton, 2002.
Harjo, Joy. "Notes." *How We Became Human: New and Selected Poems, 1975–2001*, W. W. Norton, 2002.
Harjo, Joy. "The Woman Hanging from the Thirteenth Floor Window." *How We Became Human: New and Selected Poems, 1975–2001*, W. W. Norton, 2002.
Harjo, Joy, and Cassie Premo Steele. "Crazy Brave: An Interview with Joy Harjo and Review of Her New Memoir." *Literary Mama*, Sept. 2012, http://www.literarymama.com/reviews/archives/2012/09/crazy-brave-an-interview-joy-h.html.
Harjo, Joy, and Tanaya Winder. *Soul Talk, Song Language: Conversations with Joy Harjo*. Wesleyan UP, 2011.

Hayward, Bronwyn. *Children, Citizenship and Environment: Nurturing a Democratic Imagination in a Changing World*. Routledge, 2012.

Henderson, Mae. "Toni Morrison's *Beloved*: Re-Membering the Body as Historical Text." *Toni Morrison's Beloved: A Casebook*, edited by William L. Andrews and Nellie Y. McKay, Oxford UP, 1999, pp. 79–106.

Henitiuk, Valerie. "Translating Women's Silences." *Transcultural*, vol. 7, no. 1, 2015, pp. 4–15.

Hickman, Trenton. "Hagiographic Commemorafiction in Julia Alvarez's *In the Time of the Butterflies* and *In the Name of Salomé*." *MELUS: Multi-Ethnic Literature of the United States*, vol. 31, no. 1, 2006, pp. 99–121.

Hicks, Granville. "Tormented Triangle." *The New York Times*, 14 Oct. 1956.

Hintz, Carrie, and Eric L. Tribunella. *Reading Children's Literature: A Critical Introduction*. 2nd edition. Broadview Press, 2019.

Hixson, Walter L. *American Settler Colonialism: A History*. Palgrave Macmillan, 2013.

Hodgson, Lucia. "Childhood of the Race: A Critical Race Theory Intervention into Childhood Studies." *The Children's Table: Childhood Studies and the Humanities*, edited by Anna Mae Duane, U of Georgia P, 2013, pp. 38–51.

Honeyman, Susan. *Elusive Childhood: Impossible Representations in Modern Fiction*. The Ohio State UP, 2005.

hooks, bell. *We Real Cool: Black Men and Masculinity*. Routledge, 2004.

Hopkins, Lucy. "'The Bad Man's Going to Jail': The Ethics and Politics of Childhood in *The Slap*." *Literature and Politics: Pushing the World in Certain Directions*, edited by Peter Marks, Cambridge Scholars, 2012, pp. 178–90.

Hourihan, Margery. *Deconstructing the Hero: Literary Theory and Children's Literature*. Routledge, 1997.

"*The House on Mango Street*." *Common Sense Media*, https://www.commonsensemedia.org/book-reviews/the-house-on-mango-street/user-reviews/adult.

Hoyos, Kim. "There's a Disparity in Latinx Representation in Children's Literature and These Women are Doing Something About it." *The Mujerista*, https://www.themujerista.com/the-blog/theres-a-disparity-in-latinx-representation-in-childrens-literature-and-these-women-are-doing-something-about-it.

Hughes, John. "Changing Africa." *Rotarian*, vol. 96, no. 4, 1960, pp. 12–15, 53–56.

Hughes, Langston. *The Big Sea: An Autobiography*. Hill and Wang, 1993.

Hughes, Langston. *The Dream Keeper and Other Poems*. Alfred A. Knopf, 1994.

Hughes, Langston. *Lullaby (for a Black Mother): A Poem*. Illustrated by Sean Qualls, Houghton Mifflin Harcourt, 2013.

Hughes, Langston. "The Negro." *The Crisis*, vol. 23, no. 3, 1922, p. 113.

Hughes, Langston. *Not Without Laughter*. Scribner, 1995.

Hughes, Langston. *Selected Letters of Langston Hughes*, edited by Arnold Rampersad and David Roessel, Knopf, 2015.

Hughes, Langston. *The Ways of White Folks*. Vintage Classics, 1990.

Hunnicutt, Amber. "Books for Woke Kids: Part 1." *Goodreads*, 1 Feb. 2018, https://www.goodreads.com/list/show/120601.Books_for_Woke_Kids_Part_I.

Igwedibia, Adaoma, Christian Anieke, and Kelechi Virginia Ezeaku. "Chinua Achebe's *Girls at War and Other Stories*: A Relevance-Theoretical Interpretation." *International Journal of Applied Linguistics & English Literature*, vol. 8, no. 3, 2019, pp. 78–83.

Innes, C. L. *Chinua Achebe*. Cambridge UP, 1990.

"Introduction." *The Routledge Companion to International Children's Literature*, edited by John Stephens, Routledge, 2017.

Jacobson, Matthew Frye. *Whiteness of a Different Color: European Immigrants and the Alchemy of Race*. Harvard UP, 1999.
James, Henry. "Daisy Miller." *Daisy Miller and Other Stories*, Oxford World's Classics, 2009.
Jemtegaard, Kristi. "Winter Lights & Wenceslas: A Christmas Reading List." *Parents' Choice: Children's Media and Toy Reviews*, http://archive.parentschoice.org/article.cfm?art_id=228&the_page=article.
Jeyathurai, Dashini. "The Complicated Racial Politics of Little Black Sambo." *South Asian American Digital Archive*, 4 Apr. 2012, https://www.saada.org/tides/article/little-black-sambo.
Jimenez, Laura M. "The Overwhelmingly White, Straight, and Able Face of Children's Literature." *Michigan Reading Journal*, vol. 51, no. 1, 2018, pp. 64–69.
Johnson-Roullier, Cyraina E. "(An)Other Modernism: James Baldwin, *Giovanni's Room*, and the Rhetoric of Flight." *MFS: Modern Fiction Studies*, vol. 45, no. 4, 1999, pp. 932–56.
Jones, Leroi. *Blues People: Negro Music in White America*. Harper Collins, 2002.
Karefa-Smart, Aisha. Afterword. *Little Man, Little Man: A Story of Childhood*. Duke UP, 2018.
Karefa-Smart, Aisha, and the Conscious Kid. "An Interview with Aisha Karefa-Smart on James Baldwin's *Little Man, Little Man: A Story of Childhood*." https://www.theconsciouskid.org/littlemanlittleman.
Karp, Jonathan. "The Story Behind the Sequel." *The Fortunate Pilgrim*. Ballantine, 2004.
Katanski, Amelia V. *Learning to Write "Indian": The Boarding School Experience and American Indian Literature*. U of Oklahoma P, 2005.
Kincaid, Jamaica. *Lucy*. Farrar, Straus and Giroux, 1990.
King, Thomas. *The Inconvenient Indian: A Curious Account of Native Peoples in North America*. U of Minnesota P, 2013.
Kolmar, Wendy K. "'Dialectics of Connectedness': Supernatural Elements in Novels by Bambara, Cisneros, Grahn, and Erdrich." *Haunting the House of Fiction: Feminist Perspectives on Ghost Stories by American Women*, edited by Lynette Carpenter and Wendy K. Kolmar, U of Tennessee P, 1991.
Komunyakaa, Yusef. "Langston Hughes + Poetry = The Blues." *Race in the Poetry of Langston Hughes*, edited by Claudia Durst Johnson, Greenhaven Press, 2014, pp. 49–54.
Lee, A. Robert. *Multicultural American Literature: Comparative Black, Native, Latino/a and Asian American Fictions*. UP of Mississippi, 2003.
Lee, Gabriela. "Through Screens and Streams: Digital Liminality and Identities in Philippine Young Adult Speculative Fiction." *Asian Children's Literature and Film in a Global Age: Local, National, and Transnational Trajectories*, edited by Bernard Wilson and Sharmani Patricia Gabriel, Palgrave Macmillan, 2020, pp. 311–33.
Lester, Julius. "Children's Books." *The New York Times*, 4 Sept. 1977, http://movies2.nytimes.com/books/98/03/29/specials/baldwin-little.html.
Lewis, Nghana tamu. "In a Different Chord: Interpreting the Relations among Black Female Sexuality, Agency, and the Blues." *African American Review*, vol. 37, no. 4, 2003, pp. 599–609.
Lin, Grace. *Bringing in the New Year*. Dragonfly Books, 2008.
Lindstrom, Carole. *We Are Water Protectors*. Illustrated by Michaela Goade, Roaring Brook Press, 2020.
López, Tiffany Ana. "Reading Trauma and Violence in U.S. Latina/o Children's Literature." *Ethnic Literary Traditions in American Children's Literature*, edited by Michelle Pagni Stewart and Yvonne Atkinson, Palgrave Macmillan, 2009, pp. 205–26.

Lurie, Alison. *Don't Tell the Grown-Ups: The Subversive Power of Children's Literature*. Little, Brown and Co., 1990.

Macaulay, Thomas Babington. "The Minute on Education." *Sources of Indian Traditions: Modern India, Pakistan, and Bangladesh*, edited by Rachel Fell McDermott, Leonard A. Gordon, et al., Columbia UP, 2014, pp. 69–72.

MacCann, Donnarae. *White Supremacy in Children's Literature: Characterizations of African Americans, 1830-1900*. Routledge, 1998.

MacLeod, Anne Scott. *American Childhood: Essays on Children's Literature of the Nineteenth and Twentieth Centuries*. U of Georgia P, 1994.

Marks, Janae. *From the Desk of Zoe Washington*. Katherine Tegen Books, 2020.

Marouan, Maha. *Witches, Goddesses, and Angry Spirits: The Politics of Spiritual Liberation in African Diaspora Women's Fiction*. Ohio State UP, 2013.

Martin, Kameelah L., and Donald M. Shaffer, Jr. "Black Transnationalism and the Discourse(s) of Cultural Hybridity: An Introduction." *South Atlantic Review*, vol. 82, no. 4, 2017, pp. 1–8.

Maxwell, W. H. "Critical Reading." *The Journal of Pedagogy: A Monthly Review of Educational Progress*, vol. 3, 1890, pp. 126–30.

McFarland, Ron. *Gary Soto: A Career in Poetry and Prose*. McFarland, 2022.

McGlennen, Molly. *Creative Alliances: The Transnational Designs of Indigenous Women's Poetry*. U of Oklahoma P, 2014.

McQuail, Josephine A. "'There Is Nothing as Old as a Child': Childhood and Language in Rabindranath Tagore's *The Crescent Moon*." *Rupkatha Journal on Interdisciplinary Studies in Humanities*, vol. 2, no. 4, 2010, pp. 491–503.

Mehta, Purnima. "'On the Seashore of Endless Worlds Children Meet': Childhood Loss and Mourning Reaction in Tagore's Poetry." *Rabindranath Tagore: Universality and Tradition*, edited by Patrick Colm Hogan and Lalita Pandit, Fairleigh Dickinson UP, 2003, pp. 233–49.

Mehta, Sarah L. "Deportation by Default: Mental Disability, Unfair Hearings, and Indefinite Detention in the US Immigration System." *Human Rights Watch*, 25 July 2010, https://www.hrw.org/report/2010/07/25/deportation-default/mental-disability-unfair-hearings-and-indefinite-detention-us.

Messenger, Chris. *The Godfather and American Culture: How the Corleones Became "Our Gang."* State U of New York P, 2002.

Michals, Teresa. *Books for Children, Books for Adults: Age and the Novel from Defoe to James*. Cambridge UP, 2014.

Mickenberg, Julia L. *Learning from the Left: Children's Literature, the Cold War, and Radical Politics in the United States*. Oxford UP, 2006.

Mickenberg, Julia L., and Philip Nel. "Radical Children's Literature Now!" *Children's Literature Association Quarterly*, vol. 36, no. 4, 2011, pp. 445–73.

Miller, James. "The Novelist as Teacher: Chinua Achebe's Literature for Children." *Children's Literature*, vol. 9, 1981, pp. 97–118.

Momaday, N. Scott. *Circle of Wonder: A Native American Christmas Story*. U of New Mexico P, 1999.

Momaday, N. Scott. *Four Arrows & Magpie*. Hawk Publishing, 2006.

Momaday, N. Scott. *House Made of Dawn*. Harper Perennial, 2010.

Momaday, N. Scott. *The Indolent Boys* (First Draft). Yale U Library, MS 807, Box 85.

Momaday, N. Scott. *The Names*. U of Arizona P, 1976.

Momaday, N. Scott. *Three Plays: The Indolent Boys, Children of the Sun, and The Moon in Two Windows*. U of Oklahoma P, 2007.

Montoya, Margaret E. "*Máscaras, Trenzas, y Greñas:* Un/Masking the Self While Un/Braiding Latina Stories and Legal Discourse." *Speaking Chicana: Voice, Power, and Identity*, edited by D. Letticia Galindo and María Dolores Gonzales, U of Arizona P, 1999, pp. 194–211.

Morales, Areli. *Areli is a Dreamer: A True Story*. Illustrated by Luisa Uribe, Random House Studio, 2021.

Morrison, Toni. *Beloved*. Vintage, 2004.

Morrison, Toni. "Love and Pleasure as Political Liberation." Toni Morrison Papers, Princeton U Library, Box 300, Folder 11.

Morrison, Toni. "Novel Endings." Toni Morrison Papers, Princeton U Library, Box 298, Folder 8.

Morrison, Toni. *Paradise*. Vintage, 2014.

Morrison, Toni. *Remember: The Journey to School Integration*. Houghton Mifflin, 2004.

Morrison, Toni. "*Remember* Luncheon Remarks." Toni Morrison Papers, Princeton U Library, Box 300, Folder 16.

Morrison, Toni. "What Is a Good School?" Toni Morrison Papers, Princeton U Library, Box 300, Folder 1.

Musa, Mohammed, and Ayo Oyeleye. "Nationalism, Mass Media, and the Crisis of National Identity in Nigeria." *National Days/National Ways: Historical, Political, and Religious Celebrations Around the World*, edited by Linda K. Fuller, Praeger, 2004.

Mustapha, Abolaji Samuel. "Linguistic Hegemony of the English Language in Nigeria." *Íkala: Revista de Lenguaje y Cultura*, vol. 19, no. 1, 2014, pp. 57–71.

Nagle, Rebecca. "Invisibility is the Modern Form of Racism Against Native Americans." *Teen Vogue*, 23 Oct. 2018, https://www.teenvogue.com/story/racism-against-native-americans.

Naylor, Amanda, and Audrey B. Wood. *Teaching Poetry: Reading and Responding to Poetry in the Secondary Classroom*. Routledge, 2012.

Neitzel, Jennifer. *Achieving Equity and Justice in Education Through the Work of Systems Change*. Lexington Books, 2020.

Nikolajeva, Maria. *Children's Literature Comes of Age: Toward a New Aesthetic*. Routledge, 2016.

Nodelman, Perry. *The Hidden Adult: Defining Children's Literature*. Johns Hopkins UP, 2008.

Olivares, Julián. "Sandra Cisneros' *The House on Mango Street* and the Poetics of Space." *Chicana Creativity and Criticism: New Frontiers in American Literature*, edited by María Herrera-Sobek and Helena María Viramontes. U of New Mexico P, 1996, pp. 233–45.

Olivares, Julián. "The Streets of Gary Soto." *Latin American Literary Review*, vol. 18, no. 35, 1990, pp. 32–49.

O'Sullivan, Emer. *Historical Dictionary of Children's Literature*. Scarecrow Press, 2010.

Paranjape, Makarand R. *Cultural Politics in Modern India: Postcolonial Prospects, Colourful Cosmopolitanism, Global Proximities*. Routledge, 2016.

Pardini, Samuele F. S. *In the Name of the Mother: Italian Americans, African Americans, and Modernity from Booker T. Washington to Bruce Springsteen*. Dartmouth College Press, 2017.

Parikh, Bharati A. "Heroines of Toni Morrison and Anita Desai: A Cross-Cultural Perspective." *Indian Journal of American Studies*, vol. 23, no. 2, 1993, pp. 17–25.

Parini, Jay, editor. *The Columbia Anthology of American Poetry*. Columbia UP, 1995.

Phillipson, Robert. "International Languages and International Human Rights." *Language, a Right and a Resource: Approaching Linguistic Human Rights*, edited by Miklós Kontra, Robert Phillipson, Tove Skutnabb-Kangas, and Tibor Várady. Central European UP, 1999, pp. 25–46.

Pinkney, Andrea Davis. Letter to Toni Morrison. 28 Apr. 2005. Toni Morrison Papers, Princeton U Library, Box 128, Folder 11.

Pinkney, Andrea Davis. Letter to Toni Morrison. 2 Oct. 2003. Toni Morrison Papers, Princeton U Library, Box 128, Folder 11.

Planas, Roque. "Neither Banned Nor Allowed: Mexican American Studies in Limbo in Arizona." *Fox News*, 19 Apr. 2012, https://www.foxnews.com/world/neither-banned-nor-allowed-mexican-american-studies-in-limbo-in-arizona.

Pullinger, Debbie. *From Tongue to Text: A New Reading of Children's Poetry*. Bloomsbury, 2017.

Puzo, Mario. *The Fortunate Pilgrim*. Ballantine, 2004.

Puzo, Mario. *The Runaway Summer of Davie Shaw*. Puffin Books, 1979.

Radice, William. Introduction. *Selected Short Stories*, by Rabindranath Tagore, translated by William Radice, Penguin, 2005, pp. 1–28.

Rampersad, Arnold. *The Life of Langston Hughes, Volume 1: 1902–1941—I, Too, Sing America*. Oxford UP, 2002.

Reese, Debbie. "Deanna Himanga's *Boozhoo, Come Play with Us*." *American Indians in Children's Literature*, 5 Apr. 2007, https://americanindiansinchildrensliterature.blogspot.com/2007/04/deanna-himangos-boozhoo-come-play-with.html.

"Return to Sender." *Common Sense Media*, 6 Nov. 2018, https://www.commonsensemedia.org/book-reviews/return-to-sender.

"Reviewed Books: Middle Grade." *Latinxs in Kid Lit*, https://www.latinosinkidlit.com/reviewed-books-middle-grade/.

"Reviewer's Choice: *For a Girl Becoming*." *Midwest Book Review: Children's Bookwatch*, vol. 19, no. 12, 2009, https://www.midwestbookreview.com/cbw/dec_09.htm.

Richardson, Julia. Letter to Gary Soto. 25 Jul. 2002. Gary Soto Papers, Yale U Library, MS 640, Box 14.

Richman, Paula, editor. *Ramayana Stories in Modern South India: An Anthology*. Indiana UP, 2008.

Ritter, Valerie. *Kama's Flowers: Nature in Hindi Poetry and Criticism, 1885–1925*. State U of New York P, 2011.

Roberts, Dorothy. *Killing the Black Body: Race, Reproduction, and the Meaning of Liberty*. Vintage, 1998.

Rodríguez, Cristina M., and Ruth Rubio Marín. "The Constitutional Status of Irregular Migrants: Testing the Boundaries of Human Rights Protection in Spain and the United States." *Are Human Rights for Migrants? Critical Reflections on the Status of Irregular Migrants in Europe and the United States*, edited by Marie-Bénédicte Dembour and Tobias Kelly, Routledge, 2011, pp. 10–46.

Rodríguez, María Cristina. "Political Authority Figures as Distant Memories of a Forgotten Past: Julia Alvarez's *In the Time of the Butterflies* and *In the Name of Salomé* and Cristina García's *The Agüero Sisters*." *Journal of Caribbean Literatures*, vol. 6, no. 2, 2009, pp. 55–63.

Rodríguez, Ralph E. *Latinx Literature Unbound: Undoing Ethnic Expectation*. Fordham UP, 2018.

Roediger, David R. *Working Toward Whiteness: How America's Immigrants Became White: The Strange Journey from Ellis Island to the Suburbs*. Basic Books, 2005.

Rose, Jacqueline. *The Case of Peter Pan, Or the Impossibility of Children's Fiction*. 3rd ed. U of Pennsylvania P, 1993.

Rosen, Judith. "Growing Up." *Publishers Weekly*, 21 Feb. 2005, https://www.publishersweekly.com/pw/print/20050221/40188-growing-up.html.

Roumain, Jacques. *Masters of the Dew*. Translated by Langston Hughes and Mercer Cook, Heinemann, 1978.
Roy, Nilanjana. "Mario Puzo: An Author You Can't Refuse." *Financial Times*, 6 Feb. 2019, https://www.ft.com/content/881349b8-2606-11e9-8ce6-5db4543da632.
Roynon, Tessa. *The Cambridge Introduction to Toni Morrison*. Cambridge UP, 2013.
Rudolph, Jennifer Domino. "Identity Theft: Gentrification, Latinidad, and American Girl Marisol Luna." *Aztlán: A Journal of Chicano Studies*, vol. 34, no. 1, 2009, pp. 65–91.
Ryan, Pam Muñoz. *Esperanza Rising*. Scholastic, 2000.
Safran, William. "Diasporas in Modern Societies: Myths of Homeland and Return." *Diaspora: A Journal of Translational Studies*, vol. 1, no. 1, 1991, pp. 83–99.
Sánchez-Eppler, Karen. *Dependent States: The Child's Part in Nineteenth-Century American Culture*. U of Chicago P, 2005.
Santiago, Esmeralda. *A Doll for Navidades*. Illustrated by Enrique O. Sánchez, Scholastic, 2005.
Santiago, Esmeralda. *When I Was Puerto Rican*. Da Capo, 1993.
Saro-Wiwa, Noo. "There Was a Country: A Personal History of Biafra by Chinua Achebe—Review." *The Guardian*, 5 Oct. 2012, https://www.theguardian.com/books/ 2012/oct/05/chinua-achebe-there-was-a-country-review.
Scales, Pat R. *Defending Frequently Challenged Young Adult Books: A Handbook for Librarians and Educators*. Rowman and Littlefield, 2016.
See, Sam. "'Spectacles in Color': The Primitive Drag of Langston Hughes." *PMLA*, vol. 124, no. 3, 2009, pp. 798–816.
Sen, Sukumar. "Tagore and Folklore." *Indian Literature*, vol. 4, no. 1–2, 1960–61, pp. 84–89.
Seth, Sanjay. *Subject Lessons: The Western Education of Colonial India*. Duke UP, 2007.
Séverac, Alain. "Achebe's Short Stories: Their Intertextual Relationship to His Novels." *Telling Stories: Postcolonial Short Fiction in English*, edited by Jacqueline Bardolph, André Viola, and Jean-Pierre Durix, Rodopi, 2001, pp. 241–54.
Shange, Ntozake. *ellington was not a street*. Illustrated by Kadir Nelson, Simon and Schuster, 2004.
Shange, Ntozake. "Improvisation." *A Daughter's Geography*, St. Martin's Press, 1991.
Shange, Ntozake. "Mood Indigo." *A Daughter's Geography*, St. Martin's Press, 1991.
Shange, Ntozake. "Take the A Train." *A Daughter's Geography*, St. Martin's Press, 1991.
Shin, Sun Yung. *Cooper's Lesson*. Illustrated by Kim Cogan, Children's Book Press, 2004.
Sikdar Datta, Nilanjana. "Valmiki-Ramayana—An Approach by Rabindranath Tagore." *Critical Perspectives on the Ramayana*, edited by Jaydipsinh K. Dodiya, Sarup and Sons, 2001, pp. 52–59.
Sinha, Mrinalini. Introduction. *Mother India*, by Katherine Mayo, U of Michigan P, 2000, pp. 1–62.
Slater, Andrea M. "W. E. B. Du Bois' Transnationalism: Building a Collective Identity Among the American Negro and the Asian Indian." *Phylon*, vol. 51, no. 1, 2014, pp. 145–57.
Smethurst, James E. "The Strong Men Gittin' Stronger: Sterling Brown's *Southern Road* and the Representation and Re-Creation of the Southern Folk Voice." *Race and the Modern Artist*, edited by Heather Hathaway, Josef Jarab, and Jeffrey Melnick, Oxford UP, 2003, pp. 69–91.
Smith, Katharine Capshaw. "A Cross-Written Harlem Renaissance: Langston Hughes's *The Dream Keeper*." *The Oxford Handbook of Children's Literature*, edited by Lynne Vallone and Julia Mickenberg, Oxford UP, 2011, pp. 129–46.

Smith, Katharine Capshaw. *Children's Literature of the Harlem Renaissance*. Indiana UP, 2004.
Smith, Katharine Capshaw. "Trauma and National Identity in Haitian-American Young Adult Literature." *Ethnic Literary Traditions in American Children's Literature*, edited by Yvonne Atkinson and Michelle Pagni Stewart, Palgrave Macmillan, 2009, pp. 83–97.
Smokowski, Paul R., and Martica Bacallao. *Becoming Bicultural: Risk, Resilience, and Latino Youth*. New York UP, 2011.
Socolovsky, Maya. "Cultural (Il)literacy: Narratives of Epistolary Resistance and Transnational Citizenship in Julia Alvarez's *Return to Sender*." *Children's Literature Association Quarterly*, vol. 40, no. 4, 2015, pp. 386–404.
Soto, Gary. "Braly Street." *New and Selected Poems*. Chronicle Books, 1995.
Soto, Gary. "Bulosan, 1935." *New and Selected Poems*. Chronicle Books, 1995.
Soto, Gary. *Chato and the Party Animals*. Illustrated by Susan Guevara, Puffin Books, 2004.
Soto, Gary. *Chato Goes Cruisin'* Final Draft. Gary Soto Papers, Yale U Library, MS 640, Box 14.
Soto, Gary. *Chato's Kitchen*. Illustrated by Susan Guevara, Putnam and Grosset, 1995.
Soto, Gary. *The Elements of San Joaquin*. Chronicle Books, 1977.
Soto, Gary. "The Family in Spring." *New and Selected Poems*. Chronicle Books, 1995.
Soto, Gary. "Field Poem." *New and Selected Poems*. Chronicle Books, 1995.
Soto, Gary. "Finding a Lucky Number." *New and Selected Poems*. Chronicle Books, 1995.
Soto, Gary. *Jesse*. Harcourt, 1994.
Soto, Gary. *Living Up the Street*. Laurel-Leaf Books, 1985.
Soto, Gary. *Marisol*. Pleasant Company Publications, 2005.
Soto, Gary. *Pacific Crossing*. Harcourt, 1992.
Soto, Gary. "Saturday in Chinatown." *New and Selected Poems*. Chronicle Books, 1995.
Soto, Gary. "Some Mysteries." *New and Selected Poems*. Chronicle Books, 1995.
Soto, Gary. *Why I Don't Write Children's Literature*, UP of New England, 2015.
Soto, Gary, and TeachingBooks. "Gary Soto: In-Depth Written Interview." *Teachingbooks.net*, 29 Aug. 2007, https://www.teachingbooks.net/interview.cgi?id=47&a=1.
Spaulding, A. Timothy. *Re-Forming the Past: History, the Fantastic, and the Postmodern Slave Narrative*. Ohio State UP, 2005.
Stephanson, Anders. *Manifest Destiny: American Expansion and the Empire of Right*. Hill and Wang, 1995.
Stephens, John, editor. *The Routledge Companion to International Children's Literature*. Routledge, 2017.
Sutherland, Zena, editor. *The Best in Children's Books: The University of Chicago Guide to Children's Literature, 1966-1972*. U of Chicago P, 1973.
Sweet Wong, Hertha D. "Louise Erdrich's *Love Medicine*: Narrative Communities and the Short Story Cycle." *Love Medicine: A Casebook*, edited by Hertha D. Sweet Wong, Oxford UP, 2000, pp. 85–106.
T., Danielle. "Book Review: *Esperanza Rising*, by Pam Muñoz Ryan." *Mission Viejo Library: Teen Voice*, 1 Oct. 2013, https://mvlteenvoice.com/2013/10/01/book-review-esperanza-rising-by-pam-munoz-ryan/.
Tagore, Rabindranath. *The Crescent Moon*. Macmillan, 1913.
Tagore, Rabindranath. "Crisis in Civilization." *The Essential Tagore*, edited by Fakrul Alam and Radha Chakravarty, Harvard UP, 2011.
Tagore, Rabindranath. *The English Writings of Rabindranath Tagore: A Miscellany*. Sahitya Akademi, 2006.

Tagore, Rabindranath. *Selected Short Stories*. Translated by William Radice, Penguin, 2005.
Tan, Amy. *The Joy Luck Club*. Penguin, 2006.
Tan, Amy. *The Moon Lady*. Illustrated by Gretchen Schields, Aladdin, 1995.
Tatum, Charles M. *Chicano Popular Culture: Que Hable el Pueblo*. U of Arizona P, 2017.
Taylor, Mildred. *Roll of Thunder, Hear My Cry*. Puffin Books, 2016.
Terrones, Lettycia. "*Técnica Con/Safos*: Visual Iconography in Latino Picture Books as a Tool for Cultural Affirmation." *Multicultural Literature for Latino Bilingual Children: Their Words, Their Worlds*, edited by Ellen Riojas Clark, Belinda Bustos Flores, Howard L. Smith, and Daniel Alejandro González, Rowman and Littlefield, 2016.
"Through My Eyes." *Publishers Weekly*, https://www.publishersweekly.com/978-0-590-18923-1.
Torres, Hector A. "Genre-Shifting, Political Discourse, and the Dialectics of Narrative Syntax in Gary Soto's *Living Up the Street*." *Crítica: A Journal of Critical Essays*, vol. 2, no. 1, 1988, pp. 39–57.
Torres, María de los Angeles. *In the Land of Mirrors: Cuban Exile Politics in the United States*. U of Michigan P, 2001.
Tracy, Steven. "The Dream Keeper: Langston Hughes's Poetry, Fiction, and Non-Biographical Books for Children and Young Adults." *The Langston Hughes Review*, vol. 17, 2002, pp. 78–94.
Traylor, Eleanor W. "James Baldwin and Chinua Achebe: Transgressing Official Vocabularies." *James Baldwin: America and Beyond*, edited by Cora Kaplan and Bill Schwarz, U of Michigan P, 2011.
Tribunella, Eric L. "Boyhood." *Keywords for Children's Literature*, edited by Philip Nel and Lissa Paul, New York UP, 2011, pp. 21–25.
Trites, Roberta Seelinger. *Twenty-First Century Feminisms in Children's and Adolescent Literature*. UP of Mississippi, 2018.
Trivedi, Harish. *Colonial Transactions: English Literature and India*. Manchester UP, 1993.
Tuteja, K. L., and Kaustav Chakraborty. "Introduction: Rabindranath Tagore and an 'Ambivalent' Nationalism." *Tagore and Nationalism*, edited by Tuteja and Chakraborty, Springer, 2017, pp. 1–13.
Uko, Iniobong. "The Dynamics of Culture on the Child's Personality in Chinua Achebe's *Chike and the River*." *Emerging Perspectives on Chinua Achebe*, vol. 1, edited by Ernest N. Emenyonu, Africa World Press, 2004. pp. 455–62.
UNESCO. *Tagore, Neruda, Césaire: For a Reconciled Universal*. Paris, 2011.
Uwakweh, Pauline Ada. "Negotiating Marriage and Motherhood: A Critical Perspective on the Immigration Narratives of Buchi Emecheta and Chimamanda Adichie." *Engaging the Diaspora: Migration and African Families*, edited by Pauline Ada Uwakweh, Jerono P. Rotich, and Comfort O. Okpala, Lexington Books, 2014, pp. 15–37.
Valdez, Luis. *Zoot Suit and Other Plays*. Arte Público Press, 1992.
van Lierop-DeBrauwer, Helma. "Crossing the Border: Authors Do It, But Do Critics? The Reception of Dual-Readership Authors in the Netherlands." *Transcending Boundaries: Writing for a Dual Audience of Children and Adults*, edited by Sandra L. Beckett, Routledge, 2012, pp. 3–12.
Van Winkle, Katie. "Saving Mango Street." *Rethinking Schools*. https://rethinkingschools.org/articles/saving-mango-street/.
Vogel, Shane. "Closing Time: Langston Hughes and the Poetics of Harlem Nightlife." *Criticism*, vol. 48, no. 3, 2007, pp. 397–425.
von Merveldt, Nikola. "Informational Picturebooks." *The Routledge Companion to Picturebooks*, edited by Bettina Kümmerling-Meibauer, Routledge, 2018, pp. 209–19.

Washburn, Frances. *Tracks on a Page: Louise Erdrich, Her Life and Works*. Praeger, 2013.

Washington, Harriet A. *Medical Apartheid: The Dark History of Medical Experimentation on Black Americans from Colonial Times to the Present*. Harlem Moon, 2006.

"We Are Water Protectors." *Goodreads*, https://www.goodreads.com/en/book/show/44581496-we-are-water-protectors.

Weems, Lisa. "Theorizing Resistance and Intimacy in Youth Studies." *Jeunesse: Young People, Texts, Cultures*, vol. 7, no. 2, 2015, pp. 134–47.

Weir-Soley, Donna Aza. *Eroticism, Spirituality, and Resistance in Black Women's Writings*. U of Florida P, 2009.

Wong, Sau-Ling Cynthia. "'Sugar Sisterhood': Situating the Amy Tan Phenomenon." *The Ethnic Canon: Histories, Institutions, and Interventions*, edited by David Palumbo-Liu, U of Minnesota P, 1995, pp. 174–210.

Yelchin, Eugene. "'Mama's Nightingale,' by Edwidge Danticat, and More." *The New York Times*, 21 Aug. 2015, https://www.nytimes.com/2015/08/23/books/review/mamas-nightingale-by-edwidge-danticat-and-more.html.

Zaborowska, Magdalena J. *Me and My House: James Baldwin's Last Decade in France*. Duke UP, 2018.

Zaslow, Emilie. *Playing with America's Doll: A Cultural Analysis of the American Girl Collection*. Palgrave Macmillan, 2017.

Zúñiga, Christian E. "'This Is What Is Happening to My Students': Using Book Talk to Mediate Teacher Discussion on Immigration and Social Justice." *InterActions: UCLA Journal of Education and Information Studies*, vol. 11, no. 1, 2015.

INDEX

Achebe, Chinua, 4, 10–11, 38, 56–64; Igbo society, portrayal of, 57–60, 149nn17–18; as "protest writer, with restraint," 60; Works: *Chike and the River*, 4, 38, 42, 60–64; "Chike's School Days," 149n21; *How the Leopard Got His Claws*, 60; *There Was a Country*, 38, 59–60, 149n24; "Vengeful Creditor," 38, 56–61
activists, children as, 7, 12, 103; Black children, 94–95, 103–4, 106–11; Chicanx children, 122–23; in *The Village by the Sea*, 96–101. *See also* African American childhood; Chicanx culture; childhood; children; Latinx children's literature; resistance
adaptations and rewritings, 7–8; *ellington was not a street* as, 11, 141–43; *The Moon Lady* as, 11, 138–41
adventure stories, 11–13, 148n10; activist work in, 38–39, 40, 42, 48–49; anticolonial, 38–39, 59–60, 63–64; commonalities with "adult" literature, 38–39; critique of toxic expectations for boys, 42, 46, 48–49, 55; "escape from the domestic sphere," 51, 57; gender in, 42, 46, 48–51, 55, 57–58; genre conventions of, 38–40, 51, 63; imperialist history of, 39; optimistic endings, 63; resistance to antiqueer attitudes, 43–45; "tactical maneuvers" in, 38, 43, 48. *See also* Achebe, Chinua; Baldwin, James; Puzo, Mario

African American authors and Indian writers in conversation, 18–19, 29, 94–96, 108, 111
African American childhood, 28–30; and "angelic white child," 28–29, 45, 55, 96; Black children as activists, 94–95, 106–11; Black children treated as adults, 29, 45, 49; and cultural heritage, 141–42; fracturing of families, 34; pickaninny stereotype, 28–29; and resistance to respectability politics, 12, 109, 111
African continent, 17, 30–31, 33, 56, 149n21. *See also* Nigeria
"African Dance" (Hughes), 30–31, 34, 79
African languages, colonialist approach to, 62
age-appropriateness, 7–10, 68, 75; restrictive definitions of and challenges to, 4–5, 21, 32, 37, 39, 45 46, 77, 120
agricultural labor: in California, 40, 117–18; in colonial and post-independence India, 20, 97; transnationalism of, 130–31; in Vermont, 130
Aham-Okoro, Sussie U., 58
Alexander, Kristine, 14, 103
Alvarez, Julia, 6, 13, 116, 152n4, 153n10; Works: *In the Name of Salomé*, 116, 126–29, 133–34; *Return to Sender*, 6, 116, 129–34
ambivalence, 10, 12, 93–94, 115; vs. binaristic fables of "good" and "bad"

171

immigration, 96; and boundary between fictional and nonfictional modes, 95; "development" vs. protest, 97–98; embracing for age-diverse readerships, 111; and imperial legacy, 100–101; and Jim Crow–era injustice, 106–11; in literature, as reflection of world, 95; and "non-militant" entry of African American children into formerly all-white US schools, 107, 109, 111; about postrevolutionary Cuban history, 128; about US criminal justice and immigration systems, 102–4
American Dream, mythology of, 76, 119
American Library Association, 108
Anieke, Christian, 57
anticolonial and antiracist work, 11–13, 149n18; in adventure stories, 38–39, 59–60, 63–64; belonging, redefinition of, 7, 11–12, 66, 68, 71–74, 78–83, 88, 90–92; *The Brownies' Book* as, 17–18, 29, 33; and gender, 19, 25–27, 32; precolonial history in, 17–18, 23; in Tagore, 17–27. *See also* Achebe, Chinua; Cisneros, Sandra; colonialism; Erdrich, Louise; Hughes, Langston; Momaday, N. Scott; Santiago, Esmeralda; settler colonialism; Tagore, Rabindranath
Aparicio, Frances R., 113–14
Apol, Laura, 32
archival connections between writers, 67–68, 117
Areli Is a Dreamer: A True Story (Morales), 96
artistic production, challenges to Eurocentric, 30–31
Artist of Disappearance, The (Desai), 99
Asha and the Spirit Bird (Bilan), 40
Asian women, gendered stereotypes of, 138–40
assimilation: forced linguistic and other forms of, 20–22, 41, 61, 71, 79, 81–82, 152n8; simplistic cultural narratives of, 76
"As the Crow Flies" column (*The Brownies' Book*), 17
Athique, Adrian, 22

Atkinson, Yvonne, 10
audience, 3–5; African children as, 61; authors' young family members as, 28, 45, 61, 79; age-diverse, 5, 12–13, 15, 35, 66–68, 73–75, 92, 111, 116, 137; bold readers, children as, 134–35; for canonical texts, 9; cross-cultural mix of adults and children as, 22–24; Indian readers as, 24; Indigenous children as, 79–80; linguistic effort required of, 23–24, 121; mutual meaning-making by writer and, 143; Spanish-speaking readers as, 121; white children as, 24, 29, 108, 133
Ayyıldız, Nilay Erdem, 43, 44, 47

Bacallao, Martica, 78
Balagopalan, Sarada, 20
Baldwin, James, 7, 9, 11, 64, 95; in conversation with Achebe, 42; in conversation with Puzo, 41–42; transnationalism of, 41–42, 56; Works: *Giovanni's Room*, 38, 42–46; *Little Man, Little Man: A Story of Childhood*, 7, 9, 14, 37, 41, 45–49, 54; "On Being 'White'... and Other Lies," 41–42
Balogun, F. Odun, 56, 57, 58
Baraka, Amiri, 109
Basu, Biman, 18
Beauvais, Clémentine, 6
Beckett, Sandra L., 4, 5, 9, 28, 35
belonging, 7, 11–12, 66, 68, 71–74, 78–83, 88, 90–92
Beloved (Morrison), 9, 107, 110–11, 151n7
Bernstein, Robin, 28, 29
Berry, Faith, 31
Biafran War, 60
Bilan, Jasbinder, 40
bilingualism, 66–67, 71, 78–79, 121–22
Birchbark House, The (Erdrich), 8, 68–73, 79
Birmingham, Alabama, church bombing (1963), 108
Black love, 110; self-care and self-love as political, 110, 151n8
Blint, Rich, 56
"Blues I'm Playing, The" (Hughes), 33–35
Boggs, Nicholas, 37, 45, 47

Books for Children, Books for Adults (Michals), 9
Boozhoo, Come Play with Us (Himanga), 67
Bost, Suzanne, 113–14
Bracero Program, 117
Brady, Mary Pat, 114
Breath, Eyes, Memory (Danticat), 104, 111, 151n7
Bridges, Ruby, 95, 151n2
Bringing in the New Year (Lin), 66
Brown, Monica, 78–79
Brown Girl Dreaming (Woodson), 8
Brownies' Book, The (children's magazine), 17–18, 29, 33, 37
Brown v. Board of Education, 107, 109
Bruce-Novoa, Juan, 118
brujería, 76
Bulosan, Carlos, 118–19
"Bulosan, 1935" (Soto), 118–19, 126
Burnett, Frances Hodgson, 22, 147n6
Burrows, Ed, 117
Butterworth, Michael L., 124

Cambridge Introduction to Toni Morrison, The, 3
Camo Girl (Magoon), 8
Camper, Cathy, 40, 84
canonical texts, 100; adventure stories, 7, 9, 30, 38–39, 43, 45, 47; Latinx canon, 74, 113–16
Carroll, Lewis, 39
Castro, Fidel, 128
categories: adventure story as genre, 13; age-differentiated, 3–6, 9–10, 37, 56–57, 101, 143–44; of childhood as construed by white racists, 29; cultural, 123–25, 131, 135; "human impulse" to rely on, 56
"Cathy, Queen of Cats" (Cisneros), 75–76
Cazac, Yoran, 37, 47
Celia's Robot (Chang), 8
Certo, Janine L., 32
Cesar Chavez: A Hero for Everyone (Soto), 120
"Champa Flower, The" (Tagore), 23, 27, 31
Chang, Margaret, 8
chapter books. See *Chike and the River* (Achebe); *The Runaway Summer of Davie Shaw* (Puzo)

Charles, John C., 43
Chaudhri, Amina, 8, 71, 78
Chaudhuri, Supriya, 26
Chávez, César, 119–20
Chekhov, Anton, 57
Chicanx culture, 67, 83, 115, 133, 152n8; and cross-cultural encounter, 117–23; and pre-Columbian history, 67, 83; "raza-style," 122. See also Latinx authors
Chike and the River (Achebe), 4, 38, 42, 60–64
childhood: antiessentialist vision of, 135; as category, 29; as cultural construct, 9, 14; as "primitive state" and blueprint for imperialism, 9, 19, 35, 47, 95–96. See also African American childhood; Indian child, imperialist imaginings of; Indigenous childhood; Italian American childhood; Latinx children's literature
"Child of Nature" paradigm, 39
children: African American, "non-militant" entry into formerly all-white US schools, 107, 109, 111; agency of, 14, 86–88, 91–92, 98; Black, protests by, 94–95, 103–4, 106–11; as intellectually independent, 22, 25; and politics, 9–10; racist caricatures of, 28–29; as readers, 134–35; rethinking of cultural constructs by, 68–69, 74, 82, 142; separation of from parents, 93–94, 102–3; sophistication of, 30–31, 33, 35–36, 72, 74, 77, 89, 110, 116, 131, 134, 143. See also activists, children as; African American childhood; Indian child, imperialist imaginings of; Indigenous childhood; Italian American childhood; Latinx children's literature
children's literature: academic studies on, 3–6, 9, 18–19, 47, 60, 113–14, 137, 151n7, 152n7; African American, 9–10; bilingual texts, 66–67, 71, 78–79; culturally appropriative, 114; exclusionary attitude toward, 3–5; expectations of ethical simplicity for, 97–99, 101; "Golden Age" of British and US, 38–39, 42, 147n6; imperialist

function of, 9, 19, 35, 39, 47, 61, 95–96, 147n6; Indigenous, 79; Latinx, 113–14; oversimplified approaches to, 37; pressure on authors to self-censor, 120; stereotypes of as "frivolous," 54
Children's Literature (journal), 5
chimookomanug (white people), 68–71
ciguapas (mythical creatures), 129
Cinder (Meyer), 8
Circle of Wonder: A Native American Christmas Story (Momaday), 4, 11, 87–88, 150n12
Cisneros, Sandra, 11, 12, 66, 67–68, 73–79, 150n2; website, 73; Works: *Bravo Bruno!*, 75; "Cathy, Queen of Cats," 75–76; *Hairs/Pelitos*, 11, 75, 77–79, 82–83; *Have You Seen Marie?*, 73; *The House on Mango Street*, 74–79, 82, 89, 92; "You Bring Out the Mexican in Me," 83
"civilization," concept of: alternative meanings of, 66–68; cities as supposed exemplars of, 76–77; critique and destabilization of, 69, 76, 81–82; rethinking European ideologies of, 69–72, 81–82, 86, 90; and savagery of whiteness at "Indian boarding schools," 84–85
civil rights movement, 108
Clark, Keith, 30
class dynamics, 21, 30, 138–39; of educational system, Nigeria, 56–57, 60; "European-style," 59; in Italian American communities, 51–52; in Nigeria, 56–57, 61–63; in post-independence Mumbai, 98; satire of US, 54–55; and US neoimperialism in Puerto Rico and Mexico, 89–91, 133; and white flight, 75
Clitandre, Nadège T., 105
code-switching, 51, 66–67, 89, 122
Cogan, Kim, 71
colonialism, 12; administrative dysfunction of, 25–26; African languages, treatment of, 62; in Borinquen, 89; and British constructions of Indian childhood, 19; class inequalities rooted in, 57; and domestic sphere, 26; and "mutability" of western culture, 67; in Nigeria, 58–62; and precolonial history, 17, 23, 58, 67, 87, 147–48n10; and women, propaganda about, 19–21, 24, 58–59. *See also* anticolonial and antiracist work; settler colonialism

"color-blind" literary strategies, 31
color-caste systems, 18
Common Sense Media website, 77, 134
companion texts, "adult," 4–8, 12, 41–42, 116; adventure stories, 38–39, 63–64; *Beloved* as, 110–11; Cisneros's and Harjo's poetry as, 82–84; and *ellington was not a street*, 11, 141–43; *The Fortunate Pilgrim* as, 38, 50–55, 149n13; *Future Home of the Living God* as, 72–73; *Giovanni's Room* as, 45–46, 49–50; Hughes's poetry as, 28, 33–35; *The Indolent Boys* as, 84, 87; *In the Name of Salomé* as, 129; and *The Moon Lady*, 11, 138–41; Soto's poetry as, 120; in Tagore's writings, 25–27; "Translator Translated" as, 99, 101; *When I Was Puerto Rican* as, 90–91
Conquistadora (Santiago), 91
Cooper's Lesson (Shin), 71
Coretta Scott King Award, 108
counterknowledge, 76
Crescent Moon, The (Tagore), 9, 19, 21, 95; "The Champa Flower," 23, 27, 31; children as original audience for, 27–28; cross-cultural mix of adults and children as audience for, 22–24; motherhood in, 24–25; "My Song," 24, 32; "Playthings," 21–22, 26, 30; references to violence subdued in, 19, 25–27; "The Sailor," 23; "Sleep-Stealer," 23, 27, 31; "Superior," 24; "The Unheeded Pageant," 22, 31–32; untranslated terms in, 23–24, 26–27, 66
Crisis, The (magazine), 18, 29
critical race theory, 6
critical thinking, 91–92
Cronin, Richard, 96–97
cross-cultural cross-writing, 5, 7, 12–13, 22–24, 114–16; in Alvarez's work, 125–34; and bold child readers, 134–35; in Soto's work, 117–25. *See also* Alvarez, Julia; Soto, Gary

crossover fiction, 4–5
"Cross-Writing Child and Adult"
   (*Children's Literature*), 5
Cuba, 126–28, 151n5
cultural appropriation, 114, 149n15
"cultural capital," 116
curanderismo, 76

Daisy Miller (James), 124–25
Dantica, Joseph N., Rev., 106
Danticat, Edwidge, 4, 10; Works: *Breath, Eyes, Memory*, 104, 111, 151n7; *The Dew Breaker*, 105–6; "The Funeral Singer," 105–6; *Mama's Nightingale*, 4, 11, 93–96, 101–6, 111; "New York Was Our City on the Hill," 106
Daughter's Geography, A (Shange), 141
Defoe, Daniel, 9, 39
de la Peña, Matt, 40
den Otter, A. A., 77
Department of Homeland Security, 106
Desai, Anita, 10, 109, 151n3; Works: *The Artist of Disappearance*, 99; "Translator Translated," 99–101; *The Village by the Sea*, 10, 94–95, 96–101, 111
destinarian language, 70
"development," in India, 12, 95, 97; adaptation as response to, 99
DeVere Brody, Jennifer, 45
Dew Breaker, The (Danticat), 105–6
diachronic reading, 5, 13, 114
diaspora: African, 17–18, 30–35, 42, 99, 105, 128; Haitian, 104–6; Irish, 51; Italian, 132
digital platforms, 134
Doll for Navidades, A (Santiago), 4, 88–91, 151n14
Dominican American writers, 116, 126
Dominican Republic: Alvarez and national history, 128–29; US invasion of, 126–27
Dow, Miriam, 61, 63
Dreaming in Cuban (García), 151n5
Dream Keeper, The (Hughes), 6, 11, 19, 27–35; "African Dance," 30–31, 34, 79; "The Dream Keeper," 29; human rights violations recorded in, 32–33; "I, Too," 30, 34; "Lullaby," 32; "Mother to Son," 32; "My People," 31–32; "The Negro," 32–33, 34, 99; "The Negro Speaks of Rivers," 31, 34
Du Bois, W. E. B., 9–10, 29, 33, 56, 142; and *The Brownies' Book*, 17–18; *Dark Princess*, 18
Duke University Press, 14, 37, 45
Durán, Leah, 67
Duvalier, François, 105–6
Duvalier, Jean-Claude, 106
Duyvis, Corinne, 114
Dyer Anti-Lynching Bill, 33

educational systems: assimilationist aims under colonialism, 20–22, 61, 75, 85–86; British, in India, 20–22; British, in Nigeria, 61; English, "hierarchical, bullying atmosphere," 63; in United States, racism and alienation in, 75, 91
Egypt, 17
Eisenhower, Dwight, 128
Elements of San Joaquin, The (Soto), 115, 117, 126
Ellington, Duke, 141
ellington was not a street (Shange), 11, 141–43
Emenyonu, Ernest N., 61, 149nn22–23
emotion work, 14, 103, 109–10, 111, 151n6
Erdrich, Louise, 8, 10, 11, 12, 66, 67–68, 78, 150n2; Works: *The Birchbark House*, 68–73, 79; *Books and Islands*, 68; *Future Home of the Living God*, 72–73; "Where I Ought to Be: A Writer's Sense of Place," 67, 72
Esonwanne, Uzoma, 60
Esperanzu Rising (Ryan), 13, 40
Ethnic Literary Traditions in American Children's Literature (Stewart and Atkinson), 10
Eurocentric ideals, countering of, 23, 30–32, 61, 69–70, 76, 78, 90, 97
"existential novels," 39
Ezeaku, Kelechi Virginia, 57

Falola, Toyin, 58
Fanon, Frantz, 61
Fernandez, Raul A., 117
Ferraro, Thomas J., 50

"Field Poem" (Soto), 117–18
Flynn, Richard, 5
Fond du Lac Band of Lake Superior Chippewa, 67
For a Girl Becoming (Harjo), 6, 79–84, 99, 150n5, 150nn7–9; colonizing interpretations of, 79–80; protocol and self-respect in, 80–81, 150n4
Fortunate Pilgrim, The (Puzo), 38, 50–55, 149n13
Four Arrows & Magpie (Momaday), 87
France, African Americans in, 34
Fresno, California, 118–19
From the Desk of Zoe Washington (Marks), 104
"Funeral Singer, The" (Danticat), 105–6
Future Home of the Living God (Erdrich), 72–73

García, Cristina, 151n5
Garcia Lopez, Christina, 76
gender, 151n6; aging woman, perceptions of, 50–51; in anticolonial/antiracist work, 19, 25–27, 32; Asian women, stereotypes of, 138–40; frank discussions of, 33–35; "Golden Age" paradigms, 42; masculinity, toxic, 42, 46, 48–49, 55; in Tagore's works, 24–27. *See also* women
genre reinvention, 40
gentrification, 75
Ghosh, Ranjan, 21
Gibson, Ernest L., III, 43
Giovanni, Nikki, 109
Giovanni's Room (Baldwin), 38, 41, 42–46, 48
Glazer, Lori, 106–7
global literature, 5–6, 10, 18, 27, 93–94
glocal frame of reference, 19, 28
glossaries, 65–66, 71, 121
Goade, Michaela, 40–41, 129
Godfather series (Puzo), 38, 149n13
"Golden Age" of children's literature, 38–39, 42
Gonzalez, Gilbert G., 117
Goodreads reviews, 40–41
Goswami, Supriya, 18, 147–48n9
Gothic tropes, 85, 110

Government College, Umuahia (Nigeria), 59
Graff, Jennifer M., 6
graphic science fiction series, 40
Graves, Lucia, 6
Great War, 17
Green, Martin, 50
Greenfield Review, The, 117
Gubar, Marah, 39

Hairs/Pelitos (Cisneros), 11, 75, 77–79, 82–83
Haiti, 93, 104; Alvarez's references to, 127; Danticat's family history in, 93, 106; Duvalier regime, 105
Harjo, Joy, 6, 12, 66, 68, 95; Cisneros's letter of recommendation for, 74; dedication to granddaughter, 80; protocol in writings of, 80–81, 150n4, 150n6; Works: "3 A. M.," 84; *For a Girl Becoming*, 6, 79–84, 99, 150n5, 150nn7–9; "It's Raining in Honolulu," 83; "The Woman Hanging from the Thirteenth Floor Window," 84
Harlem Renaissance, 9–10, 18
Hatchet (Paulsen), 39
Hawai'i, 83, 150n9
Heaton, Matthew, 58
Henderson, Mae, 67
heteronormativity, challenge to, 42–47
Hicks, Granville, 41
Hill, Douglass, 22
Himanga, Deanna, 67
Hintz, Carrie, 40
historical novels, 13, 40, 48, 79. See also *Birchbark House, The* (Erdrich)
Hixson, Walter L., 69, 75
Hodgson, Lucia, 6
Honeyman, Susan, 9
hooks, bell, 49
hope, 29–30, 33, 38, 58, 80, 97, 104
Hourihan, Margery, 39
House Made of Dawn (Momaday), 84
House on Mango Street, The (Cisneros), 74–79, 82, 89, 92; as "required reading," 74–75
How the Leopard Got His Claws (Achebe), 60

Hughes, Langston, 6, 11, 18, 37, 95; hopes for and candidness with Black children, 29–30, 33; poetry in *The Brownies' Book*, 29, 37; transnationalism of, 30–31, 56; *Works:* "The Blues I'm Playing," 33–35; *The Ways of White Folks*, 11, 33–34. See also *Dream Keeper, The* (Hughes)
"hunted man," 40
hybrid cultural identities, 72, 84, 87–92

"I, Too" (Hughes), 30, 34–35
identities: biracial, 8, 72, 78; forced loss of, 20–21, 61, 71, 79, 81–82, 152n8; hybrid, 72, 84, 87–92; linguistic, 62, 66–67, 71–72, 78–79, 83, 89, 92, 100, 117, 120–22, 139–40, 152n8; multicultural Indigenous, 80
Igbo society, 57–60, 149nn17–18
Igwedibia, Adaoma, 57
immigration, 93–94, 101–6, 152n2, 153n11; binaristic fables of as "good" and "bad," 96; "legally resident non-citizens," 153n11; from Mexico, 116–117; and nationalistic US ideas about language, 121; US mythology of as unfettered opportunity, 117; "utopian" expectations for, 106
imperialism, 6; and adventure stories, 39; childhood as "primitive state" and blueprint for, 9, 19, 35; faulty justifications for, 19–20, 21, 24; function of in children's literature, 9, 19, 35, 47, 61, 95–96, 147n6; linguistic hierarchy, 121, 125; questioning of industrialization as "progress" following, 97. See also neoimperialism, US
India, 10, 17; agricultural communities, 20; ambiguities of responses to imperial legacy in, 100–101; British assimilationist education in, 20–22; British constructions of childhood in, 19; "development" in, 12, 95, 97; Jallianwala Bagh massacre, 27; nationalism in, 27; women's position in, 26
Indian authors and African American authors in conversation, 18–19, 29, 94–96, 108, 111

Indian child, imperialist imaginings of, 19–27
Indigenous adventure stories, 40
Indigenous authors, 12, 67–68, 72. See also Erdrich, Louise; Harjo, Joy; Momaday, N. Scott
Indigenous childhood: and agency, 86–88; and "Indian boarding schools," US, 84–88; and protocol, introduction to concept of, 80–81
Indigenous people: Anishinabe, 68–73; "complex responses in order to survive," 86–87; encroachment of settler colonialists on lands of, 67–68; home, experiences of, 81; Kiowa, 84–88; Mvskoke, 80–81; pre-Columbian history, 67, 83, 150n4, 150n6; relocation of to urban areas, 84; "savagery" attributed to by white people, 84–85, 88; "self-respect" as form of resistance, 80–81; Trail of Tears, 132–33
Indolent Boys, The (Momaday), 84–88
Innes, Catherine Lynette, 56, 57
intergenerational conflict, 51, 138
intersectional approaches, 8, 11, 19, 30, 32, 35–36, 42, 50, 63, 90, 103, 138–40
In the Name of Salomé (Alvarez), 116, 125–29, 133–34
Irish diasporic communities, 51
Italian American childhood: adventure in 10, 50–51; and intergenerational conflict, 51; and toxic masculinity, 52
Italian Americans, 41–42, 50–55, 132, 148n6
"It's Raining in Honolulu" (Harjo), 83

Jallianwala Bagh massacre, 27
James, Henry, 124–25
Japanese culture, 120–25
Jesse (Soto), 114, 120, 152n6
Jimenez, Laura M., 114
Journal of Pedagogy, 65

Karefa-Smart, Aisha, 45, 47, 49, 148n10
Katanski, Amelia V., 86
Kennedy, John F., 105
King, Thomas, 72, 79
kinship, "counter-narratives" of, 48

Kiowa Boarding School (Anadarko, Oklahoma), 84, 150n11
Knoepflmacher, U. C., 5
Komunyakaa, Yusef, 32
Korean language, 71
Ku Klux Klan, 129

language: African languages, colonialist approach to, 62; assimilationist settler colonial practices and subversive modes of learning, 71–72; Bengali, 11, 23, 28, 147n5; bilingual texts and identities, 66–67, 71, 78–79; code-switching, 51, 66, 67, 89, 122; imperialist hierarchy of, 121, 125; Italian, 51, 75; meanings of words, 65–66, 68, 70; "national," 121–22; Ojibwa, 71; Spanish, 66, 78–79, 91, 118, 120–22; untranslated terms, 23–24, 26–27, 66
Latin America: anti-Blackness in Caribbean, 128–29; US attempts at hegemony in, 126–27. *See also* Cuba; Dominican Republic; Mexico; neoimperialism, US; Puerto Rico
Latinx authors, 12, 68; and "pan-Latino" intellectual space, 114, 116; white outsiders' expectations for, 114–15. *See also* Alvarez, Julia; Chicanx culture; Cisneros, Sandra; Santiago, Esmeralda; Soto, Gary
Latinx children, cultural "masking" expected of, 78
Latinx children's literature, 113–16; cross-cultural encounters in, 115; multiplicity of, 114–15, 129, 134
Latinxs in Kid Lit, 129–30
Lee, A. Robert, 45
Lester, Julius, 41, 45
Lin, Grace, 66
Lincoln, Abraham, 126, 131
Lindstrom, Carole, 40–41, 129
Little Black Sambo, 28–29
Little Man, Little Man: A Story of Childhood (Baldwin), 7, 9, 37, 41, 54; classified as "a child's story for adults," 45, 47; Duke University Press reissue of, 14, 37, 45; ending of, 49–50; reviews of, 41, 45
Little Princess, A (Burnett), 22, 147n6

Living, The, series (de la Peña), 40
Living Up the Street (Soto), 118, 123
López, Tiffany Ana, 129
Lowriders series (Camper), 40
"Lullaby" (Hughes), 32
Lurie, Alison, 22
lynching, 32–33

Macaulay, Thomas Babington, 23
MacCann, Donnarae, 42
Magoon, Kekla, 8
Mama's Nightingale (Danticat), 4, 11, 93–96, 101–6, 111
Marisol McDonald Doesn't Match (Brown), 78, 152n2
Marks, Janae, 104
Martin, Kameelah L., 56
masculinity, toxic, 42, 46, 48–49, 55
Maxwell, W. H., 65
McDonald, Mercedes, 79
McGlennen, Molly, 81
McKay, Claude, 34
McQuail, Josephine A., 22, 27–28
Mehta, Purnima, 28
memoir, 38, 59–60, 87, 90–91
mestizaje, 83
Mexican American studies, 75, 150n3
Mexico, 83, 116, 127, 133; Mexican American War, 75, 130, 133, 153n13. *See also* Chicanx culture; Latin America
Meyer, Marissa, 8
MFA programs, insularity of, 73–74
Michals, Teresa, 9
Mickenberg, Julia L., 7, 9, 21, 22
Midwest Book Review, 79–80
"Minute on Indian Education" (Macaulay), 23
Momaday, N. Scott, 11–12, 66, 68; Works: *Circle of Wonder: A Native American Christmas Story*, 4, 11, 87–88, 150n12; *Four Arrows & Magpie*, 87; *House Made of Dawn*, 84; *The Indolent Boys*, 84–88; *The Names*, 87
Montoya, Margaret E., 78
"Mood Indigo" (Shange), 141–43
Moon Lady, The (Tan), 11, 138–41
Morales, Areli, 96

Morrison, Slade, 3
Morrison, Toni, 3, 9, 94; Works: *Beloved*, 9, 107, 110–11, 151n7; "Novel Endings" speech, 110; "Recitatif," 3; *Remember: The Journey to School Integration*, 3, 10, 94–95, 106–11; "What Is a Good School?," 108–9; "What the Black Woman Thinks about Women's Lib," 3
motherhood: in Danticat's work, 102–3; in Hughes's work, 32; in Puzo's work, 51–52; under slavery, 110–11; in Tagore's work, 24–25
"Mother to Son" (Hughes), 32
multicultural identity, 80
multiethnic US literature, 5–6, 10, 68, 71, 115, 150n2
multiracial children, 8, 78
Multiracial Identity in Children's Literature (Chaudhri), 8
Muñoz Ryan, Pam, 13, 40, 66–67
Mustapha, Abolaji Samuel, 62
Myers, Mitzi, 5
"My People" (Hughes), 31–32
"My Song" (Tagore), 24, 32

Nagle, Rebecca, 67
Names, The (Momaday), 87
National Association for the Advancement of Colored People (NAACP), 142
nationalism, Chicanx, 123, 152n8
nationalism, US, 6, 13, 115–25; baseball rituals, 124; exaggerated cultural distinctions as foundation of, 123
nature, 23, 29, 76–77
NCAE Writers Workshop, 117, 152n5
"Negro, The" (Hughes), 32–33, 34, 99
"Negro Speaks of Rivers, The" (Hughes), 31, 34
Nel, Philip, 7, 9, 21
Nelson, Kadir, 141, 142
neoimperialism, US: throughout the Americas, 126–27; in Cuba, 128; as cultural hegemony, 100; in Hawai'i, 83; after the Mexican American War, 133; in Puerto Rico, 89–91. *See also* imperialism
Newsweek, 106–7
New York Times, The, 106

Nigeria: Biafran War, 60; class dynamics in, 56–57, 61–63; colonialism's effect on, 58–62; educational experiences in, 56–61, 63
Nikolajeva, Maria, 39
Nkrumah, Kwame, 142
nonfiction, 5–6, 18, 95, 141, 151n2. *See also* memoir

Olivares, Julián, 117
"On Being 'White'... and Other Lies" (Baldwin), 41–42
Operation Return to Sender, 130
Ortiz, Simon J., 117
"Overwhelmingly White, Straight, and Able Face of Children's Literature, The" (Jimenez), 114
OwnVoices movement, 114, 129–30, 135

Pacific Crossing (Soto), 114–15, 116, 120–25, 130, 132–33
Palacios, Sara, 78
Paranjape, Makarand R., 23
paternalism, of outsider activists, 97–98
patriotism, critique of, 131–33
Paulsen, Gary, 39
pedagogical discourses, 65–66
perspective-taking, 109
Phillipson, Robert, 121
Phoenix Award, 115
pickaninny stereotype, 28–29
picture books, 4, 73, 78, 87, 95; *Chato* series (Soto), 114. *See also Doll for Navidades, A* (Santiago); *Hairs/Pelitos* (Cisneros); *Mama's Nightingale* (Danticat); *Moon Lady, The* (Tan)
Pinkney, Andrea Davis, 106, 108
"Playthings" (Tagore), 21–22, 26, 30
poetry, 5, 11, 18; cross-written, 35–36. *See also* Cisneros, Sandra; *Crescent Moon, The* (Tagore); *Dream Keeper, The* (Hughes); *For a Girl Becoming* (Harjo); Harjo, Joy; Hughes, Langston; Soto, Gary; Tagore, Rabindranath
Power, Effie Lee, 28
precolonial history, 17–18, 23, 58, 67, 87, 147–48n10

progressivism, 126
Publishers Weekly, 75
publishing industry, 14, 106–7, 120, 139, 141; Duke University Press, 14, 37, 45; underrepresentation of Latinx identities, 113–14
Puerto Rico, 88–91, 127
Pullinger, Debbie, 21
Pura Belpré Award, 134
Puzo, Mario, 10–11; Works: *The Fortunate Pilgrim*, 38, 50–55, 149n13; *Godfather* series, 38, 149n13; *The Runaway Summer of Davie Shaw*, 6, 38, 42, 49–55, 63–64

racism, 41; constructions of childhood used to justify, 28–29; transatlantic violence of, 32–33; white fascination with, 83
Ramayana (Valmiki), 23
Raúl the Third, 40, 84
redefinition: of belonging, 7, 11–12, 66, 68, 71–74, 78–83, 88, 90–92; children as agents of, 68–69; of "civilization," 69–72, 81–82, 86, 90; of colonialism, 75–76; in cross-cultural cross-writing, 140, 142; of culturally central terms, 66, 68, 70
Reese, Debbie, 67
religion: and antiqueerness, 44; brujería and curanderismo as, 76; as "concrete abstraction," 56; Igbo, 59; Kiowa, 88; and patriotism, 124; satirical depictions of, 53; syncretic, 76, 87–88
Remember: The Journey to School Integration (Morrison), 3, 10, 94–96, 106–11
"rememory," 110
resistance: glossaries as, 66, 71; hybrid cultures of, 12; learning settler colonial languages as, 71–72; mother-child relationships as site of, 24, 32; self-respect as, 80–81; syncretic religious practices as, 76, 87–88; transnational project of, 34–36. *See also* activists, children as
respectability politics, 12, 102–3, 109, 111, 152n11
Return to Sender (Alvarez), 6, 116, 129–34

reviews, 72, 77, 104, 120, 152n2; colonizing impulses in, 79–80, 91
Rice and Beans (Muñoz Ryan), 66–67
Richardson, Julia, 120
Robeson, Paul, 142
Robinson Crusoe (Defoe), 9, 39
Roll of Thunder, Hear My Cry (Taylor), 48, 129
Routledge Companion to International Children's Literature, The, 6, 18–19
Runaway Summer of Davie Shaw, The (Puzo), 6, 38, 42, 49–55, 63–64

Sánchez, Enrique O., 88
Sanchez-Eppler, Karen, 9
San Joaquin Valley: agricultural labor in, 117–18; Fresno as urban center within, 118–19
Santiago, Esmeralda, 12, 66, 68, 95; Works: *Conquistadora*, 91; *A Doll for Navidades*, 4, 88–91, 151n14; *When I Was Puerto Rican*, 90–91
Saro-Wiwa, Noo, 60
satire, 10, 53–55, 64, 76
Schields, Gretchen, 138
Scholastic, 114, 115
sea, figure of, 96
Secret Footprints, The (Alvarez), 129
self-care and self-love as political, 110, 151n8
self-defense as recourse for communities of color, 109
self-respect as resistance, 80–81
semiautobiographical mode, 95, 101–6
sentence-level style, 71
settler colonialism, 132; destinarian language of, 70; diseases brought by, 69–71; homes stolen from Indigenous people, 81; late twentieth-century and early twenty-first-century persistence of, 73–74, 76, 81, 126; and Mexican American War, 75; resisting in Cisneros and Harjo, 73–84; resisting in Erdrich, 68–72; "vacant land," myth of, 67, 69; and white flight, 75–76. *See also* colonialism
Séverac, Alain, 56–57
Shaffer, Donald M., Jr., 56

Shange, Ntozake, 6, 137; Works: *A Daughter's Geography*, 141; *ellington was not a street*, 11, 141–43; "Improvisation," 141; "It Hasn't Always Been This Way," 141; "Mood Indigo," 141–43; "Take the A Train," 141
Shin, Sun Yung, 71
shopping mall, 22
Silko, Leslie Marmon, 117
Sí Magazine, 88
Simon, Scott, 40
Sinha, Mrinalini, 24
Slater, Andrea M., 18
slavery, 18, 31, 34, 56, 79, 110–11, 131, 151n8; as haunting, 110
"Sleep-Stealer" (Tagore), 23, 27, 31
"Sleepy" (Chekhov), 57
smallpox, 69–71
Smith, Katharine Capshaw, 5, 9–10, 18, 29, 31
Smokowski, Paul R., 78
Socolovsky, Maya, 131
Soto, Gary, 6, 13, 66; Works: "Being Mean," 118; "Braly Street," 118; "Bulosan, 1935," 118–19, 126; *Cesar Chavez: A Hero for Everyone*, 120; *Chato* series, 114; *The Elements of San Joaquin*, 115, 117, 126; "Field Poem," 117–18; *Jesse*, 114, 120, 152n6; *Living Up the Street*, 118, 123; *Marisol*, 115; *Pacific Crossing*, 114–25, 115, 116, 120–25, 130–33; "Saturday in Chinatown," 119; *Where Sparrows Work Hard*, 115, 119, 126; *Why I Don't Write Children's Literature*, 115, 152n2
Staub, Leslie, 93
Stephanson, Anders, 70
Stewart, Michelle Pagni, 10
stoic child, figure of, 46
Stowe, Harriet Beecher, 28

Tagore, Rabindranath, 6, 9, 18, 41, 95, 147nn1–2, 147n10; Bengali, writings in, 11, 23, 28; "child-poems," 19–27; children seen as intellectually independent by, 22, 25, 27–28; classical references in, 23; decolonial consciousness, 27; gender in works of, 25–27; interest in children and childhood, 20–21; nature, references to, 23–24; shortsightedness of adulthood in, 21–22; Works: "The Postmaster," 25–26; "Punishment," 26–27. See also *Crescent Moon, The* (Tagore)
Tan, Amy, 4, 137; Works: *The Joy Luck Club*, 138, 139; *The Kitchen God's Wife*, 141; *The Moon Lady*, 11, 138–41
Taylor, Mildred, 13, 40, 48, 129
Terrones, Lettycia, 66–67, 71, 79
Thackeray, William Makepeace, 39
There Was a Country (Achebe), 38, 59–60, 149n24
Through My Eyes (Bridges), 95, 151n2
Tito Puente: Mambo King/Rey del Mambo (Brown), 78–79
Tom Sawyer (Twain), 51
Trail of Tears, 132–33
transhistorical identity, diasporic, 31
"Translator Translated" (Desai), 99–101
transnationalism, 35–36; "agrarian," 130–31; of Baldwin, 41–42, 56; within cross-writing, 11, 19, 38, 41–42, 57, 68, 94–95; of diasporic communities, 17, 30–31, 33–34, 142; of Hughes, 30–31, 56; of systems of oppression, 6, 29, 35, 82–83, 126–27
trauma, historical, 128–29
Traylor, Eleanor W., 42
Tribunella, Eric L., 38, 40, 51
Trites, Roberta Seelinger, 8
Tucson, Arizona, Mexican American studies program, 75, 150n3
Twain, Mark, 51
Twenty-First-Century Feminisms in Children's and Adolescent Literature (Trites), 8

Uncle Tom's Cabin (Stowe), 28
"Unheeded Pageant, The" (Tagore), 22, 31–32
United Nations Convention on the Rights of the Child, 102
United States: anti-Haitian xenophobia, 104; Bracero Program, 117; *Brown v. Board of Education*, 107, 109; civil rights movement viewed as "commitment to justice," 108; colonial and neocolonial history, 83, 150n9; criminal justice

and immigration systems, 94, 101–6; Dominican Republic, invasion of, 126–27; fallacy of exceptionalism, 32, 70, 96, 115–16, 129, 133–34; Hawaiʻi, colonial and neocolonial history, 83, 150n9; Jim Crow, 106–11; "majority" culture, notions of, 115; and Mexican American War, 75, 130, 133, 153n13; Mexico, domination of, 75, 130; nationalism, 6, 13, 115–25; "national language," notions of, 121–22; neoimperialism in Latin America, 88–91, 126–28, 133; Operation Return to Sender, 130; relocation of Indigenous people to urban areas, 81, 84; slavery, 18, 31, 34, 79, 110–11, 131; Vietnam War, 115, 120
Ureña de Henríquez, Salomé, 116, 126
Uribe, Luisa, 96
Uwakweh, Pauline Ada, 56

Valdez, Luis, 121
VanderHaagen, Sara C., 6
"Vengeful Creditor" (Achebe), 38, 56–61
Vietnam War, 115, 120
Village by the Sea, The (Desai), 10, 94, 95, 96–101, 111
"virginity testing," 104

"wanderer" (picaresque hero), 50
Ways of White Folks, The (Hughes), 11, 33–34
We Are Water Protectors (Lindstrom), 40–41, 129
When I Was Puerto Rican (Santiago), 90–91
"Where I Ought to Be: A Writer's Sense of Place" (Erdrich), 67, 72
Where Sparrows Work Hard (Soto), 115, 119, 126
white allyship, 107–8
white authors, culturally appropriative works by, 114, 149n15
white children: and access to US educational resources, 109; as "angelic," 28–29, 45, 55, 96; as audience for activist children's literature, 24, 29, 108, 133; and "racialized good luck," 55; racism of, 95, 107; as "victors" in canonical texts, 61

white flight, 75–76
white savior myth, 19, 85–86, 105, 131
white supremacist thought, 9–10, 12, 41–42; and "angelic white child," 28–29, 45, 55, 96; Black children treated as adults, 29, 45, 49; among British imperialists in India, 20; and color-caste systems, 18; after Jim Crow, suppression of knowledge about, 95–96; Latinx authors, expectations for, 114–15; racism, fascination with, 83; "savagery" attributed to Indigenous people, 84–85, 88
Why I Don't Write Children's Literature (Soto), 115, 152n2
Winthrop, John, 70–71
women: Asian, gendered stereotypes of, 138–40; colonial propaganda about, 19–20, 21, 24, 58–59; othering of older, 51; position of in colonial India, 24, 26; position of in precolonial and colonial Nigeria, 58–59. *See also* gender
Wong, Sau-Ling Cynthia, 140
Woodson, Jacqueline, 8
words, learning meanings of, 65–66, 68, 70

Yelchin, Eugene, 104

Zoot Suit (Valdez), 121
Zúñiga, Christian E., 134

ABOUT THE AUTHOR

Photo courtesy of the author

Suzanne Manizza Roszak is an assistant professor of English at the University of Groningen in the north of the Netherlands. She is the author of *Uncanny Youth: Childhood, the Gothic, and the Literary Americas*.

www.ingramcontent.com/pod-product-compliance
Lightning Source LLC
Chambersburg PA
CBHW030625230426
43661CB00053B/2141